CW01481284

Rethinking the Boundaries of Strategy

Rethinking the Boundaries of Strategy

Edited by

Joyce Falkenberg and Sven A. Haugland

HANDELSHØJSKOLENS FORLAG

Distribution: Munksgaard International Publishers Ltd
Copenhagen

© by the authors and Handelshøjskolens Forlag 1996
Printed in Denmark 1996
Set in Plantin by Grafisk Værk A/S, Denmark
Printed by Reproset, Copenhagen
Cover designed by Kontrapunkt
Book designed by Jørn Ekstrøm

ISBN 87-16-13302-1

Series A
COPENHAGEN STUDIES IN ECONOMICS AND MANAGEMENT, NO. 8.

Preface

In June 1993, the conference «Rethinking the Boundaries of Strategy» took place at Solstrand Fjord Hotel in Western Norway. The aim of the conference was to discuss the resource based perspective of strategy, and how this perspective can be integrated in the strategy paradigm. This book is based on a selection of papers presented at the conference.

It is our belief that practitioners have long recognized the importance of resources to strategy formulation. This book contributes to this understanding by developing a theoretical understanding of why these resources can be important in a company's success, and also gives some interesting examples of the use of resources. It is our hope that this book will extend our knowledge of strategic management. The book offers a thorough background of the resource based perspective, and discusses how the resource based perspective can complement strategic analysis primarily concerned with external factors.

This book would not have been completed without the generous assistance of the Norwegian Research Centre in Organization and Management. We thank the Centre for sponsoring the conference in June 1993, and for providing secretarial services effectively carried out by Åse Netland and Elisabeth Tufta.

Bergen, February 1996

Joyce Falkenberg
Sven A. Haugland

Contents

Section Three
Applying the Resource Based Perspective

Introduction

A boundary is defined in Webster's Dictionary as «anything marking a limit, bound, border.» The title of this book, Rethinking the Boundaries of Strategy, suggests three important questions which will be addressed in this introduction. The first question, *what are the boundaries of strategy?* will be answered by looking at the limits set by the way strategy has been viewed historically. The way this question has been answered leads directly to the second question, *why do we need to rethink these boundaries?* By answering this question, we introduce the perspective taken in this book. The third question, *where are the new boundaries?* is answered by a presentation of the three sections of the book.

What are the boundaries of strategy?

We use a historical perspective of the strategy literature to determine the boundaries of strategy. Because strategy has been under continual development since its conception as a field of business administration, a historical perspective allows us to view where the boundaries have been and how they have changed.

Although there are different conjectures on the origin of strategy as a field of study, certainly the work of Ansoff (1965), Andrews (1971) and Chandler (1962) were relevant in the early determination of the boundaries of strategy. It is interesting that in focusing on these early works, we find that the boundaries of strategy were quite broad.

In many ways, the complexity of the strategy field and the resulting broad boundaries of the strategy concept were reflected in Chandler's 1962 book, *Strategy and Structure: Chapters in the History of the American Industrial Enterprise*. Strategy was defined as «the determination of the basic long-term goals and objectives of an enterprise, and the adoption of courses of action and the allocation of resources necessary for carrying out these goals» (Chandler, 1962: 13). Chandler's book described the growth process. Based on his historical description, strategy included a focus on implementation as well as formulation.

This broad perspective on strategy was also reflected in the strategy textbooks for this time, particularly *Business Policy: Text and Cases* (1965) written by a group of Harvard Business School professors which included

Learned, Christensen, Andrews and Guth. In addition, Andrews own book builds on a framework which views corporate strategy as a pattern of interrelated decisions. To make these decisions, that is, to formulate strategy, the framework included both an internal and external analysis. Implementation was then based on the formulated strategy. The boundaries of strategy were once again expanded with this focus on internal and external analysis. The strategy process model which is often used as a pedagogic tool was influenced by the work of Andrews.

About the same time, Ansoff's (1965) book on strategy was published. Two aspects of this book are important in our discussion of boundaries. First, the book reflected the need to define a product/market strategy based on competitive advantage. Ansoff used the term competitive advantage to refer to the common thread within a business among product characteristics, technology, or similarity of needs. Thus the competitive advantage would determine the firm's business, generally within a product/market perspective. A development based on the product-market perspective was the growth matrix, emphasizing present and potential product/market combinations. This emphasis on competitive advantage is today being renewed as an important element within the boundaries of strategy.

The second aspect of Ansoff's book which influenced the determination of the boundaries of strategy was the emphasis on planning. Unfortunately, this aspect resulted in the interpretation by many managers that strategy was the same as planning. Ansoff's Model of Strategy Planning (1965: 202-203) illustrates the strategy as planning idea. This resulted in a contration of the boundaries of strategy during the 1970s.

In recognizing the limiting aspect of strategy as planning, Schendel and Hofer (1979) reintroduced and synthesized the earlier work in the field of strategy in a flow process containing six major tasks for the strategic manager:

goals formulation
↓
environmental analysis
↓
strategy formulation
↓
strategy evaluation
↓
strategy implementation
↓
strategic control

This paradigm (Schendel's terminology, see his introduction to the *Strategic Management Journal* Summer 1994 Special Issue «Strategy: Search for New Paradigms») described the boundaries of strategy as they existed at the time: formulation as well as implementation; content as well as process. However, in their synthesis, the boundaries were drawn with the major focus on the external environment and relatively little emphasis on the internal environment of the firm.

The boundaries of strategy were once again redrawn with the arrival in 1980 of Michael Porter's book, *Competitive Strategy*. The book was important for the strategy field because it used the industrial economics perspective to give strategy a theoretical basis. And it was perhaps within the normal cycle, that after broadening the boundaries of strategy, it was time to develop a deeper understanding of part of strategy. In the «Porter Perspective», strategy became positioning; positioning of the company within the industry. Although Porter also emphasized that analysis of strengths and weaknesses of the firm was important, this aspect was often overlooked by those using this perspective. The Porter perspective, although narrowly bounding strategy within industrial economics, did result in an important impetus to the field.

Although the focus on the external environment was well established, a growing recognition that other factors also needed to be included within the boundaries of strategy began to develop. This resulted in a renewed emphasis on the internal organizational factors, specifically the resources and capabilities of the firm. This perspective revived the work of Penrose from the 1950s; and was brought into the boundaries of strategy by Wernerfelt in his 1984 article. This resource based perspective assumes that organizational resources can become sources of strategic advantage. Recently, this perspective has become well developed and is seen by some as a competitor to the earlier perspectives. The impetus from this perspective in redefining the field of strategy is a recognition of the importance of including this perspective in the field of strategy.

Why do we need to rethink the boundaries of strategy?

The boundaries set by the different perspectives may limit our thinking as to what strategy is. The brief survey of strategy given above suggests that although the boundaries of strategy have been under constant revision, there has been a tendency, at any one time, to view strategy within a particular perspective.

The early works as described by Ansoff, Andrews and Chandler suggests broad boundaries for the field of strategy. But these boundaries narrowed when strategy was interpreted to mean planning. The strategic management process presented by Hofer and Schendel suggests a realigning of the boundaries, but this process was soon overshadowed by the Porter perspective. Porter's focus on the external environment and on formulation influenced the field of strategy during the 1980s. Recognition of the potential for internal resources and capabilities to explain competitive advantage, brought the resource based perspective into focus.

These different perspectives, each contributing important insights, have been limited and perhaps limiting when considered individually. This has been illustrated in Mintzberg's (1994) recent book, *The Rise and Fall of Strategic Planning*. Here strategic planning is described as mesmerizing organizations. It is this over-emphasis on a single aspect of strategy which resulted in its downfall. While planning is recognized as an important activity, it is not strategy. In the same way, many singular perspectives of strategy, such as positioning or resources, while useful to help us better understand strategy, cannot alone define the boundaries of strategy.

When we, in the present book, suggest the need for redefining the boundaries of strategy, it is to emphasize the importance of integrating the external analysis and the internal analysis, integrating strategy from an industrial economics perspective and the resource based perspective. Many will argue that there is nothing new about this integration; certainly we saw that Andrews included both an internal and external focus in his process diagram from the early seventies. However, we must also recognize that the field of strategy has developed from this early perspective, most importantly by the addition of a theoretical basis to help us understand competitive advantage. In addition, the redefining of boundaries focuses attention from the particular *emphasis* on either the external environment or internal resources, and suggests that the field of strategy can benefit from an integration of the two perspectives.

Where are the new boundaries?

In this book, the new boundaries of strategy include the resource based perspective, but integrate this perspective into the field of strategy, rather than defining the field of strategy as the resource based perspective.

This distinction is important; remember how the field of strategy was narrowed, when strategy became defined as planning.

To achieve this integration, it is important to familiarize our readers to the resource based perspective. We assume that the process, planning and positioning perspectives do not need further explication. The first section of the book, Rethinking the Foundations of Strategy, provides a basic understanding of the resource based perspective. The perspective is based in Penrose's work, which is the focus of Knudsen's article, «Strategic Management and the Knowledge-Based Theory of the Firm: A Reconstruction of Edith Penrose's Theory of the Limits of the Growth of the Firm». From this historical background of the resource based perspective, we are now ready to understand how the resource based perspective has developed. Eriksen takes this focus in his article, «Firm Resources and Capabilities: A Renewed Focus for Strategic Management». How can we understand the resource based perspective? The article by Godfrey and Hill, «Grounding Strategic Paradigms: Logical Positivism, Realism and the Resource Based View of the Firm», focuses on the philosophy of science approach to answer this question.

Integration of the resource based perspective into the field of strategy and strategic issues is the focus of the second section of the book. This section begins with an overview of the theoretical foundations for strategy, in Reve's article «Toward an Integrative Model of Strategy Development: From Dynamic Clusters to Core Competencies». Change and adaptation is an area of strategy which has had as its focus the need to respond to the external environment. In «Strategic Change and Adaptation from a Resource Based Perspective» Falkenberg develops the framework for adaptation by included a resource based perspective. Strategic alliances, as depicted in network organizations, is the focus of the article, «Core Competencies in a Network Organization» by Haugland and Lunnan. In their article, core competencies are used to extend our understanding of the governance framework. The final article in this section «Rethinking the Metaphors of Strategic Management» by Løwendahl and Revang integrates the resource based perspective in the strategic challenges facing strategic leaders.

Applying the Resource Based Perspective is the third and final section of the book. In this section the focus is on specific organizational resources which can be potential contributors to sustained competitive advantage. Competencies, individual and organizational, are linked in Nordhaug's article, «Collective Competencies». Expert Knowledge is viewed as a strategic asset in the article by Grønhaug. Information systems can also be viewed in terms of their implications for strategy, although only as a secondary resource as described in the article «Information Systems as a Secondary Strategy Resource: The Case of Bank Credit Evaluations» by Fuglseth and Grønhaug. And the creation of sustainable competitive advantage in institutional markets is the focus of Gjelsvik's article, «Escaping the Iron Cage: Where it Goes and What it Takes».

References

Andrews, K. R. *The Concept of Corporate Strategy*, Homewood, IL: Irwin, 1971.

Ansoff, H. I. *Corporate Strategy*, New York: McGraw-Hill, 1965.

Chandler, A. D., Jr., *Strategy and Structure: Chapters in the History of the Industrial Enterprise*, Cambridge, MA: MIT Press, 1962.

Learned, E. P., Christensen, C. R., Andrews, K. R., and Guth, W. D. *Business Policy: Text and Cases*, Homewood, IL: Irwin, 1965.

Mintzberg, H. *The Rise and Fall of Strategic Planning*, New York: The Free Press, 1994.

Penrose, E. T. *The Theory of the Growth of the Firm*, Oxford: Blackwell, 1959.

Porter, M. E., *Competitive Strategy: Techniques for Analyzing Industries and Competitors*. New York: The Free Press, 1980.

Schendel, D. E., and C. W. Hofer, *Strategic Management A New View of Business Policy and Planning*, Boston: Little, Brown and Company, 1979.

Schendel, D. E., «Introduction to the Summer 1994 Special Issue – 'Strategy: Search for New Paradigms'», *Strategic Management Journal*, Vol. 15, 1-4, 1994.

Wernerfelt, B. «A resource-based view of the firm», *Strategic Management Journal*, 5(2), 1984, 795-815.

Section One

Rethinking the Foundations of Strategy

Rethinking the Foundations of Strategy encompasses three articles which describe the resource based perspective as one of the foundations of strategy. In order to be able to fully appreciate the role of the resource based perspective in the field of strategy, it is important first to have an understanding of what the perspective is, as well as what it contributes to the field of strategy.

Edith Penrose's book, *The Theory of the Growth of the Firm*, is generally accepted as the theoretical foundation for the resource based perspective. In the first article Christian Knudsen focuses on the main themes and arguments of Penrose's theory. Among these are the importance of variations in resources among firms within the same industry. This heterogeneity is explained by accumulation of different knowledge, both what Penrose distinguishes as objective knowledge and knowledge based on experience. It is this knowledge based on experience which is embodied in the capabilities, routines and competencies of the firm, and thus makes it difficult for other firms to imitate. Knudsen then relates Penrose's work to other theories, and focuses on the implications for research.

The second article develops our understanding of the resource based perspective by putting it in the context of strategic management. In this article Bo Eriksen focuses on the how sustainable competitive advantage can be achieved through an organization's resources and capabilities.

Anyone who has attempted to empirically test the resource based perspective has quickly realized the complications involved. The article by Paul Godfrey and Charles Hill focuses on the reasons for these problems by explicating the philosophy of science approaches of logical positivism and realism and the resulting implications for research methodology.

Strategic Management and the Knowledge-Based Theory of the Firm: A Reconstruction of Edith Penrose's Theory of the Limits of the Growth of the Firm

Christian Knudsen

This chapter introduces Edith Penrose's theory on limits to the growth of firms published in the 1950s. At that time, the neoclassical research tradition with its study of different market structures reigned supremely within economics. For the same reason, alternative research traditions, such as Penrose's resource-based theory of the firm, had little chance of coming into play.

Four decades after Penrose's book *The Theory of the Growth of the Firm* was published in 1959, this situation seems to have changed in several important respects. First, rediscovering Ronald Coases transaction cost analysis, Oliver Williamson has legitimized studies of the firms' internal organization within economics. Second, the growing technological competition and the consequent focus on dynamic competition have made change-oriented analyses of markets and firms much more relevant. Therefore, not until the early 1990s did Edith Penrose's theory seem to get a breakthrough almost similar to that of Ronald Coase's transaction cost analysis since the mid-1970s.

This chapter describes the explanatory model on which Penrose's theory of the firm builds. Then, her knowledge- and resource-based understanding of the firm is discussed together with the most important theses of her theory of what sets the limits to the growth of the firm. The article concludes with a short discussion of modern resource-based theory, in particular focusing on how this relates to Penrose's original contribution.

The explanatory structure of Edith Penrose's theory of the limits of the growth of the firm

The use of analogies and metaphors in economics

A central feature of Edith Penrose's theory is that it is built upon a change oriented and/or evolutionary model, in which the evolution or development of an organism provides an analogy for the study of the growth processes of the firm. Penrose perpetuates a tradition dating back to Alfred Marshall's theory of the life cycle of the firm. By arguing that the growth of a firm will decrease as it grows older, Marshall attempted to justify how an assumption of perfect competition could be reconciled with firms producing under increasing return to scale. On a more general level, Penrose was very critical of Marshall's life cycle theory because it used a biological model in an unquestioning way without accounting for the many negative analogies that existed between the evolution of an organism and a firm. Edith Penrose argued as follows:

> The purpose of analogical reasoning in which we consciously and systematically apply the explanation of one series of events to another very different series of events is to help us better to understand the nature of the latter, which presumably is less well understood than the former. If the analogy has really helpful explanatory value, there must be some reason for believing that the two series of events have enough in common for the explanation of one, mutatis mutandis, to provide at least partial explanation of the other. (1952: 807)

If we view a firm as if it were an organism, this involves using our knowledge of the development of biological organisms in order to gain deeper insight into the nature of firms. Given her general view of what analogy models can be used for, Penrose was far more willing than most evolutionary economists to openly recognize the lack of similarities between biological and economic phenomena. It can even be said that Penrose favored a realist interpretation of analogy models. This involved a refusal to consider these models as metaphors and pure rhetoric which need not be appraised by reference to real phenomena, and would therefore, according to Penrose, lack any explanatory content. She consequently argued that «this type of analogy must be distinguished from the purely metaphorical analogy in which the resemblances between two phenomena are used to add a picturesque note to an otherwise dull analysis, and to help a reader to see more clearly the outlines of a process being described by enabling him to draw on what he knows in order to imagine the unknown» (1952: 807). To Penrose, metaphors and analogy models are mainly useful tools for identifying new aspects of reality. However, the fact that they play such an important part in the discovery phase of a theory does not make it legitimate to treat them exclusively as linguistic or rhetorical tools in the justification phase having no reference to real phenomena. For this reason Penrose's view of analogy models appears to conflict with the rhetorical program that Donald McCloskey (1985) proposed more recently.

Edith Penrose versus Armen Alchian in the debate on biological analogies in economics

What implications were drawn by Penrose from her appraisal of metaphors and analogy models, where the use of biological analogies and metaphors within economics was concerned? We can find the answer to this question in Penrose's (1952, 1953) contributions to the debate on biological analogies, which were a reaction to Armen Alchian's article «Uncertainty, Evolution and Economic Theory» from 1950. According to Alchian, economists were not necessarily bound to an orthodox form of analysis based on the maximization principle and the concept of equilibrium, but could just as well use a more evolutionary inspired type of analysis. As Alchian wrote: «There is an alternative method which treats the decisions and criteria dictated by the economic system as more important than those made by the individuals in it. By backing away from the trees, the optimization calculus of individual units, we can better discern the forest of impersonal market forces» (1950: 19). An alternative existed, therefore, to the traditional way of building economic models up from a number of individual experiments, which resulted in numerous laws or relations at the market level via an aggregation procedure. On the basis of the law of supply and demand, so-called market experiments could be carried out in which the stability of the system under analysis could be examined, and the possibility of deducing comparative static results could be demonstrated. If, however, we inverted this traditional form of explanation by assuming that it was the system that formed the behavior of the individual agent through a selection mechanism, we could, according to Alchian, also understand apparently intentional behavior in purely causal terms without assuming that agents consciously maximize. Alchian had thus introduced a functionalist evolutionary type of explanation into economics, which seems to have had its main breakthrough since the beginning of the 1970s. Here we only need to point out Alchian & Demsetz's (1972) launch of the nexus of contract theory of the firm and Oliver Williamson's (1975) subsequent development of transaction cost theory.

To Alchian, his market selection model should be seen as a kind of basic model which was to be modified later by attributing gradually more complex learning mechanisms to its nonintentional individuals. Penrose's (1952) most important objection to Alchian's analysis was, however, that he overlooked the fact that economic systems consist of intentional individuals. In her appraisal of Alchian's economic analogies to the three main mechanisms of the theory of evolution 1) the transmission or hereditary mechanism, 2) the variation mechanism, and 3) the selection mechanism, Penrose (1952) considered it to be a problem that the concept of innovation was posed as an analogy to the concept of mutation, and therefore also to the variation mechanism. She objected as follows:

> But mutations are «alterations in the substance of the hereditary constitution» of an organism, while innovations, though they may consist of changes in the constitution of firms, more often than not are direct attempts by firms to alter their environment. In other words, innovations are directly related to the environment of firms whereas the biologists tell us that genetic mutations are apparently completely unrelated either to the environment or to the agent inducing the mutation. The biologist cannot explain why mutations take the course they do while the economist, if he can assume with some justification that the activity of firms is induced by a desire for profits, has a plausible partial explanation of innovation. (Penrose, 1952: 815)

In the biological theory of evolution it is assumed that mutations can have both positive and negative consequences; that is, they will be uncorrelated to their environment. Similarly, in Alchian's basic model, innovations are random. Penrose does not consider this point to be reasonable. Evolution in economics is therefore distinguished from evolution in biology by not being quite so blind or shortsighted, precisely because one is confronted with systems consisting of agents who are intentional, and therefore have the ability to search for new variations in certain profitable directions. While Alchian had probably placed too much emphasis on the ability of the system to form the behavior of the agent, Penrose argued that the decision-making units of a system took a more active part, being capable of conscious adaptation to new circumstances.

If, however, we are to understand the background of Alchian's and Penrose's differing conceptions of the usefulness of biological analogies within economics, we should take a closer look at their different theoretical focuses and the very different levels of analysis at which they have operated in their substantial contributions to economics. Let us start by considering how Penrose (1952) describes her method:

> The growth approach has so far been expounded in any systematic form only by the «biological economists»? by those who view firms as organisms and conclude that they grow like organisms. That variant of the growth approach leaves no room for human motivation and conscious human decision and I think should be rejected on that ground. (Penrose, 1952)

Three years later, in connection with the presentation of an early version of her theory of the limits to the growth of the firm, Penrose argued as a consequence of the above criticism that there must be developed «an alternative growth approach which, in common with the biological variant, insists that a predisposition to grow is inherent in the very nature of firms, but which, in contrast, makes growth depend on motivation in the usual case on the businessman's search for profits.» (1955: 531).

Unlike Alchian's basic model, Penrose emphasizes that there is an intentional element involved in producing innovations or variations in the economy that does not exist in biology. Penrose also considers that the biologists' understanding of the variation mechanism as a kind of black box that should not be examined too closely is not appropriate to economics. Here it should be pointed out that Penrose herself attempted to give an in-principle explanation of how innovations are continually produced in the economy by the continuous release of excess management resources within firms. The consequence of this is that Penrose is far more critical than Armen Alchian concerning the use of functional explanations or viability analyses as she describes them in economics. That is to say, explanations in which the existence of institutions or behavioral rules are explained in terms of their beneficial but unanticipated consequences. It is characteristic of this type of analysis to focus on the study of the end results of an evolutionary process, and disregard the actual process as uninteresting or impossible to study. Penrose reverses these priorities, arguing that the process of change itself should be studied from the viewpoint of an unfolding perspective, rather than studying these in separate ad hoc constructions which are tacked onto the end result or the equilibrium state.

The fact that Alchian and Penrose, who are basically positive towards the use of evolutionary models in economics, can still reach such different conclusions in the debate on biological analogies in economics is due to the character of their respective contributions to economics. These differences will be explained in the following section in terms of the distinction between what biologists refer to as, respectively, ontogenetic and phylogenetic theory.

Penrose's theory as an example of ontogenetic theory

If we compare Armen Alchian's model and Edith Penrose's theory of the limits of the growth of firms, the main difference between them appears to be that they operate on different levels of analysis. While Armen Alchian is primarily interested in studying phenomena at the industry level, or what biologists might refer to as at the population level, Penrose is primarily interested in studying the development of a firm in analogy with the study in embryology of stages of development of a single organism. In the first of these instances, biologists refer to phylogenetic theories in that they are preoccupied with explaining the evolution of one or more species on the basis of three basic mechanisms: variation, transmission and selection. In the second type of theory, where the level of analysis is not the individual species, but rather the individual organism, biologists speak of ontogenetic theory. If we take Armen Alchian's evolutionary market theory to represent a phylogenetic theory, and take Penrose's theory of the firm to represent an ontogenetic theory, not only can we recognize a number of fundamental differences between them, but of even greater importance we can now begin to speculate about how these two theories or types of theories are related to each other, and how they might supplement or support one another.

Let us start with an attempt to clarify different characteristics of Edith Penrose's ontogenetic theory of the limits to the growth of the firm. Here she argues that the gradual release of management resources is partly the cause of, and partly places limits upon, the growth of the firm.

This can be described as a specification of the generative mechanisms which fuel economic development. It is through this specification of the variation mechanism that innovations are continually produced in the economy, which are necessary in order to sustain the evolutionary process. This means that Penrose's model can be said to satisfy Ulrich Witt's definition of an evolutionary explanation, in that «evolution is considered to be the transformation of a system over time through endogenously generated change» (1991: 87). However, disequilibrium or changes to a mechanical system will always be caused by exogenous forces. By starting with Roy Bhaskar's (1975) distinction between internal and external closure it can be said that evolutionary models diverge from mechanical models by not sustaining an assumption of internal closure. That is, although all factors in the environment of a firm might remain constant, in Penrose's theory this would not (unlike standard microeconomics) exclude changes in its behavior, as the firm will continue to generate new knowledge and capabilities. Witt therefore concludes: «Hence, to the extent to which change is, in fact, caused endogenously within the economy, a theoretical approach which builds on the mechanical interpretation can, at best, provide a fragmentary understanding of the evolutionary economic process» (1975: 87).

Penrose therefore considers her own theory to be based on the study of «continuous ongoing and unfolding processes», since it focuses on the way in which the knowledge of a firm is gradually accumulated in a path-dependent and irreversible course of development, where each new step of this process is dependent upon the last, etc. In this way, her model can be seen as an example of Thorstein Veblen's cumulative causation explanation. This is an explanation in which a firm, after a period of individual and social experimentation, produces a solution to a fairly general problem. Knowledge of this solution is subsequently stored in the firm by establishing a routine or behavioral rule etc., which is handed down by being absorbed into the pool of knowledge that a firm has accumulated. This subsequently enables the transmission of the solution from period to period. Several social researchers insist that the transmission mechanism in the social sciences is a cultural and not a gene transmission mechanism: that is, the knowledge that is stored is not passed on by the genes of the individual, but through what Dawkins (1976) describes as memes, Lumsden and Wilson (1981) denote as culturgen and Nelson and Winter (1982) denote as routines.(For interesting explanations of how firms or organizations remember, Winter (1991) and Walsh & Ungson (1991) should be consulted.) At each point the firm therefore carries a pool of knowledge concerning solutions to technical, organizational and market problems with it, which creates the prerequisites for its subsequent solution of even more complex problems. Solutions to new problems are once more integrated into new routines and subsequently incorporated into the established pool of idiosyncratic knowledge. In this sense Penrose can be said to have conceptualized the firm as a transmission or hereditary mechanism through which new knowledge will gradually be accumulated from period to period, and the competence of the organization will be expanded. Penrose's theory therefore focuses explicitly on the cumulative processes of growth and change through which a firm gradually attempts to build up its resources and capabilities over time. On this point the theory is also in agreement with Nelson & Winter's evolutionary research programme, and especially their analysis of the single firm as an historical entity whose present behavior can only be understood against the background of its specific or idiosyncratic course of development.

Penrose would probably have gone as far as to argue that only by analyzing the firm from an unfolding perspective is one capable of identifying the most important strategic and managerial dilemmas which the firm will face. In general, these problems could be described as an attempt to ensure the firm a sustainable growth process, that is, a growth process in which the firm avoids ending up with a too fragmentary knowledge structure which might contribute to undermining its more long-term resource and capability development.

More generally, Penrose's evolutionary perspective of the firm involves an implicit critique of the adaptationist paradigm on which both transaction cost theory and contingency theory are built. Gould & Lewontin (1984) consider the adaptationist paradigm to be characterized primarily by its atomistic research strategy. In biology, this strategy consists of studying a single organism by analyzing it as if it consisted of a number of independent and autonomous traits. That is, each part of an organism is assumed to have been formed in isolation by a selection process, so that the organism as the end product of this process is assumed to consist only of efficient and adaptive components or traits. In accordance with this adaptationist programme, social scientists analyze organizations as if they consisted of a set of independent and autonomous component parts, each of which is assumed to be formed by the selection mechanism and therefore converges into an efficient and well adapted form. That is, a perfect fit is assumed to emerge between the organizational structure and the environment in the long term.

When both Gould and Lewontin (1984) and knowledge-based theorists take a critical stance towards the adaptationist programme and its atomistic research strategy, the main reason for this is that the basic structure of an organization is assumed to be so integrated and subject to so many development constraints that there are very strict limits to the part that the selection mechanism can play in forming the single parts of an organization. Traditional selection stories will therefore, according to this point of view, have a very limited explanatory content, and the focus should rather be on how earlier architectural constraints within an organization will tend to freeze or limit its subsequent developmental path. Gould and Lewontin therefore conclude that:

> In a complex organism, early stages of ontogeny are remarkably refractory to evolutionary change, presumably because the differentiation of organ systems and their integration into a functioning body is such a delicate process so easily derailed by early errors with accumulating effects ... If development occurs in integrated packages and cannot be pulled apart piece by piece in evolution, then the adaptationist programme cannot explain the alteration of developmental programmes underlying nearly all changes of Baupläne. (1984: 266)

In an equivalent way, the knowledge-based theory of the firm assumes that a firm is bound by certain developmental constraints in its early phases of development, which may consist of a freezing of certain functions, roles, or specialization patterns, which may bring the organization into a course and therefore restrict its later course of development. Seen from the perspective of a more change-oriented and holistic type of analysis, as found in the knowledge-based theory of the firm, the adaptationist theories may therefore be criticized for focusing too much on the individual components of an organization. It has not, on the other hand, paid sufficient attention to the limitations to which a firm is subjected in its course of development, in respect of securing an integration of its component parts and in its ability to deliberately bind itself to constraints of this developmental nature. According to Gould and Lewontin (1984), the adaptationist paradigm, and its manifestation in the social sciences, functionalism, has therefore drawn our attention away from the important classical themes concerning the developmental constraints of organizations, and Baupläne, who has been studied by morphologists.

Edith Penrose's theory of the growth of the firm

One of the main assumptions of orthodox neoclassical price theory is that both the market structure and the number of products are exogenously given. It was by abandoning these assumptions that Penrose (1959) built her theory on a radically different view of the market system, much closer to Schumpeter's view than to the *Weltanschauung* of the Arrow-Debreu model. This necessitated a radically different conception of the firm.

As a pupil of Fritz Machlup, however, Edith Penrose was careful to emphasize that this new and very different conception of the firm was not constructed to solve traditional problems in economics of how prices are determined on different types of markets, but rather to study the growth processes of firms and their limits. In accordance with Fritz Machlup's conventionalist methodological conception of economics, Penrose emphasized that the formulation of a new research programme would necessitate the development of a new type of theory. Penrose therefore insisted that it would be completely legitimate to search for such a new conception of the firm, arguing that «little is gained by tortuously trying to force an adaptation of the (neoclassical) theory of the firm merely because it has proved to be a valuable concept for a different purpose» (1959: 14). Unlike the neoclassical conception of the firm as a production function that tells us how homogeneous units of production factors such as capital, labor, etc., may be transformed efficiently into output, Penrose argued for a conception of the firm as a collection of heterogeneous resources which can produce a broader or narrower set of productive services. As Penrose herself put it:

> It is the heterogeneity, and not the homogeneity, of the productive services available or potentially available from its resources that gives each firm its unique character. Not only can the personnel of a firm render a heterogeneous variety of unique services, but also the material resources of the firm can be used in different ways, which means that they can provide different kinds of services. (1959: 75)

By emphasizing the heterogeneity of firms as opposed to their homogeneity, Penrose, together with Armen Alchian (1950), relaunches what the biologist Ernst Mayr (1976) describes as a population perspective of firms and industries which, in economics, dates back to Alfred

Marshall. In Marshall's system, an industry was seen as a collection of heterogeneous firms whose knowledge base was idiosyncratic and which had reached different stages of development, but that could be studied using Marshall's construction of a representative agent. It was this perspective of firms and industries that was gradually replaced by what Mayr described as a typological perspective as the 1930s progressed, while the Walrasian method of analysis gradually displaced the Marshallian. According to the typological perspective, all firms in the same industry were regarded as fundamentally identical and interchangeable, in that the firms were assumed to have equal access to the same technological knowledge. There was not, therefore, any substantial difference between the firms in respect of their cost curves, demand conditions etc., which could explain why one firm held a competitive advantage over others within the same industry. The only difference that could be exploited by a firm to create such a competitive advantage was either that it was able to exploit certain economies of scale compared with its competitors or had positioned itself in markets where it could exploit entry barriers or other types of market imperfections. The dominance of this typological perspective in economics and its denial that firms within the same industry are fundamentally heterogeneous was probably one of the main reasons why the theory of the firm held so little sway over more normative-oriented research in strategic management.

Variations between firms within the same industry are therefore seen as an essential, not an incidental, feature of Penrose's theory. It is presumably also this theorizing around the heterogeneity of competing firms that is one of the main reasons why her theory of the growth of firms today attracts so much attention as a possible theoretical foundation for several new schools of strategic management in their attempt to clarify how a firm can have a sustainable competitive advantage over others.

Edith Penrose sees the firm as essentially a pool of productive resources $R_1, R_2, R_3 \ldots\ldots R_n$, stretching from purely physical resources such as machines, buildings, land, etc., to immaterial resources such as patents, licenses, etc. Given that a firm is in possession of such a pool of productive resources, heterogeneity between firms in the same industry is explained by the fact that they have accumulated different knowledge throughout their existence, which determines how efficient the firm is at exploiting its resources in order to get productive services from them. More recent contributions refer to this accumulated pool of knowledge within the firm of how to transform resources into services as the competence (Teece 1980, 1982), capabilities (Winter, 1987; Chandler, 1992 etc.) or the heuristics (Nelson & Winter, 1982) of the firm. This accumulated knowledge can only be imitated with great difficulty by other firms, which may be used to explain the idiosyncratic nature of the firm being the basis of its sustainable competitive advantage.

Yet what is the nature of the knowledge that, according to Penrose, explains the sustainable competitive advantage of one firm in relation to other firms within the same industry? It is important to answer this question because other theories of the firm, especially those working on the theory of incomplete contracts (Hart 1995), start with the basic assumption that a firm can only be identified by its physical assets, since the firm will only have residual rights of control over these and not over the knowledge that has been accumulated within the firm. According to the theory of incomplete contracts, the reason for this is that the firm's pool of knowledge is accumulated as human capital. The firm will therefore never have any direct control over this knowledge, since it is owned by the individual workers, who can always deny the firm access to it. On the other hand, the firm is in a position to exercise some authority over the work force, since the management can deny the work force access to the firm's physical resources.

A theorist such as Edith Penrose would probably not accept the view of the firm that is prevalent in the modern theory of incomplete contracts, since it operates within far too narrow a view of what knowledge is. It is in this connection that Penrose has introduced a distinction between objective knowledge and knowledge based on experience, where the difference between the two depends primarily upon the way in which the knowledge accumulated by the firm is transmitted or passed on from one period to the next. Objective knowledge can usually be transmitted in code form, that is, independently of specific individuals or groups of individuals via books, blueprints, etc., while knowledge based on experience is embodied in the capabilities, routines and competence of the firm, which is why the transmission can only proceed directly between teacher and pupil in the form of learning-by-doing processes.

A fundamental characteristic of knowledge based on experience is that it does not consist of human capital as embodied in a number of individuals, but of what Coleman (1988, 1990) describes as social capital, and Prescott and Visscher (1980) describe as organizational capital. That is, it is a form of immaterial capital that has emerged from long-term team work that typically consists of coordination norms based on experience, the development of roles that stabilize expectations and functions within an organization as well as other embodied organizational routines. The concept of knowledge as it is used in relation to the capabilities, competence and heuristics of an organization is therefore inherently complex, since it essentially involves the capacity of a plurality of resources or persons in the organization to do certain things. In her only case study of the Hercules Powder Company, Penrose argued that the growth of this firm had been limited by the experience it had managed to accumulate: «To the extent that limited opportunities in existing fields force firms to go into new ones, the rate of growth is retarded by the need for developing new bases and by the difficulties of expanding as a coordinated unit» (1960: 23).

As Sidney Winter (1987) has pointed out, it is the experience-based character of the firm's knowledge, as embodied in its capabilities and competence, that makes it difficult for other firms to imitate. That is, it is the fundamentally idiosyncratic nature of this knowledge that explains why certain firms have a competitive advantage over other firms. This experience-based knowledge will, unlike Penrose's objective knowledge, be of a tacit, nonarticulate, nonobservable, systemic and complex nature. As already indicated, it will be of great importance from the perspective of Penrose's theory to establish certain dimensions regarding the nature of knowledge, since these may be essential in order to characterize the knowledge base of a firm, and therefore understand its choice of strategies.

The growth processes of the firm, management resources and sustainable competitive advantage

Unlike several other research traditions in the area of the theory of the firm, Penrose insists that both the incentives and the limits to the growth of a firm are to be found within the firm and not in its environment. Unlike, for example, Adam Smith's thesis that the size of a firm will be restricted by the market for its products, Penrose's concept of the firm as a pool of resources implies that we should emphasize internal rather than external constraints on growth:

A firm is not confined to particular products or locations by the supply of resources or the demand for products in the market, and provided that there are profitable opportunities open for the use of further or different resources obtainable in the market, the fundamental limit to the productive opportunity of the firm cannot be found in external supply and demand conditions; we must look within the firm itself. (1959: 44)

If we wish to understand what it is that distinguishes Edith Penrose's view of the accumulation of a firm's resources, we must first examine which assumptions of orthodox neoclassical theory she is challenging. The main purpose of the neoclassical theory's static analyses has always been to investigate the conditions under which the productive opportunities of a firm will be limited. We therefore assume that a firm is in equilibrium if it can be demonstrated that no changes are taking place in its external environment or in its knowledge, and consequently in its range of productive services. These two assumptions ensure that rising marginal costs must set in at some point, placing upper limits on the growth of the firm.

According to Penrose, the problem with this concept of the firm is that economists generally have not been willing to carry out an explicit analysis of the concept of knowledge, and in this way consider the influence it may have had on several economic variables. Penrose comments on this anomaly as follows:

Economists have, of course, always recognized the dominant role that increasing knowledge plays in economic processes but have, for the most part, found that the whole subject of knowledge is too slippery to handle with even a moderate degree of precision, and have made little attempt to analyze the effect of changes in the traditional economic variables upon changes in knowledge. (1959: 77)

Penrose's argument is that the productive services that a firm yields as a by-product of its activities will depend on the knowledge that the firm and its employees possess. Unlike neoclassical theory, she assumes that this knowledge will show an almost automatic tendency to increase as a result of learning-by-doing and learning by using processes. A kind of self-reinforcing process takes place within most firms, which has the character of an in-built tendency towards knowledge accumulation, and involves an increase in the capacity of the firm to secure better use of its resources for productive purposes. According to Penrose, therefore, one of the most serious limitations of the neoclassical theory of the firm is that it overlooks the fact that knowledge is typically subject to increasing return to scale. Penrose considers that a knowledge-based theory of the firm would therefore also be a theory of endogenous growth.

> Once it is recognized that the very processes of operation and of expansion are intimately associated with a process by which knowledge is increased, then it becomes immediately clear that the productive opportunity of a firm will change even in the absence of any change in external circumstances or in fundamental technological knowledge. New opportunities will open up which did not exist at the time expansion plans were made. (1959: 56).

Penrose (1955, 1959) insists that it is especially management resources that determine the opportunities and limits for the growth of the firm. Some would object that if a firm is limited in its growth by the relatively scarce services produced by the internal management resources of the firm, these services could always be purchased on the open market as an alternative, in what resource theorists later described as a strategic factor market (Barney 1986; Dierick & Cool 1989). However, Penrose explains why this opportunity is not available, or is at least extremely limited:

> Existing managerial personnel provide services that cannot be provided by personnel newly hired from outside the firm, not only because they make up the administrative organization which cannot be expanded except by their own actions, but also because the experience they gain from working within the firm and with each other enables them to provide services that are uniquely valuable for the operations of the particular group with which they are associated. (1959: 46).

That is, it is as a consequence of the fact that the accumulation of knowledge and capabilities within a single firm depends on experience-based knowledge rather than formal knowledge that the growth of the firm cannot depend on external management resources via purchases on a strategic factor market. According to Penrose, this implies that the expansion of a firm will therefore only be limited by the pace at which the firm, through its accumulation of experience, is capable of providing new excess management services. This cumulative process by which the resources of a firm are gradually expanded forms the main focus of Penrose's theory of the firm. However, the theory also implies that the strategy choices of the individual firm are always restricted by its inherited pool of capabilities (for example, in respect of the markets the firm may attempt to enter). Consequently, the choices open to a firm at a specific point in time will always depend on its previous accumulated knowledge.

Meanwhile, what course will the gradual accumulation of management resources and the provision of excess management services take? Seen from the point of view of the individual decision-maker, the process takes the following course: a firm must initially expend a great deal of time and energy solving management problems, but as its experience in dealing with these problems grows they are in fact increasingly solved by developing skills and routines. Explicit, articulated problem-solving is therefore gradually replaced by more automatic procedures which are increasingly based on tacit knowledge. The conversion of such management problems into routines, capabilities and heuristics will itself enable the gradual release of new management services, which allows decision-makers to focus their attention on new management tasks. In this way decision-makers are gradually able to expand their repertoire with new capabilities, developing the ability of the heuristic to deal with new problems. On the organizational level, therefore, the gradual release of new resources can lead to greater efficiency in solving coordination problems after an initial period of trial and error learning. This may result in the development of new types of social behavior which stabilize expectations, enabling the decision-makers to economize on their rather limited decision-making resources. When these social rules gradually develop into more or less subconscious routines, they are finally incorporated into the firm's heuristic. As Penrose puts it:

> When men have become used to working in a particular group of other men, they become individually and as a group more valuable to the firm in that the services they can render are enhanced by their knowledge of their fellow workers, of the methods of the firm, and of the best way of doing things in the particular set of circumstances in which they are working. (1959: 52)

As a firm ages it becomes more effective in dealing with its internal and external coordination problems. In order to capitalize on this learning process and the solutions the organization discovers over time, a formalization process is initiated. This can involve the establishment of standard operating procedures, the establishing of routines, the standardization of communication and the development of specialist functions which are intended to solve recurrent problems. The prerequisite of this process is that more complex problems can be broken up into smaller ones, which also enables the delegation of tasks and responsibility within the organization, etc. This formalization process is therefore a condition as well as a result of the growth process of the firm.

New firms will typically perceive their environment as chaotic and variable, since they have no experience of problems; and have not yet established any routines for dealing with them. Nor have they learnt to distinguish between important and unimportant problems. On the other hand, older organizations will usually have learnt to ignore unimportant problems and will have developed routines for solving more regularly occurring problems. They will therefore perceive their environment as more stable and predictable than younger, less experienced organizations. It is therefore the purpose of the formalization process to store solutions to the problems of a firm from one period to the next, and incorporate solutions into future, more complex situations, thus enabling the accumulation of experience in the firm. The formalization of solutions to the problems of a firm naturally results in a certain behavioral inertia and inflexibility. This is, however, a necessary prerequisite if the firm is to be at all capable of releasing new management resources for the accumulation of experience and gradually expanding the firm's choice set.

The internal growth of the firm, loss of management control and the coherence of the firm

What happens when the pace of a firm's growth exceeds that permitted by the gradual creation and releasing of management services within the organization? In these instances it may be expected that a strategic loss of control will occur, as described in the strategy literature. At the level of the individual decision-maker these losses might manifest themselves in such a way that decision-makers find it more and more difficult to find adequate solutions to the decision-making problems with which they are confronted. That is, a widening of what Heinar (1983) calls a competence-difficulty gap. At the social or organizational levels, these losses of control can take the form of tendencies towards lacking cohesion and integration in the organization, whereby uncertainty is created regarding rules for social behavior as well as concerning their domains.

We have already seen how a gradual accumulation of experience within a firm eventually enables the release of excess management services, which subsequently create the conditions for new growth and the release of new resources, etc. The question posed by Edith Penrose in this respect is to what extent growth processes also lead to efficient results?

To answer this question Penrose considers it necessary to introduce a number of new concepts such as economies of expansion, which in a more dynamic analysis are the equivalent of the traditional concept of economies of scale in orthodox production theory. The necessity of introducing this new concept is primarily a consequence of the fact that Penrose's theory is anchored in neither a traditional equilibrium nor a functional model, but instead in a endogenous growth perspective. She does not therefore focus so much on the end result that a process must lead to, but rather on the growth process itself. This is in turn a direct implication of the fact that she does not actually want to answer the question of what determines the absolute size of a firm, but rather the question of what it is that sets the limits of its growth. Penrose defines these economies of expansion as:

> The internal economies available to an individual firm which make expansion profitable in particular directions. They are derived from the unique collection of productive services available to it, and create for that firm a differential advantage over other firms in putting on the market new products or increased quantities of old products. At any time the availability of such economies is the result of the process, ... by which unused productive services are continually created within the firm. (1959: 99)

Economies of expansion are therefore totally dependent upon the productive resources available to a firm, and their exploitation can be completely independent of how large a firm is. Penrose therefore insists that there is a paradox here:

> The growth of firms may be consistent with the most efficient use of society's resources; the result of a past growth – the size attained at any time – may have no corresponding advantages. Each successive step in its growth may be profitable to the firm and, if otherwise under-utilized resources are used, ad-

> vantageous to society. But once any expansion is completed,
> the original justification for the expansion may fade into in-
> significance as new opportunities for growth develop and are
> acted upon. (1959: 103)

That is, the advantages which were originally the prerequisite of starting
the growth process will therefore tend to disappear when the firm has
grown large. Although each stage of this process can be considered optimal in isolation, this is in no way a guarantee that the final result of the
whole process will be optimal. We are therefore confronted with an
intertemporal decision-making problem, in which decisions made on a
case-by-case basis can lead us into a time-inconsistency problem. That
is, if we choose the best solution within every single period, such a case-
by-case response might lead to a suboptimal result. In an economic context this might mean that new problems are only solved in an ad hoc
way, and that the organizational structure will therefore tend to frag-
ment, which makes the coordination of the single parts of the organization more and more difficult.

From this perspective the problem is one of finding a strategy which
ensures a reasonable balance between static efficiency, understood as
the exploitation of the existing resources of the firm, on the one hand,
and on the other, dynamic efficiency, which focuses on the development
of the resources or capabilities of the firm. Every new activity that is
commenced within the firm must therefore be evaluated according to
whether it will tend to block or promote the future growth of the firm in
respect of the cumulative development of its capabilities. In some of the
more recent literature on strategic management, firms are advised to ensure balanced growth, in which the coherence of the organization is put
in focus in order to avoid its fragmentation. Strategic management can
therefore be said to imply that the firm should abstain from more short-
sighted or myopic case-by-case strategies, but should be tied to developmental constraints which should ensure the building-up of an integrating core competence.

An almost identical interpretation of Penrose's theory of the ideal
growth process of the firm is constructable on the basis of J.G. March's
(1991) discussion of how a firm should try to balance exploitation (of
existing resources) and exploration (learning new capabilities and creating new resources). As stressed by Penrose herself, and further emphasized by Levinthal and March (1993), such balancing is very difficult to
sustain. The reason is the existence of self-reinforcing processes which

undermine the possibilities of maintaining the same balance. Thus, in some cases, a firm is trapped by its success, reinforcing its exploitation of existing resources. As a result, any attempt of explorative search is suppressed and may finally stop, reducing the firm's long-term possibilities of survival. In other cases, the firm will end up in a failure trap, that is, explorative activities are self-reinforcing and lead to an endless cycle of failures.

Normative strategic implications of Penrose's theory: the firm's diversification pattern

One of the most important questions to arise from Penrose's theory is what determines a firm's pattern of diversification. As we have seen, her theory is distinct from neoclassical theory in that it does not assume that the products of a firm are given, but something partly determined by the productive resources of a firm and partly by the knowledge it has accumulated concerning the exploitation of these resources. As Penrose views the firm as a pool of resources that can be exploited in several different ways, but whose capabilities are also subject to certain constraints at any point, her theory appears to be ideally suited to answering the question of what determines and constrains a firm's diversification pattern.

It is partly because of this view of the firm that Penrose's theory is perceived today as one of the most important alternatives to Michael Porter's (1980) understanding of strategic management, which is based on a more conventional market-power conception as the foundation of the firm's competitive advantage. Penrose challenged this view of competition as early as 1959, in favor of a more Schumpeterian dynamic efficiency view in which a more important role is attributed to the position of a firm's resources than to its position in the market:

> A firm may attempt to entrench itself by destroying or preventing effective competition by means of predatory competitive practices or restrictive monopolistic devices that relieves it of the necessity of either meeting or anticipating serious competitive threats to its position ... Even when the firm exploits to the fullest possible extent the opportunities for monopolistic gain available to it, the protection afforded, though often extensive, can neither be complete nor absolute certain. For many, if not most firms, the more effective long run pro-

> tection both against direct competition as well against the in-
> direct competition of new products will lie in the firm's ability
> to anticipate, or at least to match, threatening innovations in
> processes, products, and marketing techniques. In a society
> characterized by a widespread «spirit of enterprise» and a
> highly developed technology, the threat of competition from
> new products, new techniques, new channels of distribution,
> new ways of influencing consumer demand, is in many ways
> a more important influence on the conduct of existing pro-
> ducers than any other kind of competition. (1959: 113)

Whereas Michael Porter's (1980) theory of strategic management
started from the Structure-Conduct-Performance paradigm with its relatively static conception of competition, Penrose's theory has been
based on a more Schumpeterian and therefore more dynamic conception of competition. While Porter has tended in this way to see the competitiveness of the firm as a result of its market position, knowledge-
based theorists have claimed that the causal relationship was the exact
opposite. That is, if some firms within an industry were doing well, the
reason for this was not their market position, but rather their internal
resources and accumulated capabilities.

In her case study of the Hercules Powder Company, Penrose explicitly
argues that the growth of this firm has not been restricted by the market
opportunities that were available to the firm, but rather by the ability of
the firm to exploit these opportunities with its existing resources:

> If the growth of the firm has been restrained by a «lack» of
> profitable opportunities for expansion, this merely reflects
> the lack of entrepreneurial confidence in the profitability for
> Hercules of areas of activity with which the officials of the
> firm are insufficiently familiar. Since a «technological base»
> consists not of buildings, kettles, and tubes, but of the expe-
> rience and know-how of personnel, the basic restriction
> comes down to the services available from existing personnel.
> (1960: 22)

An important implication of this is that, while Porter's conception of
strategy has largely been more short-sighted and directed towards the
external market behavior of the firm, Penrose has focused on the long-
term strategic outlook of the firm and especially on the development of

its internal resources. Market opportunities only exist for a firm if it has built up adequate capabilities within the firm to be able to take advantage of them. That is, if the firm can secure an attractive market position with its existing resources. Furthermore, Penrose's theory is different from Porter's in that it not only discusses strategy at business unit level but also at corporate level.

The importance of Penrose's contribution within the current debate on strategic management is considered below, focusing particularly on the discussion of what constitutes reasonable or less reasonable diversification strategy. In accordance with her knowledge-based view, Penrose sees the growth of firms as quite narrow in relation to the process whereby new knowledge is produced. The endogenously generated accumulation of experience that continuously takes place within the framework of the firm must therefore be seen as a process by which the firm gradually acquires the capability of expanding the area of its production opportunities by continuously creating new capabilities that enable the generation of new productive services. Unlike neoclassical production theory, but in accordance with evolutionary theory, it is the productive or technological base that a firm has created that determines its current diversification pattern and limits the directions of its future growth.

Firms that find themselves in a strong selection regime must therefore expect to be compelled to expend large resources in order to maintain and expand their existing competitiveness. In such a situation it must therefore be expected that the firm will prefer to invest in depth rather than in breadth, which if all things remain equal will tend towards the firm placing a higher priority on a related, as opposed to an unrelated, diversification strategy:

> A firm may go into many fields, but to maintain itself against competitive pressures it must be prepared to continue putting new funds into each field. This need for continuous new investment will restrict the number of fields a firm can support at any given time. The further from its existing areas of specialization it goes, the greater the effort required of the firm to attain the necessary competence not only in dealing with present production and market conditions, but also in making the adaptations and innovations necessary to keep up with competition. (Penrose, 1959: 134)

This implies that the firm will always prefer a related to an unrelated diversification profile from a strategic point of view. That is, it will prefer what is commonly referred to as «stick to your knitting» strategy in the literature of strategic management. However, sometimes it can be difficult to determine from outside what a related or an unrelated diversification strategy is, if we start as Penrose does with the resource position of a firm rather than with its market or product position:

> Yet if one examines closely the established firms with a long history of successful growth, and in particular, the genesis of their product diversification, one will find that their strength lies in the fact that they have established and maintained a basic position with respect to the use of certain types of resources and technology and the exploitation of certain types of market. (1959: 137-8)

An even more important conclusion of Penrose's theory is perhaps that every firm is limited in respect to how quickly it can diversify and acquire firms in new fields of operation. Therefore, if its growth is too fast in too many and too weakly related areas, seen in relation to the existing resource position and knowledge base of the firm, this involves a risk of undermining the competitive advantage of the firm in its already established area of specialization and will, in the long-term, threaten the very existence of the firm. Diversification into new areas should therefore take the form of careful experimentation with and development of new resources, which must not proceed faster than excess management resources can be released within the firm. These strategic instructions are a direct implication of the fact that Penrose's theory is concerned with the limits of the growth of the firm, and not with explaining its absolute size. This, in turn, is a consequence of the fact that the theory is anchored in an endogenous growth perspective rather than an equilibrium model.

Particularly in the cases where a firm grows by quickly acquiring new firms, there will be, according to Penrose (1959), a trade-off between the speed of a firm's expansion and the maintenance of effective management coordination of its constituent parts. That is, in periods of expansion through takeovers of other businesses, the firm will experience threats to, or even the collapse of, its integration or coherence. This would be the case if the acquisitions are large and can only be absorbed with great difficulty into the existing structure of the firm. To explain this, Penrose distinguished between firms which have the character of holding companies and mainly consist of financial holdings, and industrial types of firm in which there should be a high degree of administrative coordination between its constituent parts. It is especially in the building up of the first of these types, according to Penrose, the empire-builder tends to sacrifice coordination and consolidation to the pace of expansion. It is this that brings his activities closer to those of the «financier» than to those of the «industrialist» ... (1959: 189). Similarly, Dosi, Teece and Winter (1992) refer to the existence of so-called hollow corporations, whose main characteristic is that they no longer have any core competence, and therefore must be expected to disappear when there is a shift from a weak to a strong selection regime.

More recent experiences with growth through related and unrelated diversification

Especially during the 1960s and the early 1970s, the United States was, like some other industrialized economies, characterized by one of the largest waves of mergers and acquisitions so far. The number of mergers and acquisitions rose from approximately 2,000 in 1965 to 6,000 in 1969. Behind these acquisitions and the creations of large conglomerates was a belief in management mastering general capabilities and skills not requiring concrete experience with the individual firm's technology, products or market conditions. Therefore, everything else being equal, the most optimal situation would be if larger firms acquired small and medium-sized firms as the former had, or were able to attract, the best managers. At this point, the stock markets reflected trust in such general managers being capable of allocating scarce capital between the individual business units and thus diversify risk adequately.

However, during the 1980s it became increasingly clear that these arguments did not hold. A series of studies demonstrated that more focused and less diversified firms did better. Such scholars as Wernerfelt and Montgomery (1988), found that more focused firms in general scored higher on Tobin's q than more diversified firms. (Tobin's q is defined as the ratio between a firm's market value and the replacement value of its assets. Tobin's q is thus a measurement for the value created in a firm.) Against this, Alfred Chandler (1990) argued in *Scale and Scope. The Dynamics of Industrial Capitalism*:

> Such unprecedented diversification created another new phe-
> nomenon in the evolution of the managerial industrial enter-
> prise: it often led to a separation, that is, a breakdown of com-
> munications, between top management at the corporate office
> – the executives responsible for coordinating, managing, and
> planning and allocating resources for the enterprise as a whole
> – and the middle managers who were responsible for main-
> taining the competitive capabilities of the operating divisions
> in the battle for market share and profits. (1990: 623)

Chandler gave two reasons for this breakdown of communications or
loss of control. First, top management in the large divisionalized headquarters often had too little product-specific knowledge of or experience
with the acquired firms or divisions. As a result, they experienced it as
increasingly difficult to compare the investment plans of single divisions. Second, the large number of acquisitions implied that many of the
largest firms' headquarters not merely were to allocate resources among
10 or, at worst, 25 divisions, as was the case before the Second World
War, but now had to have specific knowledge of 40-70 divisions and in
some cases more. As a consequence, headquarters were turned into hierarchies, groups of divisions were each managed by their vice director,
who had a staff of employees to assist him. Thus, the management in
many headquarters no longer had direct and trust-based contact with
the managers of the individual divisions but had to make their decisions
based almost exclusively on impersonal statistical data.

According to Chandler (1990), the major consequence of the acquisitions in the 1960s was that «top managers were beginning to lose the
capabilities needed to maintain a unified enterprise whose whole was
more than the sum of its parts» (1990: 623-4). That is, due to its deficient knowledge of the individual units' products, technologies and
markets, top management found it increasingly difficult to address its
function as internal capital market and hence secure the coherence of
the firm. This was, in part, a consequence of cross-divisional comparisons making it increasingly difficult to prioritize the business units' investment projects, and in part due to the fact that only to a limited extent did they succeed in exploiting the synergy effects, or the co-specialization of assets, which was the rationale behind having different product areas and competence areas in the same organization.

The consequence of the deficient knowledge of the management in
multidivision firms also questioned their ability to function effectively as

internal capital markets and secure a reasonably degree of coherence between the firm's various business units. In the late 1970s and the early
1980s, a vast increase in sell-offs succeeded the previous wave of mergers
and acquisitions. An increase so dramatic that some banks and financial
institutions, which had earlier established mergers and acquisitions departments, now hired so-called deconglomeration experts. In many cases, the sell-offs were initiated by the companies themselves as the majority of the acquisitions proved unprofitable (Ravenkraft & Scherer, 1987).
In other cases, conglomerate companies were subject to hostile takeovers and then stripped: that is, the previous incoherent conglomerates
were reorganized into homogeneous units, more appropriate from a resource perspective. Only this way was it possible to reestablish the firms'
internal capital markets on the condition, however, that top management
had sufficient specific knowledge about the individual divisions to handle
resource allocation better than the capital market.

The modern resource-based theory

Just as Ronald Coase's article «The Nature of the Firm» from 1937 did
not attract much attention until the 1970s, Edith Penrose's resource-
based theory from the 1950s seems to have a similar renaissance during
the 1980s and the 1990s. Important contributions to this are Wernerfelt
(1984), Lippman and Rumelt (1982), Rumelt (1984), Barney (1986;
1991) and Dierickx and Cool (1989). However, as pointed out by Foss,
Knudsen and Montgomery (1995), there seems to be a series of major
differences between Penrose's own contributions and later contributions to the resource-based theory. Penrose's key explanandum was the
single firm and its growth pattern, whereas contemporary resource theorists have shifted focus from the single firm to the market level. The key
question to which they have tried to find an answer is how the individual
firm within an industry can keep on making above normal profits in the
long run. Contemporary resource-based theory can, thus, be characterized as an equilibrium theory of industries of heterogeneous firms. Even
though one changes analytical level from the firm to the market by primarily wishing to explain why market competition does not eliminate
above-normal profits, contemporary resource-based theory is still based
on Penrose's view of the firm.

Already in 1974, Richard Rumelt demonstrated that variations in
profits within the same industry were greater than profitability variations between industries. The implication of this result was that it be-

came increasingly difficult to sustain the implicit assumptions of the Structure Conduct Performance-paradigm that firms in the same industry were fundamentally uniform. According to this typological view of systems, sustained competitive advantages, or above-normal profits could only be explained by certain firms having been able to position themselves within more attractive industries of high entrance barriers. Against this, proponents of the resource-based theory argued that the reason for a firm's sustained competitive advantages was not its market position but rather its resource position (Wernerfelt, 1984). Thus, the explanation of above normal profits changed from an external, market power explanation to an internal, efficiency explanation.

Therefore, the major problem of contemporary resource-based theory has been to explain why competition between firms in an industry does not eliminate all above normal profits, as, the theory of perfect competition assumes. According to Lippmann and Rumelt (1982), a series of mechanisms make it difficult for less successful firms to imitate the more successful ones. These imitation barriers make it possible to sustain heterogeneity and variation between firms within the same industry. At firm level, such isolation mechanisms correspond to the SCP-paradigm's entry barriers at industry level and to mobility barriers at industry-group level. And the underlying explanation of these imitation barriers is the causal ambiguity, that is, there is a basic uncertainty about the nature of the causal relations between action and outcome. Concretely, such causal ambiguity implies that less successful firms will be unable to uncover why a successful firm makes above-normal profits and thus replicate its behavioral pattern.

According to Reed and Defilippi (1990) causal ambiguity can be explained in terms of two factors. First, the competence, capabilities and heuristics applied by the firm to exploit its various resources aimed to produce services or products are often tacit knowledge. Thus, a firm may know how to exploit various resources without necessarily being able to articulate this knowledge, that is, converting know-how knowledge into know-that knowledge and thus eliminate causal ambiguity. Even though the element of tacit knowledge always is reducible, it can never be completely eliminated as Hayek points out: «... all we can talk about and probably all we can consciously think about presupposes the existence of a ... system of rules which operates us but which we can neither state nor form an image of» 1978: 62).

Second, a firm's ability to perform certain activities will be characterized by causal ambiguity because the firm's capabilities, or competence, are complex. As it appeared from Penrose's knowledge-based theory, a firm's capabilities must always be understood as the result of an historical process of which the first, simple activity constituted the building block for the subsequent more complex activities. Thus, performing such a complex activity will always depend on an underlying capability to combine various single activities to form a coherent and complex pattern. As Rumelt (1995) formulates it: «The general viewpoint adopted here is that competencies are hierarchical in structure and exist in *layers*, the existence of a higher layer being dependent upon competent execution of lower layers ... Returning to the firm, one could define skills in layer 1 as being basic manufacturing operations, selling activities, etc. Layer 2 might then be defined as the condition of these skills into a coherent business. Layer 3 would then be the coordination among related businesses and layer 4 the adaption of this pattern to local conditions throughout the world» (1995: 128). And exactly because of the complex and cumulative nature of the capabilities it will not be immediately possible for competitors to imitate this.

In keeping with this, a further development of Penrose's resource-based theory must include the modeling of the firm's growth process as a cumulative and complex process.

References

Alchian, A. (1950): Uncertainty, Evolution and Economic Theory. *Journal of Political Economy 58*: 211-221.

Alchian, A. & H. Demsetz (1972): Production, Information Costs and Economic Organization. *Quarterly Journal of Economics 63(5):* 777-795.

Barney, J.B. (1986): Strategic Factor Markets. *Management Science 32*: 1231-1241.

Barney, J.B. (1991): Firm Resources and Sustained Competitive Advantage. *Journal of Management 17:* 99-120.

Bhaskar, R. (1975): *A Realist Theory of Science.* Leeds: Leeds Book Ltd.

Chandler, A. (1990): *Scale and Scope. The Dynamics of Industrial Capitalism.* Cambridge, MA: Harvard University Press.

Chandler, A. (1992): Organizational Capabilities and the Economic History of the Industrial Enterprise. *Journal of Economic Perspectives 6*: 79-100.

Coase, R.H. (1937): The Nature of Firm. *Economica 4:* 386-406.

Coleman, J.S. (1988): Social Capital in the Creation of Human Capital. *American Journal of Sociology 94*: 95-120.

Coleman, J.S. (1990): *Foundation of Social Theory.* Cambridge, MA: Harvard University Press.

Dawkins, R. (1976): *The Selfish Gene.* New York: Oxford University Press.

Dierickx, I. & K. Cool (1989): Asset Stock Accumulation and Sustainability of Competitive Advantage. *Management Science 35*: 1504-1511.

Dosi, G., D. Teece & S.G. Winter (1992): Toward a Theory of Corporate Coherence: Preliminary Remarks. In G. Dosi, R. Giannetti and P.A. Toninelli (eds.): *Technology and Enterprise in a Historical Perspective.* Oxford: Clarendon Press.

Foss, N.J., C. Knudsen & C.A. Montgomery (1995). An Exploration of Common Ground: Integrating Evolutionary and Strategic Theories of the Firm. In C. Montgomery (ed.): *Resource-Based and Evolutionary Theories of the Firm: Towards a Synthesis.* Boston: Kluwer.

Gould, S.J. & R. Lewontin (1984): The Spandrels of San Marcos and the Panglossian Paradigm: A Critique of the Adaptionist Programme. In E. Sober (ed.) (1984): *Conceptual Issues in Evolutionary Biology.* Cambridge, MA: Bradfords Books, 252-270.

Hart, O. (1995): *Firms' Contracts and Financial Structure.* Oxford: Clarendon Press.

Hayek, F.A. (1978): *New Studies in Philosophy, Politics, Economics, and the History of Ideas.* Chicago: University of Chicago Press.

Heinar, R. (1983): The Origin of Predictable Behavior. *American Economic Review 73*: 560-595.

Levinthal, D.A. & J.G. March (1993): The Myopia of Learning. *Strategic Management Journal 14*: 95-112.

Lippman, S.A. & R.P. Rumelt (1982): Uncertain Imitability: An Analysis of Interfirm Differences in Efficiency under Competition. *Bell Journal of Economics 13*: 418-438.

Lumsden, C.J. & E.O. Wilson (1981): *Genes, Mind and Culture: The Coevolutionary Process.* Cambridge, MA: Harvard University Press.

March, J.G. (1991): Exploration and Exploitation in Organizational Learning. *Organization Science 2*: 71-87.

Mayr, E. (1976): *Evolution and the Diversity of Life.* Cambridge, MA: Harvard University Press.

McCloskey, D. (1985): *The Rhetoric of Economics.* Madison, WI: University of Wisconsin Press.

Moore, J. (1992): The Firm as a Collection of Assets. *European Economic Review 36*: 493-507.

Montgomery (1988): Diversification, Ricardian rents, and Tobin's *RAND Journal of Economics, Vol 19:* 623-632.

Nelson, R. & S. Winter (1982): *An Evolutionary Theory of Economic Change.* Cambridge, MA: Harvard University Press.

Penrose, E.T. (1952): Biological Analogies in the Theory of the Firm. *American Economic Review 52*: 804-819.

Penrose, E.T. (1953): Rejoinder. *American Economic Review 43*: 603-609.

Penrose, E.T. (1955): Limits to the Growth and Size of Firms. *American Economic Review, Papers and Proceedings 45:* 531-543.

Penrose, E.T. (1959): *The Theory of the Growth of the Firm.* Oxford: Oxford University Press (2nd edition 1995).

Penrose, E.T. (1960): The Growth of the Firm, a Case Study: The Hercules Powder Company. *Business History Review 34*: 1-23.

Porter, M. (1980): *Competitive Strategy: Techniques for Analyzing Industries and Competitors.* New York: The Free Press.

Presscott, E.C. & M. Visscher (1980): Organizational Capital. *Journal of Political Economy 80*: 446-461.

Ravenskraft, D.J., & F.M. Scherer (1987): *Mergers, Sell-offs and Economic Efficiency*. Washington, DC: Brooking Institution.

Reed, R. & R.J. DeFilippi (1990): Causal Ambiguity, Barriers to Imitation and Sustainable Competitive Advantage. *Academy of Management Review 15:* 88-102.

Rumelt, R. (1974): *Strategy, Structure and Performance* Division of Research. Harvard Business School, Boston, Ma.

Rumelt, R. (1984): Towards a Strategic Theory of the Firm. In R.B. Lamb (ed.): *Competitive Strategic Management*. Englewood Cliffs, NJ: Prentice-Hall: 556-570.

Rumelt, R. (1995): Inertia and Transformation. In C.A. Montgomery (ed.): *Resource-Based and Evolutionary Theories of the Firm: Towards a Synthesis*. Boston: Kluwer Academic Publishers.

Teece (1980): Economics of Scope and the Scope of the Enterprise. *Journal of Economic Behavior and Organization Vol 1:* 223-247.

Teece, D.J. (1982): An Economic Theory of Multiproduct Firms. *Journal of Economic Behavior and Organization 3:* 39-63

Walsh, J.P. & G.R. Ungson (1991): Organizational Memory. *Academy of Management Review 16*: 57-91.

Wernerfelt; B. (1984): A Resource-based View of Firms. *Strategic Management Journal 5:* 171-181.

Wernerfelt, B. & C.A. Montgomery (1988): Tobin's q and the Importance of Focus in Firm Performance. *American Economic Review 78(1)*: 246-250.

Williamson, O.E. (1975): *Markets and Hierarchies*. New York: The Free Press.

Winter, S.G. (1982): An Essay on the Theory of Production. In S.H. Hyman (ed.): *Economics and the World around It*. Ann Arbor: University of Michigan Press.

Winter, S.G. (1987): Knowledge and Competence as Strategic Assets. In D.J. Teece (ed.): *The Competitive Challenge: Strategies for Industrial Innovation and Renewal*. Cambridge: Ballinger: 159-184.

Winter (1991): «Survival, Selection, and Inheritance in Evolutionary Theories of Organization» in J.V. Singh (ed): *Organizational Evolution: New Directions*. London: Sage.

Witt, U. (1991): Reflection on the Present State of Evolutionary Economic Theory. In G.M. Hodgson & E. Screpanti (eds.): *Rethinking Economics. Markets, Technology and Economic Evolution*. Aldershot: Edward Elgar, Gower House.

Firm Resources and Capabilities: A Renewed Focus for Strategic Management[1]

Bo Eriksen

An emerging research program in strategy content research is the resource-based view of the firm. This may eventually become an important research focus for research on strategic management. The resource-based view of the firm draws its intellectual roots from the works of Penrose (1959), Chandler (1962) and, to a certain extent, the early business policy scholars such as Andrews (1971). The resource-based model has, by some authors, been termed a strategic theory of the firm (Rumelt, 1984; Conner, 1991) and shows much promise of becoming a cornerstone of a theory of the firm that is unique to the field of strategic management. To a certain extent, the resource-based view of the firm marks a renewed focus upon the firm's distinctive capabilities, a focus shared with the early business policy scholars, but within a more rigorous framework.

This paper reviews some of the literature and draws some implications for the formulation of business strategies. An attempt is made to operationalize the concept of firm resources and capabilities. The potential for developing a resource-based theory of the firm is also discussed. The main argument of the paper concerns the desirable properties of valuable resources. It is suggested that the firm's competitiveness rests upon the control of scarce resources and capabilities that are difficult to imitate or substitute. The desired characteristics of the resources and capabilities that may give the firm competitive advantage are those

1. I acknowledge most valuable comments from Associate Professor Laurids Hedaa, Management Research Institute, Copenhagen Business School; Professor Børge Obel and Assistant Professor Carsten Koch, Department of Management, Odense University; Assistant Professor Nicolai Juul Foss, Associate Professor Christian Knudsen and Jesper Mikkelsen, Institute of Economics and Strategy, Copenhagen Business School, Denmark.

of a high degree of asset specificity, of complexity, a high productive capacity and a high degree of flexibility.

The resource-based view of the firm

Much recent research in the strategy content literature focuses on the economics of strategy and borrows many analytical tools from microeconomics. The dominant line of research in the economics of strategy draws its intellectual roots from the neoclassical theory of the firm, the structure-conduct-performance paradigm in industrial organization and the new industrial organization. The most prominent articulation of this comes from Porter (1980) who proposed an approach to formulating competitive strategies which is based on the structure-conduct-performance link. Building upon this premise, and with the industry as the unit of analysis, Porter's (1980) five forces framework tends to underemphasize the important role that the firm's unique resources and capabilities may have as a source of competitive advantage. Industry analysis focuses: «... on the *what*, rather than the *why*, of competitive advantage» (Hamel, 1991: 4). That is, the focus is mainly on the status quo of the market positions of the incumbents within a given industry. The main criticism of the structure-conduct-performance view is that the proposed chain of causality views market structure as an effect, rather as an outcome.

The firm in the neoclassical theory of the firm in many ways does not resemble the real-world firm. The real-world firm often operates in many product markets, and the firm changes over time, for example, through internal growth or by merger. Thus the real-world firm seldom experiences the restrictive and static conditions of the neoclassical theory of the firm. In the resource-based view, firms are viewed as essentially heterogeneous, and the firm's endowment of resources and capabilities is seen as the source of its competitive advantage, and therefore as the main source of economic rents. In this respect, the resource-based view of the firm is somewhat related to the views of early scholars in business policy who asserted that competitive advantage grows out of the firm's distinctive competence (Andrews, 1971). However, the basic assumptions between the early view and the resource-based view differ somewhat, and the resource-based view offers a more rigorous analysis of the properties that resources should exhibit in order to generate sustainable economic rents.

As a response to the limitations of the neoclassical theory of the firm, Penrose (1959) set out to formulate a theory of the growth of firms that recognized that the firm is continuously changing, and many resources are deployed in several product markets. She defined the firm as: «... more than an administrative unit; it is also a collection of productive resources, the disposal of which between different uses and over time is determined by administrative decision» (Penrose, 1959/1972: 24). This definition is, by and large, the basic premise of the resource-based view of the firm: that the firm is a collection of idiosyncratic and heterogeneous resources and resource conversion mechanisms under managerial discretion (Rumelt, 1984).

The important point is that the firm's resource endowment determines which strategies the firm is able to pursue in the product market. According to Wernerfelt (1984):

> Resources and products are two sides of the same coin. Most products require the services of many resources, and most resources can be used in several products. By specifying the size of the firm's activity in different markets, it is possible to infer the minimum necessary resource commitments. Conversely, by specifying a resource profile for a firm, it is possible to find the optimal product-market activities. (p. 171)

The resource-based approach has mostly been concerned with theoretical work, and applied work is more scarce. The most prominent area of applied work is that of corporate diversification strategy, but the resource-based view has also been applied in the case of multinational corporations and the case of intangible resources. The main problem of the resource-based view is that little is known about what valuable resources are and their sources.

What are resources and capabilities?

Penrose (1959) defines the firm's resources as the basic inputs into the production process. This equals resources with factors of production. According to Wernerfelt (1984), the resources of the firm can be defined as assets controlled by the firm; more precisely, «... as those (tangible and intangible) assets which are tied semipermanently to the firm» (p. 172). Such factors as the firm's knowledge base, which is intangible and difficult to articulate and codify, may also be considered a resource for the firm (Dierickx & Cool, 1989; Winter, 1987). Such authors as Rubin (1973) define a resource as «... a fixed input which enables the firm to perform a particular task.» (p. 937). Further, as De Gregori (1987) emphasizes, it may be inappropriate to view resources as fixed, since resources are created and more often than not change during the course of time as a consequence of technological and organizational improvements. This point was also emphasized by Penrose (1959) in her analysis of the growth of firms. By performing a set of activities repeatedly, firms, in a learning-by-doing manner, become increasingly able to perform these tasks, and then create excess resources that are available for further expansion.

Resources and capabilities are strongly interrelated. For practical purposes, there may be little value in distinguishing between resources and capabilities, as the line between the two seems quite blurred. In order to distinguish between the two, capabilities may be thought of as the ability to organize teams of resources for productive activities, whereas resources may be viewed more as the basic inputs to the activities in question (Grant, 1991). This definition of capabilities is close to the notion of core competence that has been proposed by Hamel and Prahalad, (1990).

The starting point for identifying the firm's resources is a very broad general classification of resources. Grant (1990) offers a more detailed classification of resources where six classes are offered: financial resources, physical resources, human resources, technological resources, reputation and organizational resources. The technological resources may be patents, trade secrets etc., while reputation may exist in the form of brand names or a reputation for good customer service. The organizational resources may be exemplified by the collective capabilities and tacit knowledge that exist in an organization. To Grant's (1991) classification may be added information resources (Itami & Roehl, 1987); for example, superior information about customer needs, provided by maintaining close relationships with key customer groups, may improve the efficiency with which a firm serves its customers.

Capabilities are clearly important for a firm's competitiveness, since these are often more difficult to develop, substitute, or imitate, and as this process takes time and capital and is somewhat uncertain.

The firm's resources and capabilities may be seen as the building blocks of its competitive advantage. Such mainstream strategy theory as Porter's (1985) value chain concept seems to focus upon the activities the firm performs as the unit of analysis and not explicitly upon the resources and capabilities required to perform these activities, and only briefly on the concept of resources and capabilities. Discretionary control over scarce resources and capabilities is the reason why a firm performs a given set of activities more efficiently than others. Thus the combination of a firm's resources and capabilities enables it to perform the activities upon which it competes. This is illustrated in Figure 1. Access to certain resources and capabilities is the necessary condition for performing the activities, which in turn leads to value creation for the customers and competitive advantage *vis-à-vis* competitors. It is important to note that capabilities and resources are interrelated. The firm's skills are tied to a bundle of resources. For example, functional skills in handling a certain machine are tied to the specific requirements of the machine as well as the general work flow in the organization (Penrose, 1959).[2]

Figure 1. A simple resource-based model of the firm

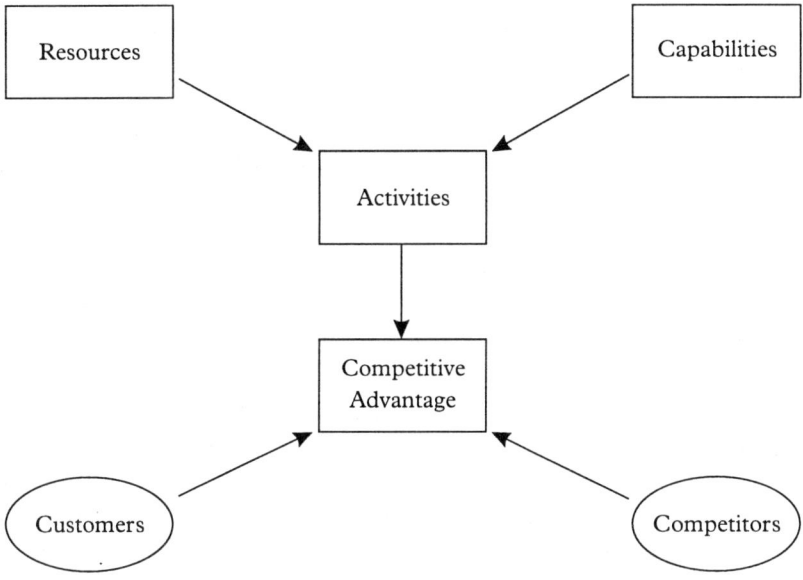

Firm resources and profitability

Much of the research effort, particularly the empirical work, has focused on the performance issues of the resource-based view. Therefore, a brief

2. Note, though, that these considerations do not necessarily tell us anything about who should own the asset(s) in question. This matter is best viewed in the context of contracts and incentives. See Milgrom and Roberts (1992) for a general introduction to these topics.

examination of the link between performance and resources is in order. Most of the empirical work has explored the diversification-performance link, the main hypotheses being that there is a positive correlation between profitability and diversification relatedness. Representative bodies of work include Wernerfelt & Montgomery (1988), who explored the relative performance contributions of industry, market share and focus effects; Montgomery & Wernerfelt (1988), who explored the performance implications of diversification relatedness; Montgomery & Harihan (1991) who examined the link between the direction of growth and the firm's resources; and Amit & Livnat (1989) who examined the links between business cycles, diversification relatedness and performance.

The resource-based perspective holds that there is a link between the firm's profitability and its resources. In this sense, the resource-based view is related to the Chicago school of industrial economics with its emphasis on efficiency differentials between firms (Conner, 1991). The possession and deployment of superior resources and capabilities will lead to a sustainable competitive advantage, which in turn leads to superior returns. The firm earning superior returns possesses a bundle of resources and capabilities enabling it to become more efficient than its competitors. The corresponding rent concept is Ricardian rents, as opposed to the monopoly rents pursued in the structure-conduct-performance approach to strategy, where the source of rents is market power (Teece, Pisano & Shuen 1990; Peteraf 1993; Grant 1990).[3] However, deployment of the firm's resources and capabilities in a new way may also cause a technological lead or another type of first mover advantage that creates an advantage which may be limited in time. Then, the rent concept is Schumpeterian (Teece, Pisano & Shuen 1990). One must note that the causal structure of the resource view and the structure-conduct-performance approach are different. The structure-conduct-performance hypothesis proposes that industries are fundamentally attractive, and that industry structure should therefore be the unit of analysis (Porter 1980). The resource-based view, as well as the Schumpeterian version termed dynamic capabilities by Teece, Pisano & Shuen (1990), hold that it is firms and their unique endowments that are attractive. The firm is the primary unit of analysis.

---

3. Ricardian rents are due to unique inputs rather than output restriction in the final product market (Teece, Pisano & Shuen 1990). Ricardian rents are wholly determined by the demand for the services of these unique inputs.

In order to examine these questions, Rumelt (1991) analyzed the variance components of firm profitability in two samples of data over four years from 457 and 1070 corporations respectively, and found that «... stable industry effects accounted for only 8% of the variance in business unit returns» (p. 168). Further, Rumelt found that «... stable business unit effects account for 46% of the variance» (p. 168). Rumelt's investigation concerns itself with the relative contributions to profitability from different factors; as he phrases it: «My intention here is to suppress concern with *causal* mechanisms and focus instead on the question of *locus*» (p. 169). Rumelt's conclusions seem to indicate that the locus of business profitability is the firm's endowment of resources and capabilities. This indicates that the starting-point of the analysis should not be the firm's position in the industry, but rather the factors contributing to the firm's competitive position, that is, its resources and capabilities.

This proposition has an important implication for the understanding of the basic means of strategy. Strategy, in its structure-conduct-performance version, is a matter of obtaining market power, which in turn should result in higher prices as a consequence of output restriction. In the resource-based version, rents should accrue to the firms that are able to control and develop scarce and valuable resources at less than their opportunity cost. In their study of the United States brewing industry, Montgomery and Wernerfelt (1991: 958) found that «... on the average, gains in market share were associated with the destruction, rather with the creation of firm value...» This result substantiates a hypothesis that firms should rather seek Ricardian rents than monopoly rents. This may be because Ricardian rents are more difficult to compete away than pure market power (that may be bought, say by acquisition or excessive marketing expenditure).[4] A reason why Ricardian rents may be more difficult to compete away lies within the fact that the further supply of the scarce resources may be difficult; and for competitors it may be difficult to identify exactly which resources and capabilities are the critical and scarce ones, as well as determining which combinations of these are efficient.

Further, there may be substantial ambiguity as to how particular types of resources and capabilities are created. Some even have characteristics of externalities such as corporate culture. Corporate culture may be seen as a social capital which is an effect of complex and repeated patterns of

---

4. The basic argument behind this is the existence of competitive bidding for market share in an auction-like game.

social interaction, and which is both difficult to create consciously as well as being difficult to copy. If corporate culture supports other types of competitive advantage, say low manufacturing cost, then the whole bundle may be difficult to imitate (Barney, 1986b).

Entrepreneurial rents should also be included in the resource-based concept of business strategy since innovative behavior allows the firm to adapt to (or perhaps even shape) environmental changes (Rumelt, 1987). Entrepreneurship, or innovation, is a crucial ingredient in business strategy, as this is the process by which new resources and capabilities are created and deployed. Entrepreneurial rents may become Ricardian rents if the innovation in question cannot be imitated or substituted, or is subject to decay. However, few resources can avoid these effects in the long run. Examples, such as the Coca-Cola brand, are rare but do exist. An important corollary to this example is that Coca-Cola invests heavily in its brand name to prevent its decay. Furthermore, competitors attempt to imitate or substitute Coca-Cola's brand name. Examples include Pepsi-Cola, 7-UP and various others around the globe. Such competition limits the returns to the Coca-Cola brand name.

Not all resources will have the same profit potential since some resources are more scarce, unique or valuable than others, and some are more difficult to imitate (Lippman & Rumelt, 1982). Thus it may be more difficult to base sustained competitive advantage on access to cheap and abundant financial resources, given a reasonably effective capital market, as opposed to organizationally embedded skills which are very difficult to imitate and carry a high degree of causal ambiguity. What protects the rent-earning firm are isolating mechanisms that prevent competing firms from imitating the firm's resources (Lippmann & Rumelt, 1982; Rumelt, 1984; Rumelt, 1987).

Barney (1991) proposes four empirical indicators that may help to determine whether the firm's resources may be the foundation of a sustainable competitive advantage. First, are the firm's resources valuable in the sense that «... they enable a firm to conceive of or implement strategies that improve its efficiency and effectiveness?» (p. 106) Second, are the resources rare, that is, are the resources or combinations of them unique or proprietary to the firm? Third, how easily can the resources be imitated by competitors? Finally, how easily can the resources be substituted? In addition, the resources and capabilities should be durable, as in the case of physical assets (Amit & Schoemaker, 1993), or must be reproducible, as in the case of the more intangible assets such as technological skills.

The scope of the firm and appropriate rents

In the resource-based view, the firm may be seen as a rent-seeking entity and a repository of knowledge and capabilities. The attractiveness of the resource endowment determines the level of rents the firm will enjoy. However, it is not under all conditions that the firm is able to appropriate the available economic rents from its endowment. Other factors may be important in deciding the optimal scope of the firm. In this section, a synthesis between the resource-based view and the transaction cost perspectives is attempted to get closer to a resource-based theory about the optimal scope of the firm.

The theory to be advanced is one that combines the idiosyncratic nature of the firm's endowment of resources and capabilities (for example, asset specificity, relatedness, complexity and tacitness) with the existence of transaction costs and opportunistic behavior.

The very nature of the firm's endowment may render the breaking up of activities impossible, as a technologically separable surface cannot be said to exist. First of all, assets are mostly specific to the firm, for example, because they are dedicated to a special purpose or because they are tied to a unique organizational context. This limits the range of possible productive applications outside the organization. Accentuating this is the fact that resources and capabilities may be interdependent, tying any individual resource to an idiosyncratic use within the firm. Further, some activities are best performed by a closely knit team possessing cross-functional capabilities (Demsetz, 1988). In this case, scale economies of management and organization can be said to exist. The activities to be performed may be so complex that an intersubjective common language for communicating about how to perform a given set of activities can only be developed internally, and not by arm's-length relations. This complexity is characterized by a certain routineness and tacitness that can only be efficient within a single organization that reproduces and refines these complex patterns of behavior. Given that firms are rent seeking, then the rationale for the existence of firms can be said to be the exploitation of scale economies of management and/or organization of highly specific and interconnected resources and capabilities. If there are scale economies of management and organization and there is some difficulty in distributing the residual rents among the different factors, then a rationale for common ownership of a diverse set of resources also exists.[5] This argument borders on a transaction cost argument, since it reduces costly multilateral bargaining to a less costly bilateral bargaining.

Further, firms may, in some key areas, know more than it is possible to write into a contract (Kogut & Zander, 1992).

This explanation of the firm's efficient boundaries seems to fit best with the firm's horizontal scope and explains why related diversification is generally more profitable than unrelated diversification (Amit & Livnat, 1989; Montgomery & Wernerfelt, 1988; Wernerfelt & Montgomery, 1988). In the case of unrelated diversification, no firm-specific skills (other than perhaps general management skills) are transferred, few assets are interrelated and little value is added by common organization. In the case of related diversification, the opposite may hold true. In some cases, the existence of cross-functional vertical skills may make it economically attractive to integrate vertically. Examples include relations between marketing and production, where the need to adjust production levels to frequent changes in demand may make the integration of these activities into one organization advantageous.

The boundaries of the firm that will emerge as efficient from the considerations above will, in some cases, differ from those that are due to purely contractual arguments as the focus is on realizing productivity gains through internal organization. The existence of transaction costs due to bounded rationality, opportunism, asset specificity, small numbers bargaining, asset co-specialization, etc. (Williamson, 1985) may prevent the full appropriation of the economic rents that are created by the firm's resources and capabilities. Therefore, transaction cost considerations may be a valuable complement to the above-mentioned resource-based considerations.

Several phenomena may be attributed to this. First, strong complementarities between different types of resources may exist. For instance, the boundaries that are efficient according to production and information economies may include manufacturing and development, with sales and distribution as complementary assets (Teece, 1986). But given that distribution channels are dominated by a few (collusive) firms, then these may appropriate the firm's economic rents if the firm has no other

---

5. This difficulty may be due to the fact that it is impossible to assign residual profits according to the marginal contribution of each resource-owner when significant profitability effects caused by the existence of, for example, social capital (say culture) or team effects are present. If there were to be excessive bargaining over the right to residual profits, then the resource owners would suffer losses from incurring influence costs and the outcome would be less efficient. Further, if the existence of opportunism is included in the analysis, there may be extremely high transaction costs in bargaining the prices of the marginal outputs between the actors. See also Milgrom and Roberts (1992).

way of marketing its products. The complementarity phenomenon has been observed in several industries where innovators that did not possess competitive complementary assets were surpassed by imitators who did possess such complementary assets (Teece, 1986). Second, and related to the first, asset specificity and sunk investments may provide an incentive to integrate vertically since the firm may be subject to opportunistic behavior from its trading partners.

In summary, two explanations may be distinguished when discussing the optimal scope of the firm in a resource-based context. The first is a production/information economic explanation for the scope of the firm. Internal organization is superior to arm's length dealing because it is costly and difficult to communicate about matters related to production. This is caused by the complexity of performing team production, tacitness of knowledge, etc. The second is a transaction cost explanation. Here the firm internalizes functions to guard against misrepresentation and opportunistic behavior by transaction partners, as well as strategic (imitative) moves by competitors with strong endowments of complementary assets. As Demsetz (1988) concluded, firms need to minimize both transaction costs and the costs of internal organization, that is, realizing productivity advantages from internal organization. Where the resource-view distinguishes itself from the transaction cost explanation is the latter's central assumption about transactions taking place between technologically separable entities. Given the assumed importance of boundary-spanning competence (such as tacit knowledge or the informal structure in an organization that functions as a coordination mechanism between diverse functions in a firm) in the resource-view, the technologically separable entities are not fully separable, and the boundaries of the firm are not drawn as straight as the transaction cost approach would suggest.

It must be noted though, that alternatives to achieving uncertainty (transaction cost) reduction by integration of activities do exist (the implicit assumption being that it is impossible to write complete contracts). For example, there may be a strong degree of interdependence between the firm and its trading partners. Christensen (1987) has described this in a simple conceptualization. In this model three types of skills (resources) are considered: core skills, which are the core resources of the firm on which it bases its competitiveness, supplied skills are those delegated to other firms; and cross skills, which are the synergies that arise because of the combination of the firm's core skills and the supplied skills of other firms. In a resource-based context, the cross skills represent a gray area where a transition between what is considered inside the firm and what is considered outside the firm takes place. Cross skills may be considered as resources to which the firm has access, but to a large extent reside outside the organization. In effect, cross skills represent a relationship-specific investment on both sides. This investment is normally considered to be sunk, and therefore lost, if the relationship is terminated as a result of opportunistic behavior. Further, a termination of a relationship due to opportunistic behavior may force the culprit to incur a loss of reputation that will hurt his future dealings with other trading partners.

The acquisition and accumulation of resources

Given the assertion that the sources of economic rents are embedded in the firm's portfolio of resources and capabilities, the interesting question becomes: how does the firm get access to these? Since few firms are born with superior resource and capability endowments, it seems reasonable to assume that these must be created, and that this creation takes time and money. If resources are not created, then they must be accessed in another way, typically through acquisition. It is important to note, though, that an implicit assumption in the resource-based view is that some initial resource endowment exists. This point will be treated more extensively later on.

Barney (1986a) introduces the important concept of strategic factor markets, which are markets where the firm acquires the resources needed for the implementation of strategies: «All strategies that require the acquisition of resources for implementation have strategic factor markets associated with them» (p. 1232). With this concept as the foundation, Barney outlines the conditions for achieving economic success; «... the size of the returns to product market strategies will depend on the cost of the resources necessary to implement them» (p. 1232). The central requirement for achieving consistent above-average performance is «... that firms that wish to obtain expected above-normal returns from product market strategies must be consistently better informed concerning the future value of those strategies than other firms acting in the same strategic factor markets. We also argue that other apparent sources of advantage in strategy implementation are, in fact, either a manifestation of these special insights into the future value of strategies, or a manifestation of the firm's good fortune and luck» (p. 1232). Barney's point is that «... environmental analysis, by itself, cannot create the required insights, while in some circumstances, the analysis of a firm's unique skills and capabilities can» (pp. 1232-33). The assumption behind Barney's argument is similar to that of rational expectations theory in macroeconomics. If all agents within a market have similar knowledge of how to value an asset, then the only way to buy this asset for less than its economic value is to hold superior information necessary to assess its value. In the context of strategy, this information is more likely to be derived from insights about the firm's resources and capabilities than about the market. In Barney's model, the key to gaining sustainable competitive advantage is the possession of superior insight.

In a critique of Barney's (1986a) framework, Dierickx and Cool (1989) proposed that firms do not necessarily acquire the resources they need in strategic factor markets, simply because many resources are nontradable. «The implementation of a strategy may require assets which are nonappropriable. ... In addition, the successful implementation of a strategy often requires highly firm-specific assets, as opposed to undifferentiated inputs» (p. 1505). Instead, they propose that many assets are accumulated instead of traded; «... the idiosyncratic nature of firm-specific assets precludes their tradability on open markets. Being nontradable, the firm-specific component is accumulated internally» (p. 1505). Untradeability may be caused by such factors as complexity, tacitness, asset specificity, asset complementarity, time compression diseconomies, etc.

The resources and capabilities, which are acquired in strategic factor markets, can often not be readily used by the firm. The resources and capabilities that are supplied externally must go through a process of transformation where they are adapted to the specific conditions of the individual firm. That is, they develop asset specificity to the firm, enabling the firm to appropriate quasi-rents from them.[6]

The framework proposed by Barney (1986a) and Dierickx and Cool (1989) can be seen as complementary. Following this line of thought, four points may be distinguished: a) firms are able to acquire some of the resources they need to implement strategies in strategic factor markets, b) to earn superior returns from these strategic resources, the strategic factor markets must be subject to market failure to the advantage of the firm, c) firms hold a stock of these strategic assets at any point in time and d) firms accumulate the nontradable assets over time. Following this

6. The term quasi-rents is associated with Klein, Crawford and Alchian (1978). Quasi-rents are the difference between the value of an asset in its best and second best use. Sometimes quasi-rents are also termed Pareto rents.

logic, the resources that are acquired externally may be of critical importance for the well-being of the firm, but they are not a sufficient condition for the well-being of the firm unless there is persistent market failure. Market failure is unlikely to persist as competing firms will attempt to imitate the strategies of successful firms or try to substitute the strategic resources with other resources. The firm must also have an accumulated stock of internally developed resources since these resources are those likely to be best protected by isolating mechanisms. These resources may be termed the core resources (and capabilities) of the firm and are those which are central to the sustained rent earning ability of the firm. Also, these resources, when they are complementary to the acquired resources, may help to increase market failure in the strategic factor markets by creating and sustaining a monopsony for the firm.

Path dependence and environmental influences

The firm depends on attracting resources from its environment. If the firm is unable to attract critical resources such as skilled labor, clever scientists, financial resources, etc., it will be unable to compete effectively, as suggested by resource-dependence theory (Pfeffer & Salancik, 1978). Further, the firm must also deploy its resources correctly; that is, the firm must create products or services that are valued in the marketplace. The firm competes both in factor markets and in end-product markets. Thus the firm is dependent on its environment both on the input-side and on the output-side. In this sense, environmental analysis matters since «... environmental change may change the importance of resources to the firm» (Mahoney, Pandian & Pandian, 1992: 371).

Accumulating the right set of resources and capabilities is clearly an important issue since the firm is considered to be path dependent in the resource-based view of the firm (Dierickx & Cool, 1989; Penrose, 1959/1972). Once a portfolio of resources and capabilities is built up, the firm will be committed to a limited set of actions for some time (Ghemawat, 1991). This is because the firm's tangible and intangible investments are sunk, and because markets for these, sold as a bundle or as individual factors, are either highly imperfect or nonexistent.[7] This fact characterizes almost any credible business strategy available to firms.

---

7. It should be noted, though, that Ghemawat (1991) emphasizes the entry-deterrent effect of the firm's sunk investments.

The question of how the firm chooses its resource-accumulation paths becomes important. First, the managers who decide about the direction of resource-accumulation can be assumed to be boundedly rational (Simon, 1957). Second, there are behavioral biases involved in managerial decision-making. Typically, managers employ a set of decision heuristics in the face of an uncertain and complex future (Amit & Shoemaker, 1993; Bazerman, 1986). One manifestation of this is that managers enact their environment (Weick, 1969), that is, they choose which parts of their environment to include and which parts to ignore in their judgment of environmental influences. Third, as Leonard-Barton (1992) suggested, the nature of the firm's core resources and capabilities may constrain the necessary development of new resources and capabilities. Core capabilities may indeed become core rigidities. These considerations also add a further dimension to the commitment literature associated with Ghemawat (1991).

Given these assumptions about the nature of managerial decision-making, the channels through which information about the current and future state of the firm's environment is transmitted become important. For example, studies of innovation networks indicate that close ties between suppliers and customers are vital for the success of innovation efforts (Freeman, 1991). The logic behind this is that these networks are relayers of some of the most important sources of information about the current and future states of the environment and the firm's relations to this. The network may in fact be considered as an enactment of the firm's environment. Information provided through the network is internalized and subsequently reflected in the firm's actions. The network may influence the firm's search routines, and thus be vital in setting the direction of strategy. Information relayed through the network should be that which the firm is most likely to act upon, since the network is the most prominent manifestation (enactment) of the firm's environment. Also, networks may be bearers of some critical capabilities for the firm, and as such they represent the firm's external capabilities.

The properties of resources and capabilities

In the preceding sections, the resource-based view has been explored with respect to the properties that resources must exhibit in order to become the foundation of sustained competitive advantage. In this section these dimensions are further operationalized, and some imperfect measures to achieve this operationalization are suggested.[8] This operationalization may be used on individual resources, but is most appropriately employed on bundles of resources and capabilities.

The question of what actually constitutes the rent earning factors of the firm is one of the key issues to be dealt with. As should be apparent from the previous discussion, the firm's rent-earning capacity is caused by the attractiveness of its core resources and capabilities. These are assumed to be the resources and capabilities that enable the firm to realize a value creating strategy at a lower cost than its cost of capital. Resources and capabilities that would be likely to endow the firm with such advantages are assumed to be rare or unique and durable, imperfectly imitable and difficult to substitute (Barney, 1991).

However, these guidelines have few normative implications. In this section, the notion of what characterizes resources and capabilities with high rent-earning potential will be made more operational.

What characterizes those resources and capabilities that are rare or unique is asset specificity (Williamson 1985: 95-96). That is, assets that are in some way dedicated to a particular purpose, site, customer or organizational context. The central feature in the context of competitiveness is that the firm has some degree of discretion over the use and development of such assets. Since specific assets are often specific to the individual firm, they have the potential of being rare or unique. Whether the specific assets are valuable in a steady-state environment depends upon the services they can render relative to the competition and the customers' tastes and needs. Asset specificity is also central to the idea of strategic commitment, but that the firm's accumulated investments in specific assets are mainly viewed as entry deterring investments (Ghemawat, 1991). Along these lines, it should be noted that investment in specific assets reduces the firm's mobility (Lustgarten & Thomadakis, 1987), and asset specificity may actually be considered one of the most important factors in determining the firm's degree of path dependence.

In an evolving competitive environment, though, resources and capabilities may be imitated by competitors, and if the firm's specific investments are to remain valuable then they must be well protected against imitative efforts by competitors. Therefore, it is necessary to examine what types of isolating mechanisms are associated with specific assets.

8.   One of the central problems in the resource-based view is that of operationalization. There is, as yet, no clear definition of what valuable resources are ex ante. For a sympathetic critique of the resource-based view, see Porter (1991).

Following Teece (1986), there are two basic mechanisms for protecting the firm's know-how: legal mechanisms and strategic mechanisms. Examples of legal mechanisms are patents, trademarks and copyrights. According to Teece (1986), among appropriability regimes, where legal mechanisms are adequate protection mechanisms, so-called tight appropriability regimes are the exception rather than the rule. Therefore, the firm must look towards strategic mechanisms to ensure maximal appropriation from its resources and capabilities.

What, then, characterizes resources and capabilities that are difficult to imitate? Kogut and Zander (1992) and Winter (1987) offer some dimensions for evaluating the firm's knowledge. Their main argument, relating to the imitability of knowledge, is that knowledge that can be characterized as information is relatively easy to imitate, and knowledge that can be characterized as know-how is relatively difficult to imitate. The latter may be caused by its tacitness, inarticulability, unteachability, unobservability in use, complexity and its systemic nature (Winter, 1987). These dimensions may be reduced as elements contributing to the complexity of the firm's know-how. That is, complex knowledge (know-how) is difficult to imitate. The notion of complexity may be extended to the firm's total endowment of resources and capabilities. The uniqueness of a firm's organization, for instance, caused by its history, may result in an increased complexity concerning its resources and capabilities.

Thus, the firm's core resources and capabilities may be characterized by two dimensions: their degree of complexity and their degree of specificity. This is illustrated in Figure 2, and the resources and capabilities that are most central to the firm's competitiveness are likely to be those which are highly specific and highly complex. The value of complex and specific resources and capabilities is likely to be directly proportional to their degree of specificity and complexity. Figure 2 shows that, as resources and capabilities become more specific to the firm, they also become less mobile. This point is consistent with some of the research on strategic groups and mobility barriers (Lustgarten & Thomadakis, 1987), and the literature on commitment (Ghemawat, 1991) where specialized asset investments constrain firms from changing their strategies. This is also supported by Dierickx and Cool (1989). They claim that resources and capabilities are often accumulated, and that this accumulation takes time, therefore making it difficult to change strategic posture in the short term: «It takes a consistent pattern of resource flows to accumulate a desired change in strategic asset stocks» (p. 1506).

Figure 2. Classification of resources according to specificity and complexity

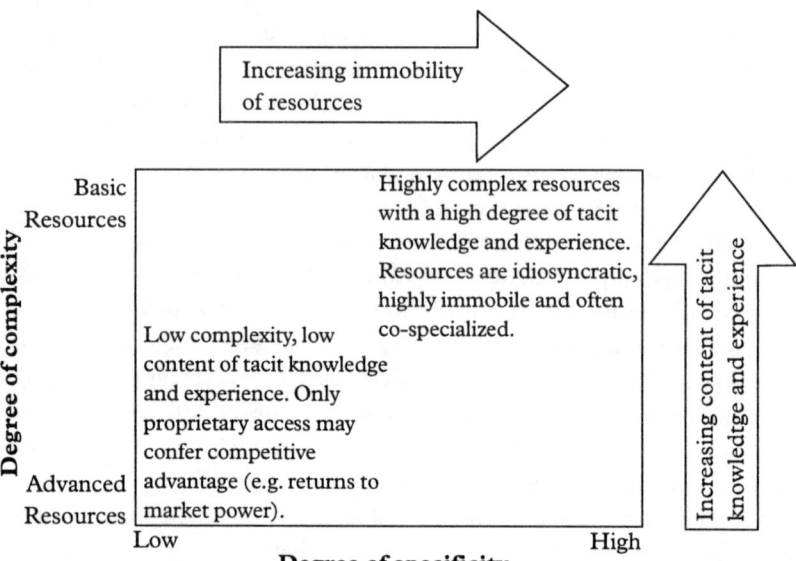

The upper-right quadrant of Figure 2 represents higher-order resources and capabilities, and, as we move from the bottom-left quadrant, skills and capabilities become increasingly important. Thus, skills and capabilities may be thought of as higher order resources.

The more higher-order resources employed to implement a given strategy, the less likely it is that the strategy will be imitated as these will be protected by the strongest isolating mechanisms (Lippmann & Rumelt, 1982); and then the more a strategy is based on higher order resources, the more sustainable the strategy should be *ceteris paribus*. A further, and quite important, point is that it takes time to create specialized and complex resources. An analogy to the sports world is that top athletes must train intensively for many years before they are able to achieve world-class performances in a single discipline. In the same manner, it takes time for a firm to build a world-class portfolio of resources and capabilities.

Not only should the firm have access to an attractive portfolio of resources, but the two central dimensions of attractiveness are their complexity and specificity, as discussed above. For these resources to be valuable requires a demand for their services. However, in a dynamic setting where firms are growing, a basic demand for the services that the firm's resources can render is not a sufficient condition for core resources and capabilities to be valuable.

A central issue is whether the firm will be able to expand its resource endowment. This is dependent upon two conditions: a) the productive capacity of the firm's endowment, and b) the flexibility of the firm's endowment. This is illustrated in Figure 3. If the firm has access to resources that are flexible, that means they are able to produce services that may be applied across a wide range of purposes. And if these resources have a high productive capacity, that means their productive capacity may be expanded as demand for their services increases. Then these two dimensions are likely to be proportional to the value of the firm's resource endowment. The firm's growth opportunities are also likely to be greater. Furthermore, if the firm's core resources and capabilities are inflexible and cannot be expanded easily, then its opportunity set is reduced and the firm will be more path dependent.

The two dimensions hold some implications for strategic management. For example, one might hypothesize that the success of a strategy is contingent on the availability of a certain type of skills, a case where high productive capacity would indicate that more of these skills could be made available. Further, the flexibility of the firm's endowment may be important in the context of diversification strategy. Then it is crucial that the firm's endowment of resources and capabilities may render services that are applicable in this new context. Otherwise, new resources must be created.

Wernerfelt (1989) describes three types of resources that have differing capacities. First, fixed resources, such as plant and equipment, have a fixed long term capacity, for example, a machine has an absolute limit as to how much it can produce. Second, «blueprints», such as brand names, patents and reputations have an almost infinite capacity, only limited by the opportunity for profitable reinvestment.[9] A brand name may become self-reinforcing as a function of the proliferation of sales and brand awareness. A household name such as Coca-Cola should illustrate this point. Finally, cultures have a limited short run capacity, but an almost unlimited long-term capacity. The latter resources typically fall under the heading organizational resources, and are characterized by a certain degree of tacitness, complexity and causal ambiguity (Reed & De Fillippi, 1990). An ideal situation for the firm would be to

---

9. One should assume that at some point, such resources will exhibit declining returns to scale, as demand for the services decrease. Further, one could also envision a situation where there is an increasing cost of organizing further activities.

possess resources with infinite productive capacities and increasing returns to scale.

Some resources have a high degree of flexibility and can be deployed for many different uses (Chatterjee & Wernerfelt 1991). Therefore, the flexibility of resources has important implications for the horizontal scope of the firm. Flexibility is often closely related to the degree of specificity in the sense that less specific resources will be highly flexible and vice versa. Financial resources may be put to many different uses, whereas physical resources, such as plant and equipment, usually have limited alternative uses, even at a cost. However, some resources are firm-specific and flexible at the same time. This is the case for a resource such as a brand name which can be extended to many different uses. Consider Kraft and their many different food products under the Kraft name (processed cheese, cream cheese, salad dressing, barbecue sauces, pasta dishes, etc.). It is necessary to distinguish between resources that are specific to a use (such as production machinery) and resources that are specific to a certain organization.[10]

Classifying resources according to their flexibility and productive capacity may yield some useful insights. It may be difficult to base the firm's strategy on resources with a low degree of flexibility and a fixed productive capacity unless this resource base endows the firm with a distinct cost advantage. Further, expansion is difficult and can only be undertaken if there is a possibility of adding to the existing stock of this particular resource. This is not without problems. For instance, new plant capacity can only be added in large increments. These types of resources are generally also more sensitive to environmental changes since they are likely to be more difficult to redeploy. Highly flexible resources with an unlimited capacity may be employed to support an expansive strategy, since these resources may be leveraged and stretched more easily (Hamel, 1991). Figure 3 illustrates the idea of looking at the productive capacities and flexibility of the firm's different resources. The problems that are most likely to be highlighted from such an analysis are those concerning the firm's growth possibilities both in terms of expanding its sales of existing products as well as diversification opportunities.

---

10. Resources that are specific to an organization may be usefully described by two dimensions. The first is property rights that protect the resource-owner from competition: for example, patents. The second is the specific nature of the resources that prevent imitation: for example, corporate culture and other types of social capital.

Figure 3. Resources classified according to degree of flexibility and productive capacity

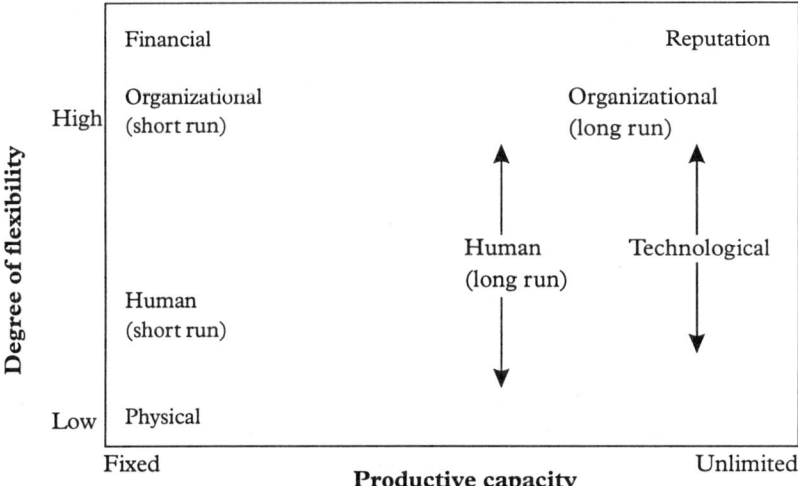

Assessment of the flexibility and productive capacity of the firm's resource base may provide corporate management with a better idea of how well the chosen strategy will perform under different environmental conditions. This is important since under conditions of high environmental uncertainty, inflexible resources are, *ceteris paribus*, more risky than flexible resources.

Conclusions

One of the most important differences between the structure-conduct-performance perspective on strategy and the resource-based perspective is the orientation towards strategic change. The industrial organization perspective assumes that reorientation is relatively uncomplicated and assets are easily redeployed, whereas the resource-perspective assumes that the firm is constrained by its past commitments. Inherent in the previous discussion lies the fact that the resource-based concept of strategy is different from the structure-conduct-performance paradigm. The latter derives its conception of strategy from the so-called design school (Andrews, 1971), and assumes a rational, omniscient decision-maker. The environmental opportunities and threats are predictable and the firm's strategy variables are controllable. These premises have been criticized as being highly dubious. The resource-based view derives its concept of strategy from behavioral and environmental assumptions that are seemingly more realistic. The behavioral assumption is one of bounded rationality, and there is considerable causal ambiguity as to what the specific source of competitive advantage is.[11] Strategic change is most often incremental as the firm is constrained by its previous commitments and time-compression diseconomies (Dierickx & Cool, 1989; Leonard-Barton, 1992). Further, there is considerable uncertainty about environmental developments, and managers can only hope to have average insights into the environmental developments (Barney, 1986a). Finally, due to the complex nature of many of the firm's resources, there is considerable uncertainty as to how they are created: How does one go about creating a valuable culture? At best, these resources can be created by indirect actions.[12]

The firm's strategy is based on the deployment of resources. Thus, in order to implement a given strategy, the firm must possess a certain set of resources and capabilities. Resources may be thought of as both assets and skills. Further, they may be more or less easy to identify and articulate. Thus, financial resources are relatively easy to identify, whereas organizationally embedded skills, supported by a cohesive corporate culture, are very difficult to identify and articulate, thus creating a situation of uncertain imitability (Lippman & Rumelt, 1982).

The role for the manager, following the resource perspective, seems to be to identify and articulate which resource base the firm has access to? internally and externally, and which of the firm's current and planned activities are supported by this resource base. Additionally, the manager must identify which resource gaps exist and how to best fill these (Grant, 1990).

Resources are acquired or accumulated, and at any given time the firm holds a stock of resources which forms the basis of the firm's current competitive advantage or disadvantage. The rate and direction of resource accumulation and acquisition determines the firm's future competitive position. Table 1 is an attempt to depict the position of the

---

11. Nevertheless, most literature on the resource-based view does not have an explicit rationality assumption. The interpretation of the resource-based view given here is one of bounded rationality. This interpretation does not conflict with the general ideas of the resource-based view, as many of the contributions could be attributed with an implicit assumption of bounded rationality. The assumption of bounded rationality may provide a more realistic perspective on firms and strategy.
12. One might propose that the ability to create resources of this type can be ascribed to a phenomenon similar to that which von Clausewitz (1984) termed genius.

six general classes of resources suggested by Grant (1991) relative to the properties discussed in the paper. Information resources are not considered in this table, as they are virtually impossible to generalize about. For example, Arrow's paradox holds that the value of information is only apparent to the buyer or user after the transfer has taken place.

Table 1. Classification of resources according to different criteria

Resource	Degree of specificity	Complexity	Productive capacity	Flexibility	Mode of access
Financial	Low	Basic	Fixed	High	Acquisition
Physical	Varying	Often basic	Fixed	Low	Acquisition
Human	Typically high	Varying across functions	Fixed in the short run Unlimited in the long run	Varying with specialization	Accumulation or acquisition
Technological	Varying	Advanced	Unlimited/ high	Varying with specialization	Accumulation or acquisition
Reputation	High	Advanced	Unlimited/high	High	Accumulation
Organizational	High	Advanced	Fixed in the short run Unlimited in the long run	High, but often varying	Accumulation

Two simple analytical tools were proposed for assessing the characteristics of the firm's resource portfolio. First the manager may use the framework outlined in Figure 2 to assess the firm's portfolio of resources and capabilities, and then determine whether the resources and capabilities confer any competitive advantage. Those resources that are likely to provide the firm with sustainable competitive advantage are likely to be those that are highly firm-specific, which is considered a measure for scarcity, and complex, which is considered a measure of inimitability. Secondly, the manager may assess the resources potential for exploitation by employing the framework outlined in Figure 3. Does the resource have a limited productive capacity, and how flexible is the resource? The classification scheme in Table 1 may aid the manager in this process. The general characteristics of each resource class are highlighted according to some of the issues that may be of importance for the sustainability of the firm's strategies.

References

Amit, R. & J. Livnat (1989): Efficient Corporate Diversification, Methods and Implications. *Management Science 35(7):* 879-897.

Amit, R. & P. Shoemaker (1993): Strategic Assets and Organizational Rent: *Strategic Management Journal 14(1):* 33-46.

Andrews, K.R. (1971): *The Concept of Corporate Strategy.* New York: Dow-Jones Irwin.

Barney, J.B. (1986a): Strategic Factor Markets: Expectations, Luck and Business Strategy. *Management Science 32(10):* 1231-1241.

Barney, J.B. (1986b): Organizational Culture: Can It Be a Source of Sustained Competitive Advantage? *Academy of Management Review 11(3):* 656-665.

Barney, J.B. (1989): Asset Stocks and Sustained Competitive Advantage: a Comment. *Management Science 35(12):* 1511-1513.

Barney, J.B. (1991): Firm Resourses and Sustained Competitive Advantage. *Journal of Management 17(1):* 99-120.

Bazerman, M. (1986): *Judgment in Managerial Decision Making.* New York: Wiley and Sons.

Chandler, A.D. (1962): *Strategy and Structure: Chapters in the History of American Industrial Enterprise.* Cambridge: M.I.T. Press.

Chatterjee, S. & B. Wernerfelt (1991): The Link Between Resources and Type of Diversification: Theory and Evidence. *Strategic Management Journal 12(1):* 33-48.

Christensen, P.R. (1987): Industriel Fleksibilitet og Lokalisering i et Netværksperspektiv. *NordRefo??.*

Conner, K.R. (1991): A Historical Comparison of Resource-Based Theory and Five Schools of Thought within Industrial Organization Economics: Do We Have a New Theory of the Firm? *Journal of Management 17(1):* 121-154.

De Gregori, T.R. (1987): Resources Are Not; They Become: an Institutional Theory. *Journal of Economic Issues 21:* 1241-1263.

Demsetz, H. (1988): The Theory of the Firm Revisited. *Journal of Law, Economics, and Organization 4:* 141-161.

Dierickx, I. & K. Cool (1989): Asset Stock Accumulation and Sustainability of Competitive Advantage. *Management Science 35(12):* 1504-1511.

Freeman, C. (1991): Networks of Innovators: a Synthesis of Research Issues. *Research Policy 20,* 499-514.

Ghemawat, P. (1991): *Commitment*. New York: The Free Press.

Grant, R.M. (1990): The Resource-Based Theory of Competitive Advantage. *California Management Review 33(3)*: 114-135.

Hamel, G. (1991): *Breaking the Frame: Strategy as Stretch and Leverage*. London: London Business School.

Hamel, G. & C.K. Prahalad (1990): Core Competence. *Harvard Business Review*, May-June: 79-91.

Itami, H. & T.W. Roehl (1987): *Mobilizing Invisible Assets*. Cambridge, MA: Harvard University Press.

Klein, B., R.G. Crawford & A. Alchian (1978): Vertical Integration, Appropriable Rents and the Competitive Contracting Process. *Journal of Law and Economics 21:* 257-285.

Kogut, B. & U. Zander (1992): Knowledge of the Firm, Combinative Capabilities and the Replication of Technology. *Organization Science 3:* 382-397.

Lamb, R.B. (1984): *Competitive Strategic Management*. Englewood Cliffs, NJ: Prentice Hall.

Leonard-Barton, D. (1992): Core Capabilities and Core Regidities in Managing New Product Development. *Strategic Management Journal 13, Summer:* 111-125.

Lippman, S.A. & R.P. Rumelt (1982): Uncertain Imitability: An Analysis of Interfirm Differences in Efficiency under Competition. *Bell Journal of Economics 13*: 418-438.

Lustgarten, S. & S. Thomadakis (1987): Mobility Barriers and Tobin's q^*. *Journal of Business 60*: 519-537.

Mahoney, J.T., J.R. Pandian. (1992): The Resource-Based View within the Conversation of Strategic Management. *Strategic Management Journal 13(5)*: 363-380.

Milgrom, P. & J. Roberts (1992): *Economics, Organization and Management*. Englewood Cliffs, NJ: Prentice-Hall.

Montgomery, C.A. & B. Wernerfelt (1988): Diversification, Ricardian Rents, and Tobin's q. *RAND Journal of Economics 19(4)*: 623-632.

Montgomery, C.A. & B. Wernerfelt (1991): Sources of Superior Performance: Market Share Versus Industry Effects in the U.S. Brewing Industry. *Management Science 37(8)*: 954-959.

Montgomery, C.A. & S. Harihan (1991): Diversified Expansion by Large Established Firms. *Journal of Economic Behavior and Organization 15*: 71-89.

Penrose, E. (1959): *The Theory of the Growth of the Firm*. Oxford: Oxford University Press.

Penrose, E.T. (1972): *The Theory of the Growth of the Firm*. Oxford: Basil Blackwell (1st edition appeared in 1959).

Peteraf, M.A. (1993): *The Cornerstones of Competitive Advantage: a Resource-Based View*. Strategic Management Journal 14: 179-191.

Pfeffer, J. & G.R. Salancik (1978): *The External Control of Organizations: a Resource Dependence Perspective*. New York: Harper and Row.

Porter, M.E. (1980): *Competitive Strategy*. New York: The Free Press.

Porter, M.E. (1985): *Competitive Advantage*. New York: The Free Press.

Porter, M.E. (1990): *The Competitive Advantage of Nations*. New York: The Free Press.

Porter, M.E. (1991): Towards a Dynamic Theory of Strategy. *Strategic Management Journal 12*: Winter, 95-117.

Reed, R. & R.J. De Fillippi (1990): Causal Ambiguity, Barriers to Imitation, and Sustainable Competitive Advantage. *Academy of Management Review 15*: 88-102.

Rumelt, R.P. (1984): Towards a Strategic Theory of the Firm. In R.B. Lamb (1984): *Competitive Strategic Management*. Englewood Hills, NJ: Prentice Hall, Ch. 26: 556-570.

Rumelt, R.P. (1987): Theory, Strategy, and Entrepreneurship. In D.J. Teece (ed.): *The Competitive Challenge*. Cambridge: Ballinger.

Rumelt, R.P. (1991): How Much Does Industry Matter? *Strategic Management Journal 12(3)*: 167-186.

Rubin, P.H. (1973): The Expansion of Firms. *Journal of Political Economy 81*: 936-949.

Simon, H.A. (1957): *Administrative Behavior*. New York: Macmillan.

Teece, D.J. (1986): Profiting from Technological Innovation. Implications for Integration, Collaboration and Public Policy. *Research Policy 15*: 285-305.

Teece, D.J., G. Pisano & A. Shuen (1990): Firm Capabilities, Resources and the Concept of Strategy. Working Paper no. EAP-38. Berkeley: University of California at Berkeley.

von Clausewitz, C. (1984): *On War*. Princeton, NJ: Princeton University Press.

Weick, K.E. (1969): *The Social Psychology of Organizing*. Reading, MA: Addison-Wesley.

Wernerfelt, B. (1984): A Resource-Based View of the Firm. *Strategic Management Journal 5*: 171-181.

Wernerfelt, B. (1989): From Critical Resources to Corporate Strategy. *Journal of General Management 14(3)*: 4-12.

Wernerfelt, B. & C.A. Montgomery (1988): Tobin's q and the Importance of Focus in Firm Performance. *American Economic Review* *78(1)*: 246-250.

Williamson, O.E. (1985): *The Economic Institutions of Capitalism.* New York: The Free Press.

Winter, S.G. (1987): Knowledge and Competence as Strategic Assets. In D.J. Teece (1987): *The Competitive Challenge.* Cambridge: Ballinger, Ch. 8: 159-184.

Grounding Strategic Paradigms: Logical Positivism, Realism and the Resource Based View of the Firm

Paul C. Godfrey & Charles W.L. Hill

The question that lies at the heart of research in the strategic management field is: why do firms succeed and why do they fail (Porter, 1991)? Or put in the language of economics: why do some firms earn positive abnormal returns while others earn negative abnormal returns? In recent years a new paradigm that provides an answer to these questions, referred to by its proponents as the resource-based view of the firm, has been taking shape in the strategic management literature (Barney, 1986a, 1986b, 1991; Conner, 1991; Dierickx & Cool, 1989; Mahoney & Pandian, 1992; Prahalad & Hamel, 1990; Reed & DeFillippi, 1990; Wernerfelt, 1984). This emerging paradigm offers an explanation of firm success and failure that appeals to many strategic management scholars. Indeed, judged by the recent, rapid, rise in theoretical and empirical papers that are framed within the context of the resource-based view, the strategic management field may at this time be undergoing a Kuhnian paradigm shift towards the resource-based view.

The objective of this paper is not to review the resource-based view critically, nor is it to compare and contrast the resource-based view with alternative views of strategy such as the industrial organization perspective, since this has already been done (Conner, 1991; Mahoney & Pandian, 1992). Rather, the objective of the paper is to examine the epistemological foundations upon which the resource-based view is built. Our central concern is that scholars working within the framework provided by the resource-based view have neglected these foundations. As a result, they risk applying inappropriate methodologies to test the resource-based view. Like much management research, the epistemological foundations of most strategy research, and particularly that framed within the industrial organization paradigm, are to be found in the philosophical tradition of logical positivism (or logical empiricism as it is sometimes called). What we will argue, however, is that the resource-based view of the firm, by virtue of its theoretical construction, is based upon a very different philosophical tradition, that of realism. Moreover, we will argue that this fact has important implications for research methodology. Applying the methodological paraphernalia of logical positivism to a theory whose foundations are so firmly based in a realist philosophy of science is an exercise only likely to end in frustration. If researchers wish to test the resource-based view empirically, they must develop methodologies and research programs that clearly reflect the re-alist nature of the theory. Thus, this paper is not about strategy; it is about philosophy as it applies to a strategic management paradigm.

The resource-based view of the firm

A number of comprehensive reviews of the resource-based view can al-ready be found in the literature, and we certainly do not intend to add to these (Barney, 1991; Conner, 1991; Mahoney & Pandian, 1992). Rather, our intention is to highlight features of the resource-based view that are important from a philosophy of science perspective. For our purposes, the resource-based view can be reduced to four propositions: (1) due to differences in resource endowments, no two firms are alike, (2) heterogeneity in resource endowments explains firm level differenc-es in performance, (3) barriers to imitating firm-specific resource en-dowments explain the persistence of performance differences over time, and (4) competition is a process in which the creation of new resources within the firm, or innovations in the way existing resources are em-ployed, explains the creation and dissipation of firm level abnormal re-turns over time. We shall consider each proposition in turn.

Firm heterogeneity

Central to the resource-based view is a conception of the firm as a collec-tion of heterogeneous resources. This perspective goes back to Penrose (1959) who argued that each firm is a collection of physical resources (plant, equipment, land, raw materials, etc.) and human resources (un-skilled and skilled labor, clerical, administrative, financial, legal, technical and managerial staff). According to Penrose, for certain resources:

> Each unit may be so unique that any classification, except one that makes each unit a separate resource, must disregard

some heterogeneity; this is the case for human beings, land, and certain other types of resources. (1959: 75)

This manifestly Ricardian view implies that, due to the heterogeneous nature of certain resources, the resource endowments of each firm are unique (no two firms are alike).

This view was added to by Nelson and Winter (1982), who focused upon the heterogeneity of firm-specific organizational routines. Organizational routines are the routines that organizations use to coordinate their human and physical resources and put them to productive use. They are seen by scholars working on the resource-based view as a special type of resource. Following Nelson and Winter, advocates of the resource-based view argue that, due to the idiosyncratic nature of individual firm histories, no two firms have the same set of organization routines; each firm is unique (this argument is based upon the historical notion of path dependence).

Nelson and Winter (1982) also argued that organizational routines are complex phenomena that defy easy articulation. They drew a comparison with individual skills, which are similarly difficult to articulate. For example, while we can say unequivocally that Boris Becker is a highly skilled tennis player, specifying why he is highly skilled is a different matter (it may be due to some unspecified combination of factors such as height, weight, agility, peripheral vision, eye-hand coordination, the way his brain processes information, etc.). Nelson and Winter's point is that even Boris Becker can probably not articulate why he is so skilled, since the causes are complex and, in part, are to be found deep within his brain in the way information is received and processed.

For Nelson and Winter, and the scholars that follow them, organizational routines are the organizational counterpart of individual skills. Like individual skills, organizational routines are depicted as having a deep structure that defies easy identification and articulation, even for members of the organization. Thus, organizational routines have a substantial tacit dimension.

Heterogeneity and performance

According to the resource-based view, differences in performance among firms primarily reflect differences in firm-specific resource endowments, including differences in organizational routines or as Barney (1986) puts it, organizational culture can be a source of competitive

advantage. While this perspective does not negate the traditional industrial organization view that industry structure influences firm performance, it does suggest that the variance in firm performance explained
by industry structure is relatively minor compared with the variance explained by firm-specific resource endowments (for empirical evidence
to this effect see Hansen & Wernerfelt, 1989; Rumelt, 1991). Thus, at
any point in time, competitive advantage and positive abnormal returns
are captured by the firms whose unique resources (including organizational routines) result in the efficient production of outputs that are
highly valued by consumers.

Persistence of performance differences

When a firm's resource endowment allows it to efficiently produce unique
and valuable outputs, the resultant positive abnormal returns act as a signal to other enterprises, who will then try to imitate the firm's resources.
Ultimately, the process of imitation will result in the firm's positive abnormal returns being competed away until only normal returns can be
earned. The speed with which this process occurs, however, is depicted as
being a function of the height of barriers to imitation. In turn, the height
of barriers to imitation is depicted as being a function of observability.

Observability refers to the fact that many firm-specific resources may
be difficult for competitors to observe (and hence imitate). This is particularly true of intangible resources such as managerial know-how, technical know-how, and organizational routines. Two reasons have been
given to explain the lack of observability of such resources: (1) the target
resource may be hidden so deeply within the organization that outsiders
cannot easily discern it, and (2) when the target resource is an intangible
such as organizational routines or know-how, it may have a significant
tacit dimension that makes it difficult to articulate, even for the firm that
possesses it (Lipperman & Rumelt, 1982; Nelson & Winter, 1982; Reed
& DeFillippi, 1990). Thus, the more unobservable the resources of a
successful firm are, the higher barriers to imitation will be, and the longer
it will take for that firm's positive abnormal returns to be competed away.

Competition as a process

Like Austrian economics, the resource-based view depicts competition
as a process that is driven by endogenously created innovations and/or
exogenous shocks (Jacobsen, 1992). In this formulation, the equilibri-

um conditions emphasized in the formal models of neoclassical and industrial organization economists have no correspondence in reality. Resource-based theorists argue that a firm comes into possession of unique and valuable resources due to: (1) fortuitous accident (luck), (2) entrepreneurial perceptions, (3) research, or (4) some combination of these (Barney, 1986a; Kirzner, 1979). As we have just seen, due to barriers to imitation, the positive abnormal returns that these unique and valuable resources gain for a firm are initially protected. Resource-based theorists push this insight one step further, however, arguing that imperfect attempts to imitate a firm's unique and valuable resources (imperfect because the resources are not directly observable) may result in mutations that are themselves more valuable than the target resources. As a consequence, imperfect imitation can itself be a source of innovation and competitive advantage for the would-be imitator (Alchain, 1950; Nelson & Winter, 1982). Thus, competition is depicted as an ongoing process with its own internal logic in which equilibrium conditions are never reached.

Logical positivism and realism

Almost all of the work in the philosophy of science in English during the present century has either been produced within the tradition of logical positivism, or has been written as a response to it (Boyd, 1991a). Realism is no exception to this; indeed, modern realism emerged in the early twentieth century as the dominant response to the philosophical problems that a major branch of twentieth century physics, quantum mechanics, created for logical positivism. Since then the debate between logical positivism and realism has been waged continuously in the philosophical literature (for an anthology that covers the main contributions to this debate over 60 years see Boyd, Gasper & Trout, 1991). Despite this lengthy discourse, the debate has not yet been resolved. It is not our intention in this paper to weigh into this debate by arguing in detail for one stream in the philosophy of science more than another. Rather, we wish to show that: (a) logical positivism and realism represent different approaches to the philosophy of science, and that (b) the resource-based view of the firm is a realist theory. To achieve these objectives, herein we compare and contrast logical positivism and realism on three critical epistemological issues: the problem of meaning, the problem of truth, and the problem of causality and confirmation.

Logical positivism

Logical positivism can trace its genealogy back to the seventeenth and eighteenth century enlightenment thinkers, Locke, Berkeley, and Hume (Russell, 1946). The clearest and most lasting of these philosophical contributions was made by David Hume, who was the chief advocate of the doctrine of empiricism. Brown (1970) traces the development of logical positivism from Hume to Wittgenstein. Hume's lasting contribution was to argue that empiricism is the foundation of meaning, while Wittgenstein gave the paradigm its formalistic orientation towards truth. As a school, the logical positivists reached their pinnacle in the middle of the twentieth century in the so-called Vienna Circle (Brown, 1970). Logical positivists espouse a verificationist theory of meaning, a formalistic theory of truth, and a view that holds that causality is imagination.

Verificationist theories of meaning

The central doctrine of logical positivism is the verificationist theory of meaning (Boyd, 1991; Brown, 1970; Hacking, 1983). This is the thesis that a proposition (theoretical statement) is meaningful if, and only if, its elements can be empirically verified. The emphasis on verification can be traced back to Hume in whose system «all perceptions of the mind resolve themselves into two distinct kinds, which I shall call IDEAS and IMPRESSIONS» (Hume, 1739: 1). Impressions are based upon sensory data, and include emotions and passions. Thus, to see an apple is an impression in the mind. Ideas are the faint images of impressions which are brought into the memory. When an individual remembers that they saw an apple yesterday, they are creating an idea in their mind of an apple. The crux of Hume's empiricism, therefore, is the thesis that no ideas can be formed independently of impressions. Given this, it follows that only the objects in the world that can be empirically verified have meaning. Put another way, central to logical positivism is the thesis that all genuine knowledge is based upon sensory observation, whether that be direct observation, or observation aided by instruments (Hacking, 1983).

Wittgenstein (1922) builds upon Hume's notion to include the role of language in ordering and giving meaning to the world. For Wittgenstein, words serve to create representations in logical space of the physical reality. Indeed, «the proposition is a picture of reality, for I know the state of affairs presented by it if I understand the proposition» (Wittgenstein, 1922: 67). The basis of knowledge comes from understanding, and the basis of understanding for Wittgenstein, like Hume, is sensory impression.

The verificationist theory of meaning has two key implications for the development of scientific theories. First, only the statements whose elements have empirically verifiable meanings can qualify as propositions (and all scientific theories are propositions). Second, as a direct consequence of the first, there are no elements in a proposition, or theory, which are purely theoretical. Purely theoretical elements cannot be verified, and thus have no meaning. There is no value added to knowledge by the inclusion of a purely theoretical element, one that cannot be verified by empirical observation in determining the truth of a proposition. Only terms that can be empirically observed, and which, therefore, have meaning, are necessary and useful in establishing the truth of a proposition.

Logical positivists apply the verificationist theory of meaning to the problem of demarcation, that is, to the problem of distinguishing between science and non-science. According to this approach theories that contain purely theoretical elements, whose meaning cannot be verified through sensory observation, are non-scientific theories. Thus, logical positivism has often been associated with attacks on metaphysics (for example, religion), and attempts to show that, in contrast to true science, such inquiries cannot result in real knowledge (O'Hear, 1989).

Much of the methodological apparatus of current management research is securely rooted in the verificationist construction of meaning. The notions of theory testability and falsifiability are grounded in the verificationist theory of meaning. The stress placed on operational techniques, such as interrater tests for reliability, construct validity and triangulation, serve as positivist means of verifying that theoretical constructs can be converted into observational measures with common meanings (Bacharach, 1989). Further, the widespread use of proxy variables in management research highlights the depth of the verification assumption; using a substitute variable is better than no variable at all. This practice is particularly prevalent in the industrial organization-based strategy literature, where variables such as firm scale and advertising expenditures are used as proxies for such key industrial organization constructs as barriers to entry.

From the perspective of logical positivism, the resource-based view of the firm is seriously deficient. The reason for this is quite obvious:

according to the resource-based view, certain key resources, such as the organizational routines of the firm, are, by definition, unobservable. The resource-based view depicts certain valuable resources as being hidden deep within the firm where outsiders cannot discern them. Moreover, the resource-based view argues that resources can have a significant tacit dimension, and as such are difficult to articulate, even for the firm that possesses them! Thus, a logical positivist would argue that since the nature, and even the existence, of such resources cannot, by definition, be verified through observation, the construct has no meaning. To the logical positivist, therefore, the resource-based view is not a scientific theory; it is an exercise in metaphysics.

Formal theories of truth

The logical positivists assess the truth value of propositions by their logical form. While this approach goes back to Russell and Wittgenstein, its most recent defense has been Hempels (1962), who has championed the deductive-nomological model of explanation. This model can be set out schematically as follows:

$$L_1, L_2, \ldots\ldots\ldots, L_n \qquad \text{(general laws)}$$
$$C_1, C_2, \ldots\ldots\ldots, C_n \qquad \text{(background conditions)}$$

$$E(\text{phenomena to be explained})$$

According to this approach, a proposition has truth value if the phenomena it is seeking to explain, E, can be deductively derived from a set of general laws, $L_1, L_2, \ldots\ldots, L_n$, and background conditions, $C_1, C_2, \ldots, C_n$. The deductive-nomological approach to warranted assertability suggests that the truth value of scientific theories depends upon the syllogistic form of the theory and not upon the substances of general laws, background conditions and phenomena to be explained. The deductive-nomological approach has come to dominate the practice of the social sciences. Indeed, the major precursors of the current academic consensus in sociology, anthropology, and economics. Weber and Durkheim, Radcliffe-Brown and Malinowskl, Menger, Jevons, and Walrus, all regarded subsumption under the general laws as the essence of scientific explanation, and took the discovery of such laws to be the means for making the social sciences truly scientific (Miller, 1991).

Current social science research is laden with a predilection for warranted assertability based on the syllogistic form of theories and models. Economics stakes its claim as a true science because its core propositions can all be reduced to mathematical equations whose truth depends upon form, not content. The increasing use of the logic tools of economic analysis, and particularly game theory, by strategic management researchers provides an illustration of the reliance of the field on formal models within the context of the deductive-nomological approach to warrant the claims to truth of propositions (Camerer, 1991; Saloner, 1991). Similarly, the population ecology approach to organizational sociology relies heavily upon formal models to provide justification for its theories (Hannan & Freeman, 1989).

In contrast, the resource-based view contains an implicit rejection of the thesis that the truth value of a proposition can be assessed by its syllogistic form. The view of competition as a process implies a rejection of the truth value of formal equilibrium models of neoclassical and industrial organization economics on the grounds that these models do not correspond to reality. Thus, from the perspective of the resource-based view, the critical test of the truth value of a proposition is not whether it has a syllogistic form consistent with the deductive-nomological approach; it is whether the proposition has a basis in reality. Note, however, that rejection of the truth value of propositions constructed following the deductive-nomological approach does not imply that such propositions are without merit. Even if they do not correspond to reality, they may be useful if they help us to understand reality (this is an attribute that many claim for neoclassical and game theory models, Camerer, 1991; Postrel, 1991).

Causality and confirmation

Explanation is an important goal of scientific inquiry. For the logical positivist, however, explanation is limited by our inability to determine causality. The argument goes back to Hume (1739), who outlined criteria in which two events, e_1 and e_2, would have to meet in order for a causal relationship between e_1 and e_2 to exist. According to Hume, e_1 and e_2 must be constantly conjoined in a specific temporal sequence. That is, every time e_1 occurs e_2 must also occur. There must also exist a necessary connection between e_1 and e_2; there must be something about e_1 from which e_2 necessarily follows. Building upon his central premise that all ideas are based upon sensory impressions, Hume argues that while we can observe the constant conjunction of e_1 and e_2, we cannot observe the necessary connection between the two:

> Reasons can never shew us the connexion of one object with another, tho' aided by experience, and the observation of their constant conjunction in all past instances. When the mind, therefore, passes from the idea or impression of one object to the idea or belief of another, it is not determin'd by reason, but by certain principles, which associate together the ideas of these objects, and unite them in the imagination. (Hume, 1739: 93, original spelling)

Thus, for Hume, causality is an imagination of the mind, driven by custom and principle rather than knowledge. While we may speculate about what causes e_1 and e_2 to be related, such speculations are invariably metaphysical because we can never observe the mechanism that links e_1 and e_2. The mechanism is unobservable, and, therefore, lacks meaning. So while Newton can postulate that gravity is the mechanism that causes an apple to fall to earth, Hume would counter that we do not know this since we cannot observe gravity.

The version of Hume that prevails in twentieth century positivism is somewhat different. This account is based upon the deductive-nomological model discussed in the previous section. It holds that an event e_1 causes an event e_2 when there are general laws, L and statements C describing conditions antecedent to e_2 such that from L and C, together with a statement reporting the occurrence of e_1, a statement describing the subsequent occurrence of e_2 can be deduced (Boyd, 1991b). For the positivist, confirmation of a body of general laws, L_1 to L_n consists solely in the experimental confirmation of the observable predictions about e_2 deducible from them given an initial event, e_1, and a set of background conditions, C_1 to C_n. Thus, the deductive-nomological model allows the positivist to attribute the conjunction of two events, e_1 and e_2, to a causal relationship if e_2 can be *a priori* deduced from L_1 to L_n, C_1 to C_n and e_1, and if this predication is empirically confirmed.

It must be emphasized, however, that, for the positivist, confirming a theory through empirical observation is not equivalent to proving it to be true. Popper (1959) believes that ultimate empirical proof of a theory is impossible. A theory may have a truth value by virtue of its syllogistic form, but science is not capable of proving that the theory is a true reflection of the empirical world, and that the postulated causal mechanism has a correspondence in reality. The reasons for this are well known and are based upon the infinite scope of the universe and our inability to know for sure that the future will be similar to the past (Popper, 1959). Thus, at best, positivists believe that we can only speak of theories as being well corroborated, meaning that they have survived repeated empirical attempts to prove their predictions false (that is, their predictions have been repeatedly confirmed).

This skeptical ideology has become an underlying principle of management research. Popper's *Logic of Scientific Discovery* (1959) is used and cited as authoritative in doctoral seminars and training for those entering the field of management research. Critiques of theory development in the field are emphatic that proof of theories is not possible, and that falsification is the core assumption in the generation of theories and hypotheses (Bacharach, 1989; Montgomery, Wernerfelt, & Balakrishnan, 1989; Whetten, 1989).

Realism

Although realism dates back to Kant, the philosophy gained momentum in the middle of the twentieth century as the epistemological problems created by quantum theories in physics were debated in philosophical circles (Aronson, 1984; Puttnam, 1990). Quantum theory proved problematic for positivism since the theoretical entities of quantum mechanics, electrons, neutrons, quarks, etc., are inherently unobservable. This is because the very act of trying to observe these entities actually changes their state. Thus, all we can observe are the effects of quantum entities (such as the vapor trails that quantum entities leave in the cloud chambers of linear accelerators). Since positivists have a thorough-going hostility to unobservable or purely theoretical entities, quantum mechanics presented a head-on challenge to the positivist philosophy of science. This is the challenge that realism addresses. Analogous to the previous section, we will examine the realist position with regard to the problem of meaning, which goes beyond verification, the problem of truth, which emphasizes correspondence, and the problem of causality and confirmation.

Beyond verification

The hallmark of realism is a belief that theories of science give us knowledge about the unobservable, and that under certain circumstances we may have good reason for believing statements about unobservable entities to be true. This is clearly the antithesis of positivism, with its insistence that no knowledge of unobservable phenomenon is possible (that is, only objects that can be observed have meaning), and that theories based upon unobservable entities are not scientific but metaphysical. According to realists, when a well confirmed scientific theory appears to describe unobservable theoretical entities, it is almost always appropriate to think of its theoretical terms as really referring to unobservable features of the world, which exist independently of our theorizing about them, and of which the theory is probably approximately true (Boyd, 1991a). So, for example, according to realists the quantum theory of physics suggests that atoms are made up of very small entities with various properties. The evidence that we have that such entities exist independent of our theorizing about them is not based upon observation of the entities themselves, since they are unobservable, but upon observation of their effects.

In this sense, the resource-based view of the firm is a realist theory. Several key theoretical entities in the resource-based view are, by definition, unobservable. Their existence can only be verified through their observable effects. Thus, following the logic of the resource-based view, a scholar might argue that if it can be shown that firm-specific positive abnormal returns decay only slowly over time, this can be taken as evidence for the existence of barriers to imitation (that is, if barriers to imitation were absent, any positive abnormal returns would soon be competed away). Indeed, from this perspective the height of barriers to imitation can be inferred from the length of time that it takes positive abnormal returns to be competed away. It should be emphasized that a positivist would completely reject such an explanation. For those who accept the realist position, however, it is interesting to note that there is a growing body of sophisticated econometric evidence that is consistent with the resource-based view of competition as a process in which positive abnormal returns decay only slowly (Cubbin & Geroski, 1987; Jacobsen, 1988).

As an aside, it should be noted that the resource-based view is far from alone in its appeal to realism. Despite the dominance of positivism, implicitly realist theories can be found throughout the social sciences. For example, key theoretical constructs of the new institutional economics, such as transaction costs and agency costs, are inherently unobservable. The existence of such costs has never been directly verified in the numerous empirical studies now published on the topic. Rather, their existence is inferred from their impact upon governance mechanisms and organizational form, which are observable (Williamson, 1985). Similarly, one of the founders of modern management theory, Barnard (1938), defined the organization as a pure construct, which in itself was unobservable and could only be defined through its visible effects in the behavior and speech of organizational actors. Ransom, Hinnings & Greenwood (1980) weave a similar argument for the foundations of organization structure and the process of organizational structuring. In their view, structuring is founded on interpretive schemes, shared values and mutual understanding between members, which are unobservable and unspoken. These schemes surface only intermittently as verifiable elements, and are articulated only to justify a structural configuration.

Correspondence theories of truth

Realists adhere to a correspondence theory of truth, according to which propositions are true if, and only if, they correspond to actual conditions in the real world (Boyd, 1991a; Horwich, 1990). The argument goes back to Tarski (1935) who used symbolic logic to demonstrate that what makes a proposition true is whether or not it corresponds to the facts (see Boyd, 1991a for a summary of Tarski's argument). This view stands in direct conflict with the formal theory of truth, in which the truth value of a proposition is assessed by its syllogistic form, as opposed to its substance. The realist conception is that the truth value of a proposition can only be assessed by its substance – it is only true if its substance corresponds to that of the real world.

As already noted, accepting the realist position raises questions about the utility of formal model building based upon the deductive-nomological approach that has become so characteristics of economics, and which now seems to be invading other social sciences. Many game theorists, for example, will state that their model «proves» a certain proposition to be true (that is, it proves that the proposition has truth value). A realist would counter that just because a proposition adheres to the logic of the deductive-nomological approach, it is not true unless it corresponds to reality. A striking example of this is Postrel's (1991) use of game theory to demonstrate that given certain background conditions, it is rational for bank managers to set their pants on fire in public (the so-called flaming trousers conjecture). Postrel's point is that game theory is no more than a logical tool, and as such it can be misused to produced absurd propositions that nevertheless have the correct syllogistic form. Only if the proposition corresponds to reality does it have truth value.

Causation and confirmation

Earlier we saw how the deductive-nomological approach to warranted assertability has been used by positivists to assign a causal ordering to two events occurring in conjunction. It is of note then, that many philosophers, including, but not limited to, realists, have argued that the deductive-nomological approach faces serious problems (Boyd, 1991b; Gasper, 1991). First, critics question whether it is possible to specify which general statements count as genuine general laws without references to unobservables or causal factors. The «law» of gravity implies the existence of gravity waves and gravity waves have not, as yet anyway, been observed. They are unobservable (at least given current instrumentation). Thus, realists argue that the deductive-nomological model, which is an attempt to dispense with unobservables, in fact invokes unobservables. Given this, argue realists, why not admit that unobservable mechanisms cause two events (e_1 and e_2) to appear in conjunction?

A second problem with the deductive-nomological approach concerns so called asymmetries of explanation. For example, given the laws of optics, the position of the sun, and the height of a certain flagpole, we can calculate the length of the shadow the flagpole will cast. Here, the deductive-nomological model confirms our intuition that the height of the flagpole explains the length of the shadow. But given the length of the shadow and the other information, we can just as well calculate the height of the flagpole, and yet it would be wrong to say that the length of the shadow explains the height of the flagpole.

Another problem with the deductive-nomological model, which is particularly relevant to its application in social science settings, is its lack of depth. While the deductive-nomological model might be used to predict a particular phenomena, it might not explain it. For example, let us suppose it were possible, given general laws and background conditions, to predict the outbreak of World War 1 on the basis of the information about the assassination of the Archduke Ferdinand in Sarajevo. Such a prediction would not constitute a satisfactory explanation of the outbreak of war since the events cited in the model would at best be immediate triggers of the conflict, and not its deep cause. It is likely that if the war had not broken out in this way, then the deep causes would have bought about the war in some other way. A satisfactory explanation should incorporate these deep causes, but a formulation based upon the deductive-nomological approach may fail to do so.

A final problem with the deductive-nomological approach is that it is possible to have explanations that do not conform to the logical structure of the deductive-nomological model. In particular, we can often propose plausible explanations for events without invoking general laws. For example, the absence of a mass-based working class political organization in the United States has been explained in terms of such factors as constitutional design, geography, uneven economic development, racism, ethnic and religious divisions, and state repression (Cohn & Rogers, 1986). The explanation is reasonable and seems worth taking seriously, but it invokes no general laws.

These criticisms of the deductive-nomological approach should resonate with those who advocate the resource-based view of the firm. The explanation of firm performance found in the resource-based view is a deep and context-specific one. It does not appeal to any general laws and, accordingly, it does not follow the structure of the deductive-nomological model. In the resource-based view each firm's resource endowment is depicted as being a unique product of its human and physical resources and its organizational routines, which in turn are depicted as being a product of the firm's own unique organizational history. Since each firm is, by definition, unique, it follows that the particular composition of a firm's resource base cannot be explained by reference to the deductive-nomological model. No covering laws are being invoked here to explain why a firm has the resource endowment that it does. Indeed, unlike the game theoretical approach to strategy, the resource-based literature is characterized both by its lack of formal model building along the lines of the deductive-nomological approach, and by the richness and depth of its narrative.

However, the criticisms of the deductive-nomological model do leave realists with something of a problem. If the deductive-nomological model is to be rejected, what is to be put in its place? For the realist the answer is quite straightforward. Just as we should be realists about the existence of unobservable entities, it is argued that we should be realists about causality (Boyd, 1991b). Realists argue that it is incomprehensible for us to conceive of events occurring without an underlying causal structure. For the realist, causation is viewed as one of the fundamental ordering principles of nature. The heavy skepticism of positivists regarding causation is viewed as unwarranted, and thus rejected.

As for theory confirmation, here too realists part company with the skepticism of positivists. While the realist would not disagree with Popper's (1959) assertion that we cannot ever conclusively prove a theory to be true, the realist argues that we can have good reasons for believing that a theory is approximately true. Therefore, we may be justified in acting as if it were true. The realist approach here is commonly known as the inference to the best explanation. The thought underlying the inference to the best explanation is that if a theory consistently explains some data better than any other theory explains them, we thereby have a good reason to act as if it were true. Moreover, realists argue that our belief in a theory can be stronger when it explains a diverse set of phenomena. It would be an absurd coincidence, indeed, if a wide variety of different kinds of phenomena were all explained by a particular theory, and yet that theory were not true. Thus, the argument from coincidence supports a good many of the inferences that we make to the best explanation (Cartwright, 1991).

Realists also point out, with some justification, that the inference to the best explanation is the only common sense position to take. After all, our design of bridges, airplanes, atomic power stations, computers, and space vehicles is guided by theories that we believe to be approximately true, even if we cannot ever conclusively prove them to be so.

Yet again, this formulation should prove attractive to proponents of the resource-based view. After all, while we can never conclusively prove the resource-based view to be true, recent empirical evidence does seem to suggest that a resource-based perspective explains the data on both the source of performance variations across firms (Hansen & Wernerfelt, 1989; Rumelt, 1991) and the persistence of abnormal returns over time (Cubbin & Geroski, 1987; Jacobsen, 1988) far better than does either the neoclassical or industrial organization perspectives. If empirical work continues to confirm this pattern, we may have grounds for acting as if the theory were true. Confirmation of such a theory would be particularly important for a field like strategic management, which seeks to do more than just explain phenomena, but also to generate normative rules that can help individual firms.

Conclusion: some methodological implications

We have argued that the resource-based view of the firm is grounded in a realist philosophy of science. The key to understanding this is the reliance of the resource-based view upon theoretical entities that are, by definition, unobservable. A positivist would reject the resource-based view as being metaphysical, but if one accepts the realist position with regard to verification, truth, causality and confirmation, the resource-based view qualifies as a valid scientific theory. It should be pointed out that the resource-based view is in good company here. One of the most successful and influential theories of physics, quantum mechanics, is also firmly grounded in a realist philosophy of science. While the skeptical positivist argues that quantum mechanics flirts dangerously with metaphysics, the theory's robustness and utility cannot be denied, and for the realist this is enough. It is at least possible that ultimately, the same might be said of the resource-based view of the firm.

By way of conclusion, let us sketch out two important methodological implications of the philosophical groundings of the resource-based view. The first point to emphasize is that, ultimately, the resource-based view of the firm will stand or fall not on the basis of whether its key constructs can be verified, but upon whether its predictions correspond to the reality observed for populations of firms. What scholars need to do is to theoretically identify what the observable consequences of unobservable resources are likely to be, and then go out to see whether such predictions have a correspondence in the empirical world. The analogy here is with quantum mechanics, which has been confirmed not by observing sub-atomic entities (since they are unobservable), but by observing the trail left by sub-atomic entities in the cloud chambers of linear accelerators. Good models for the kind of large sample econometric work that needs to be done can be found in empirical studies looking at the persistence of abnormal returns over time (Cubbin & Geroski, 1987; Jacobsen, 1988), and at the relative contribution of industry and firm-specific (resource-based) factors in explaining performance variations across firms (Hansen & Wernerfelt, 1989; Rumelt, 1991).

A second point is that the description of the firm found in the resource-based view is complex, deep and historical. Since each firm is viewed as a unique entity, explaining the cause of superior (or inferior) performance at the level of the individual firm calls for clinical work of the type that is currently unfashionable in management literature. Note that we are not advocating a return here to the type of unstructured and atheoretical case study work that characterized the early strategic management literature. Rather, we are arguing that there is value, in terms of explanation, in viewing the firm as a natural laboratory in which the theoretical propositions of the resource-based view are already being tested. The challenge facing researchers is to take a collection of firms

that face a similar environment (for example, firms in the same industry), to establish how these firms differ with regard to their resources,
and to link these differences to barriers to imitation and the persistence
of performance differences across time. Such work should follow the
methodological ground rules for comparative clinical work laid out by
Eisenhardt (1989), Leonard-Barton (1990) and the like (for a recent example of such work see Collis, 1991). Die-hard positivists will view such
work with skepticism, claiming that generalization from a small sample
is unacceptable. While recognizing the limits of clinical work, the realist
should not be put off by this. If repeated clinical studies across a wide
variety of contexts yield empirical results that are consistent with the resource-based view, then in following a realist philosophy of science we
may legitimately claim that the theory corresponds to reality. The key
here, however, is the need for repeated clinical studies. For only with
enough repetition across contexts will advocates of the resource-based
view be able to invoke the coincidence argument; that is, a theory that
has been confirmed across such diverse situations must stand a good
chance of being true and, therefore, we should act as if it were true.

References

Alchain, A.A. (1950): Uncertainty, Evolution, and Economic Theory. *Journal of Political Economy 58*: 211-222.

Aronson, J.L. (1984): *A Realist Philosophy of Science*. London: Macmillian Press.

Bacharach, S.B. (1989): Organizational Theories: Some Criteria for Evaluation. *Academy of Management Review 14*: 496-515.

Barnard, C.I. (1938): *The Functions of the Executive*. Cambridge, MA: Harvard University Press.

Barney, J.B. (1986a): Strategic Factor Markets: Expectations, Luck and Business Strategy. *Management Science 32*: 1231-1241.

Barney, J.B. (1986b): Organizational Culture: Can it be a Source of Sustained Competitive Advantage? *Academy of Management Review* 11: 791-800.

Barney, J.B. (1991): Firm Resources and Sustained Competitive Advantage. *Journal of Management 17*: 99-120.

Boyd, R., P. Gasper & J.D. Trout (1991): *The Philosophy of Science*. Cambridge, MA: MIT Press.

Boyd, R. (1991a): Confirmation, Semantics and the Interpretation of Scientific Theories. In R. Boyd, P. Gasper & J.D. Trout (eds.): *The Philosophy of Science*. Cambridge, MA: MIT Press.

Boyd, R. (1991b): Observations, Explanatory Power, and Simplicity: Towards a Non-Humean Account. In R. Boyd, P. Gasper & J.D. Trout: *The Philosophy of Science*. Cambridge, MA: MIT Press.

Brown, H.I. (1970): *Perception, Theory, and Commitment*. Chicago: Precedent Publishing.

Camerer, C.F. (1991): Does Strategy Research Need Game Theory? *Strategic Management Journal 12*: 137-152.

Cartwright, N. (1991): The Reality of Causes in a World of Instrumental Laws. In R. Boyd, P. Gasper & J.D. Trout (eds.): *The Philosophy of Science*. Cambridge, MA: MIT Press.

Cohn, J. & J. Rogers (1986): *The Rules of the Game*. Boston: South End Press.

Collis, D.J. (1991): A Resource Based Analysis of Global Competition. *Strategic Management Journal 12*: 49-68.

Conner, K.R. (1991): A Historical Comparison of Resource Based Theory and Five Schools of Thought Within Industrial Organization Economics: Do We Have a New Theory of the Firm? *Journal of Management 17*: 121-154.

Cubbin, J. & P. Geroski (1987): The Convergence of Profits in the Long Run: Inter-Firm and Inter-Industry Comparisons. *Journal of Industrial Economics 35*: 427-442.

Dierickx, I. & K. Cool (1989): Asset Stock Accumulation and Sustainability of Competitive Advantage. *Management Science 35*: 1504-1511.

Eisenhardt, K.M. (1989): Building Theories from Case Study Research. *Academy of Management Review 14*: 532-550.

Jacobsen, R. (1988): The Persistence of Abnormal Return. *Strategic Management Journal 9*: 415-430.

Jacobsen, R. (1992): The «Austrian» School of Strategy. *Academy of Management Review 17*: 782-807.

Hacking, I. (1983): *Representing and Intervening*. Cambridge: Cambridge University Press.

Hannan, M.T. & J. Freeman (1989): *Organizational Ecology*. Cambridge, MA: Harvard University Press.

Hansen, G.S. & B. Wernerfelt (1989): Determinants of Firm Performance: the Relative Importance of Economic and Organizational Factors. *Strategic Management Journal 10*: 399-411.

Hempel, C.G. (1962): Explanation in Science and History. In R. Colodny (ed.): *Frontiers of Science and Philosophy*. Pittsburgh: University of Pittsburgh Press.

Hume, D. (1739): *Treatise of Human Nature*. Buffalo: Prometheus Books.

Horwich, P. (1990): *Truth*. Oxford: Basil Blackwell.

Kirzner, I.M. (1979): *Perception, Opportunity, and Profit*. Chicago: University of Chicago Press.

Leonard-Barton, D. (1990): A Dual Methodology for Case Studies: Synergistic Use of a Longitudinal Single Site with Replicated Multiple Sites. *Organization Science 1*: 248-265.

Lipperman, S. & R.P. Rumelt (1982): Uncertain Imitability: an Analysis of Inter-Firm Differences in Efficiency under Competition. *Bell Journal of Economics 13*: 418-438.

Mahoney, J.T. & J.R. Pandian (1992): The Resource Based View within the Conversation of Strategic Management. *Strategic Management Journal 13*: 363-380.

Miller, R.W. (1991): Fact and Method in the Social Science. In R. Boyd, P. Gasper & J.D. Trout (eds.): *The Philosophy of Science*. Cambridge, MA: MIT Press.

Montgomery, C.A., B. Wernerfelt & S. Balakrishnan (1989): Strategy Content and the Research Process: a Critique and Commentary. *Strategic Management Journal 10*: 189-197.

Nelson, R.R. & S.G. Winter (1982): *An Evolutionary Theory of Economic Change*. Cambridge, MA: Belknap Press.

O'Hear, A. (1989): *An Introduction to the Philosophy of Science*. Oxford: Oxford University Press.

Penrose, E.T. (1959): *The Theory of the Growth of the Firm*. Wiley.

Prahalad, C.K. & G. Hamel (1990): The Core Competence of the Corporation. *Harvard Business Review*. May-June: 79-90.

Popper, K.R. (1959): *The Logic of Scientific Discovery*. London: Hutchinson.

Porter, M.E. (1991): Towards a Dynamic Theory of Strategy. *Strategic Management Journal 12*: 95-117.

Postrel, S. (1991): Burning Your Britches Behind You: Can Policy Scholars Bank on Game Theory? *Strategic Management Journal 12*: 153-155.

Puttnam, H. (1990): *Realism with a Human Face*. Cambridge, MA: Harvard University Press.

Ransom, S., B. Hinnings & R. Greenwood (1980): The Structuring of Organizational Structures. *Administrative Science Quarterly 25*: 1-17.

Reed, R. & R.J. DeFillippi (1990): Causal Ambiguity, Barriers to Imitation, and Sustainable Competitive Advantage. *Academy of Management Review 15*: 88-102.

Rumelt, R.P. (1991): How Much Does Industry Matter? *Strategic Management Journal 12*: 167-186.

Russell, B. (1946): *A History of Western Philosophy*. New York: Simon & Schuster.

Saloner, G. (1991): Modeling, Game Theory, and Strategic Management. *Strategic Management Journal 12*: 119-136.

Tarski, A. (1935): Der Wahrheitsbegriff in den formalisierten Sprachen. *Studia Philosophica 1*: 261-405.

Wernerfelt, B. (1984): A Resource Based View of the Firm. *Strategic Management Journal 5*: 171-180.

Whetten, D. (1989): What Constitutes a Theoretical Contribution? *Academy of Management Review 14*: 490-495.

Williamson, O.E. (1985): *The Economic Institutions of Capitalism*. New York: Free Press.

Wittgenstein, L. (1922): *Tractatus Logico-Philosophicus*. London: Routledge.

Section Two

Including the Resource Based Perspective in the Field of Strategy

The integration of the resource based perspective within the boundaries of strategy is the focus of this section. In the first article, Torger Reve focuses on the theoretical foundations of the field of strategy. The article, building on the work of Porter's indusrial economics perspective adds the resource based perspective to give increased understanding of the field of strategy. In this way the article captures both the external and the internal dimensions of strategy.

Change and adaptation continue to be essential issues in the field of strategy. The traditional explanations of an organization's ability to change are supplemented by the resource based perspective in Joyce Falkenberg's article. This addition results in a more complete explanation of an organization's ability or disability to make necessary changes and adaptations.

The importance of strategic alliances within the field of strategy has gained recognition during the past decade. In their article, Sven Haugland and Randi Lunnan extend the established theoretical framework developed by Williamson, Eccles and Bradach, etc. by focusing specifically on the governance of interorganizational relationships which differ in their similarity to the focal company's core competence.

The resource based perspective is one of many challenges forcing a change in the way we think about strategic management. Bente Løwendahl and Øyvind Revang focus on the role of knowledge and skills in post-modern conditions.

Toward an Integrative Model of Strategy Development: From Dynamic Clusters to Core Competencies

Torger Reve

Strategic management has more than most other fields been subject to changing management trends. Adaptive as it is, strategic management has changed its focus from planning to intuition, from top-down to bottom-up, from external to internal. Typically, it does not take long before the pendulum swings back, however, from emerging to analytical strategies, from participative to managerial involvement, and from internal competence to competitive position. This paper argues against the adaptive foci of strategy. Strategy, as all other fields, has certain givens. The firm should gain a competitive position in the market, and the firm should develop a unique competence base internally to be able to sustain its competitive advantage at a profit.

In order to capture both the external and the internal dimensions of strategy, an integrative model of strategy development is advanced, starting with the macro forces of competition and ending with the micro variables of the core competence of the firm. The integrative model draws heavily on Porter's works on strategy (1990, 1985, 1980), but it also incorporates the more recent resource-based approaches to strategy (Itami, 1987; Prahalad & Hamel, 1990; Barney, 1991).

In the first section of the paper, strategy is defined in terms of its two inherent components: External position and internal base. In the following section, a coherent approach to strategy analysis is presented. The strategy analysis proposed starts with two levels of external analysis: (1) industry analysis (Porter, 1990) and (2) competitive analysis (Porter, 1980). It continues with two levels of internal analysis: (1) value chain analysis (Porter, 1985) and (2) strategic core analysis (Reve, 1990; Barney, 1991). The four levels of strategic analyses are hierarchically nested, focusing on how macro and micro forces of strategy interact. The result is an integrative model of strategic development applicable at the business level.

The strategy development approach advanced in this paper has been successfully applied in several Scandinavian corporations, and some of the practical experiences in using this approach to strategy development are shared in the paper. Unlike most other integrative approaches to strategy development advanced by consultants, the integrative model presented in this paper also has a sound theoretical base, moving the field of strategy into the arena of empirical social science research.

Strategy as external competitive position

Strategy is primarily concerned with how firms can obtain sustainable competitive positions in the marketplace. This means that firms have to offer products and services that meet customer preferences, are profitable and better than those offered by their competitors. The basic idea is captured by what McKinsey refers to as the value triangle (Figure 1), where the company and its competitor rivals offer superior value to targeted customers at the same time as they have to perform better on costs.

Figure 1: Value triangle

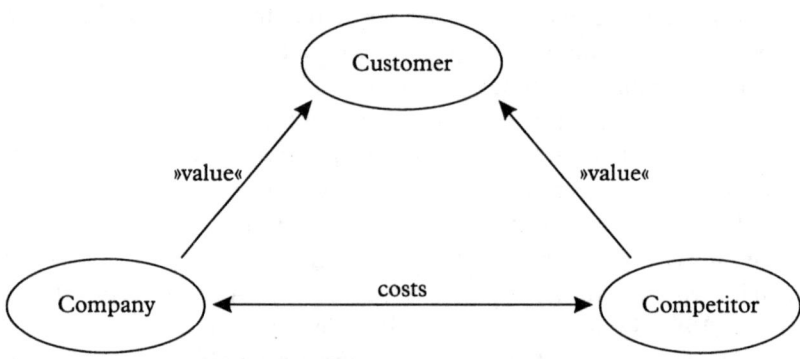

The idea of strategy as external competitive position goes back to classical writers on strategy as exemplified by Ansoff's (1965) growth matrix (Figure 2).

Strategy as competitive positioning paved the way for industrial organization economics (Caves, 1967; Porter, 1980), which has come to dominate much of the theoretical underpinnings of strategy. Basically, strategy deals with how firms can position themselves in concentrated

Figure 2: Growth matrix

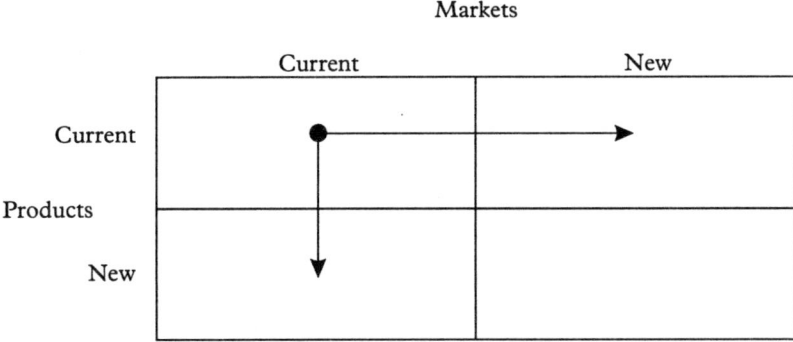

and differentiable markets. The main strategy message is to exploit imperfections in the product market, thus gaining monopoly rent from market power.

Strategy as internal resource base

Firms can only obtain sustainable competitive positions in the marketplace when they master a unique bundle of resources that provide a superior cost position or a differential advantage in their core offerings or both. Behind the core offerings (products, services and reputation) of the firm are core resources and core skills uniquely controlled by the firm, as illustrated in Figure 3.

Figure 3: Core triangle

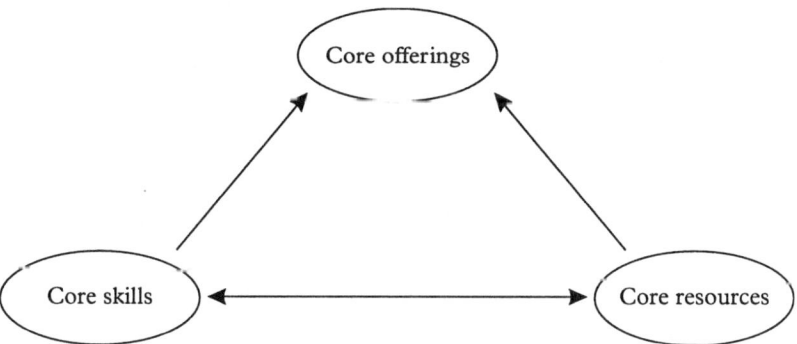

In the same way as the firm can position itself in the competitive marketplace as illustrated in Figure 2, the firm needs to establish a corresponding internal resource base of competence and technology, as illustrated in Figure 4.

Figure 4: Resource matrix

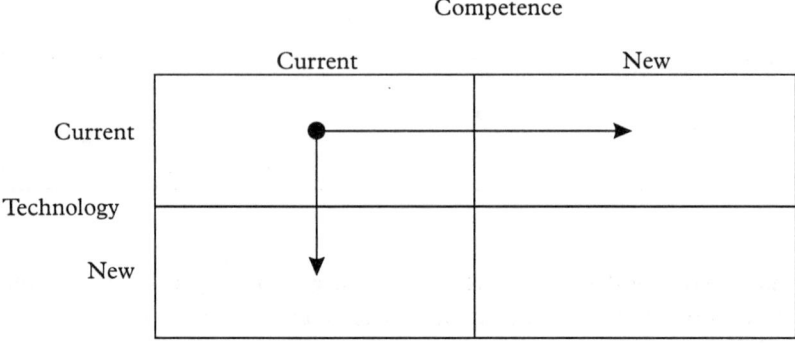

What is important to note when comparing the growth matrix (Figure 2) and the resource matrix (Figure 4) is that a new position in the growth matrix requires a new position in the resource matrix. New products may require new technology, while new international markets may require new competence in marketing and management. Thus, expanding the external competitive position requires a corresponding expansion in the internal resource base of the firm. On the other hand, acquiring new resources and skills may open a new competitive position given that the firm is able to commercialize its offerings.

The theoretical underpinnings of the resource-based approach to strategy come from several sources, including Schumpeterian economics (1934), evolutionary economics (Nelson & Winter, 1982), transaction costs economics (Williamson 1985) and business history (Chandler, 1990). The main strategy message is to exploit imperfections in the factor market, thus gaining entrepreneurial rent due to core competence.

Strategy as internal and external contracting

In a previous paper following some of the same logic (Reve 1990), the firm was defined as a set of internal and external contracts. Consistent with what has been said in the two previous sections, strategy becomes a set of internal contracts with core skills and complementary resources, which have to correspond to a set of external contracts with customers and competitors. The type of contracts will vary greatly from employment relationships for core skills, to relational contracts with key customers, to pure rivalry with the main competitors. The contracting model of strategy is conceptually illustrated in Figure 5.

Figure 5: Strategy as contracting

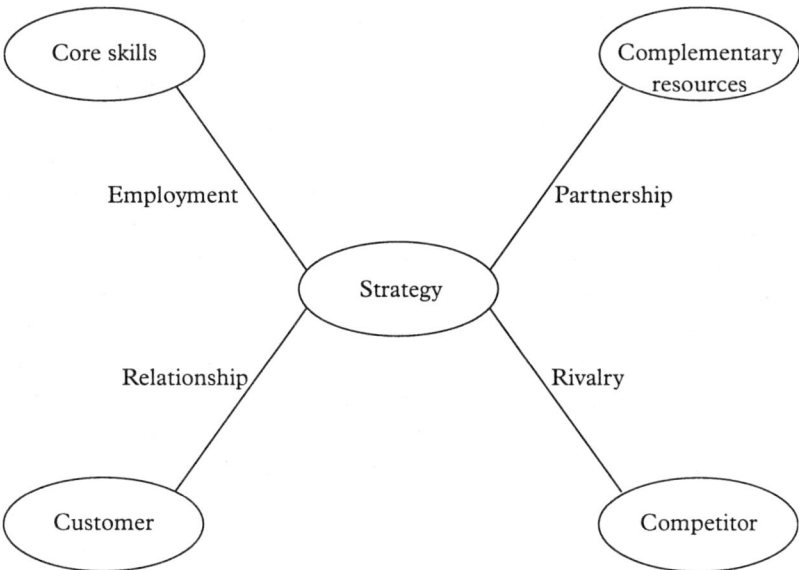

The contracting idea of strategy is adapted from transaction cost economics (Williamson 1985), arguing for hierarchical governance when asset specificity is high and market governance when asset specificity is low, with bilateral governance in the intermediate ranges. Macneil (1980) introduces the concept of relational contracts building exchange on a high amount of trust and solidarity when interdependence between the contracting parties is high. Thus, contracting is here used in its generic sense and is not restricted to formal or written contracts. The key feature is the nature of the relationships the firm forms.

Referring to the conceptual model presented in Figure 5, the firm will write employment contracts with its core skills and form partnership contracts with suppliers of complementary resources. Similarly, the firm will try to establish close relationships with its key customers, transforming market contracts to relational contracts, while its competitors are typically kept at arm's length rivalry.

Kay (1993) puts it very clearly when he defines strategy as the effective match between the external relationships of the firm and its own distinctive capabilities. Thus, strategy becomes the firm's unique set of skills, resources and relationships. The critical ability of the firm is to generate and configure skills, resources and customers and develop efficient contracts and relationships. Part one deals with the effectiveness of the firm, while part two deals with efficient organization and management.

The matching of the external competitive position and the internal resource base typically remains the weakest link in strategy development both theoretically and practically. That is also the way it should be if firms are to have any chance of maintaining their relative competitive advantages over time. Thus there will always remain an important element of creativity and commercial entrepreneurship in strategy.

In the following four sections of the paper a more systematic approach to strategic analysis is presented, going from macro to micro. The analytical approach taken builds on the concept of strategy as external competitive position and internal resource base as developed above. Although each of the elements discussed is well known from the strategy literature, their integration is new (Reve, 1990).

Industry analysis

Firms compete in industries with a horizontal and vertical structure and with certain demand characteristics. To analyze the forces of industrial competitiveness, Porter (1990) has proposed the famous diamond model as adapted in Figure 6.

The diamond model captures the demand conditions in the product market, the factor conditions in the factor market, as well as the structure and dynamics of the competitive arena in which the firm operates. In addition, the model points to the importance of related and supporting industries, getting at the vertical structure and the knowledge conditions of the industry. Finally, the diamond model includes the influence of government (taxes, subsidies and regulations) and external chance factors (environmental, political and social). The many arrows in the model indicate interaction effects.

Porter's diamond model has been repeatedly used for analyzing the competitiveness of countries, regions and industries. A consistent find-

Figure 6: Industry analysis

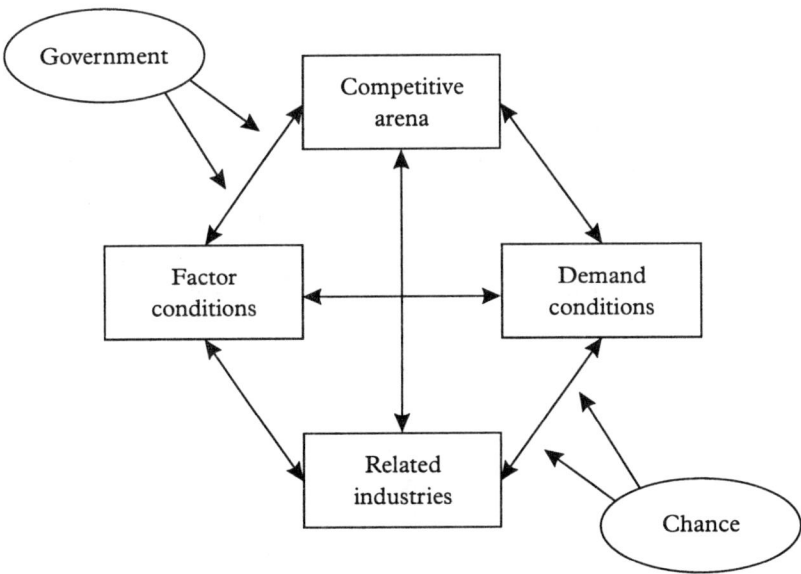

ing is that firms have a competitive advantage if they are part of dynamic industrial clusters. Industrial clusters are geographical concentrations of rival and cooperating firms sharing the same industrial knowledge base. In dynamic industrial clusters, continuous knowledge-upgrading processes take place, stimulating firms to innovate and adapt to changing market needs. In economic terms, positive knowledge externalities exist (Krugman, 1993) leading to industrial growth and innovation.

Based on several large studies of industrial competitiveness in Europe (Reve, Lensberg & Grønhaug, 1992; Reve & Mathiesen, 1994), a dynamic industrial cluster can be defined by 3 by 4 elements from the diamond model. The elements that stimulate industrial competitiveness are summarized in Figure 7.

In industry analysis the cluster conditions of an industry are evaluated. This tells the firm how much competitive pull it can obtain from its industrial milieu. It also says something about the quality of the firm's location and the industrial knowledge base to be exploited. We are talking about the Silicon Valley or Hollywood effect, to use two of the most famous examples, but most industries have similar knowledge fields on a smaller scale. There is no need to go into more detail about the impor-

Figure 7: Industrial competitiveness factors

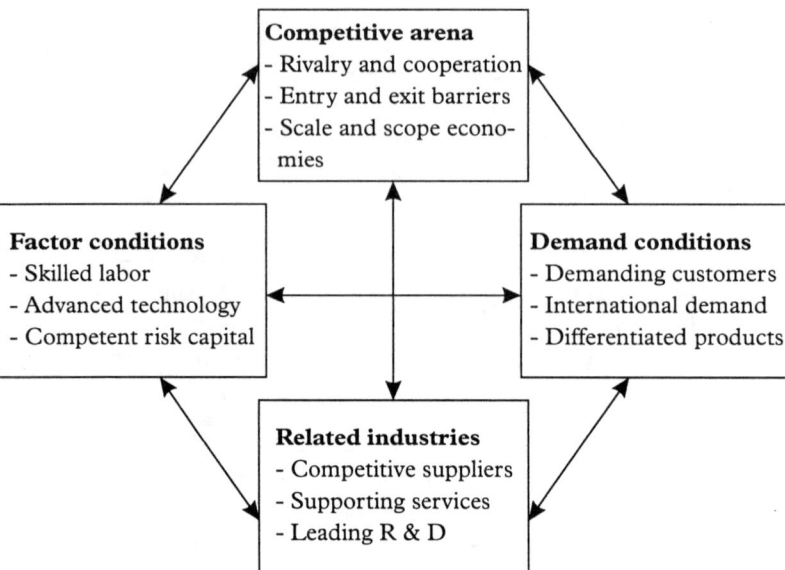

tance of industrial clusters here; their effects have been well document-ed in the strategy and industrial policy literature.

Industry analysis following the diamond model has emphasized the importance of demanding customers, competitive suppliers, advanced research and development milieus, specialized and motivated labor, skilled risk capital and technological rivalry. In other cases, structural holes in the industrial milieus have been identified, for example, lack of a machine industry and other suppliers, low research and development intensity and lacking rivalry among firms. Several firms in the Norwe-gian maritime industry, competing globally, have defined belonging to the Norwegian maritime cluster as one of their primary competitive ad-vantages. Consequently, they are increasingly aware of how they can contribute to the continuous upgrading of the Norwegian maritime mi-lieu. Other applications of industry analysis at the firm level include an oil company evaluating a new international entry and a Scandinavian auto parts company analyzing the dynamics of the European auto in-dustry.

An inherent problem in applying industry analysis from the firm perspective is the conflict between what is good for the industry and what benefits the individual firm in the short run. The degree of competitive rivalry is such a factor, and the same holds good for demanding customers. Lack of rivalry may create monopoly profits, but at the same time the industry may lose its ability to innovate. This is an additional argument for an anti-trust policy.

Competitive analysis

Industry analysis was primarily concerned with macro variables, and little attention was devoted to an analysis of the competitive position of individual firms. The latter is what competitive analysis is all about. In terms of the integrated model of strategy development, the competitive arena box is opened and individual firms are positioned in the various markets.

An appropriate tool for competitive analysis is Porter's five forces model (1980) as presented in Figure 8.

Figure 8: Competitive analysis

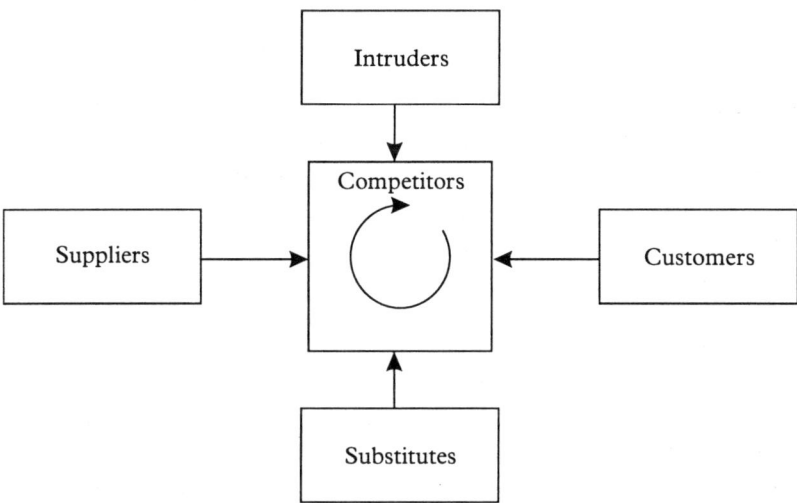

The five forces model includes an analysis of the relative positioning of the competitors within the defined market niche, as well as a similar analysis of the input and output markets of suppliers and customers. In addition to an analysis of market concentration, market shares and relative competitive positions, the competitive dynamics can be further analyzed using game theory (Tirole, 1988). An important element in the analysis of the vertical market structure is the relative power dependence between suppliers and producers, between producers and intermediaries and final customers. The bargaining balance between market actors largely determines prices and terms of trade. At the same time, market structures are subject to change due to mergers and acquisitions among existing actors, and the entry of new actors. The latter are referred to as intruders or potential competitors in Figure 8, and these should always to be included in a competitive analysis. Barriers to entry and exit here need to be analyzed.

Finally, substitutes that may replace or improve existing products or production and distribution processes should be taken into account. Typically, this means an analysis of technological change, which may bring about considerable strategic alterations.

There are two major dimensions in the competitive analysis advanced (Porter, 1980). The first is the vertical market dimension from suppliers, competitors and customers, including intermediary levels. This is the ongoing business dimension typically receiving most attention in strategic analysis. The second dimension is the change dimension, typically resulting from intruders and substitutes. These include new commercial or technological concepts, and there is often a certain resistance towards such change from the established industrial actors.

At a more detailed level, competitive analysis may be supplemented by competitor analysis, that is, detailed analysis of individual competitors. There is always room for market research and more detailed studies of consumer behavior. Similar methodology may also be used for the key input markets.

The experience from using competitive analysis in business is generally very positive. The model is widely applied in industry. The five forces model provides a simple and consistent language for analyzing the competitive position of firms, and the model builds on microeconomic theory and theories of imperfect markets. The challenge is to come up with the appropriate competitive moves when the analysis shows that the competitive situation changes. A weakness of Porter's five forces model is that it devotes too little attention to government and general environmental change. It concentrates too much on how to establish and maintain barriers to entry, and this may lead firms to be reactive rather than proactive in their strategic behavior.

Value chain analysis

The two previous strategic analyses, industry analysis and competitive analysis, have focused on the environmental forces and the external competitive position of the firm. There has been little or no detail about the firm. Typically, firms have been described in terms of size and market shares. Firms have been little more than production functions, although some tend to behave in a smarter way than others.

In the same way that the competitive arena in industry analysis was opened up for a more detailed competitive analysis, value chain analysis is introduced into the competitive arena to provide more micro detail and to give firms faces and organization. By bringing in value chain analysis, we move from external analysis to internal analysis, which is consistent with our initial discussion of the strategy concept.

Value chain analysis was developed by Porter (1985) based on an old idea of the successive vertical stages of value creation that exist in any industry.

A value chain consists of primary value activities such as incoming logistics, production, outgoing logistics, marketing and service, and an infrastructural overlay of managerial activities. The generic value chain as suggested by Porter (1985) is illustrated in Figure 9.

Figure 9: Generic value chain

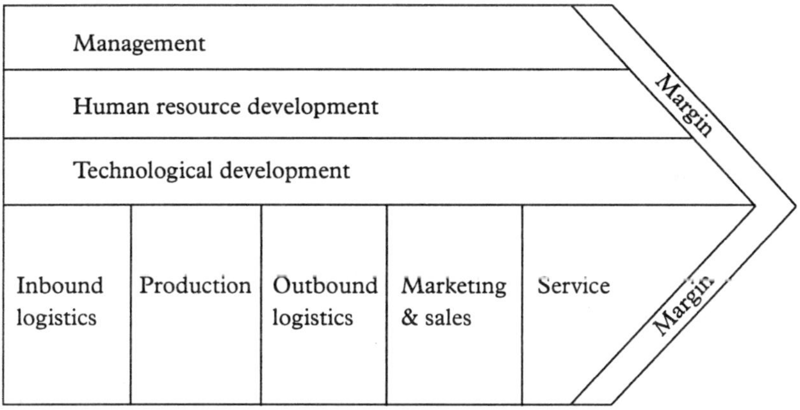

In practice, much more detail is provided by the value chains developed. Again a nested methodology is used as each set of value activities paves the way for a more detailed value chain until all business functional activities are laid out. Theoretically, each step in a value chain represents an homogeneous bundle of transactions with given asset characteristics (Williamson, 1985). This makes it possible to ask the fundamental questions about organization: Which value activities should be governed internally and which should be obtained in the market? Thus value chain analysis is a good tool for make-buy analysis, but there are also intermediary forms of partnership and alliances which should not be overlooked (Reve, 1990).

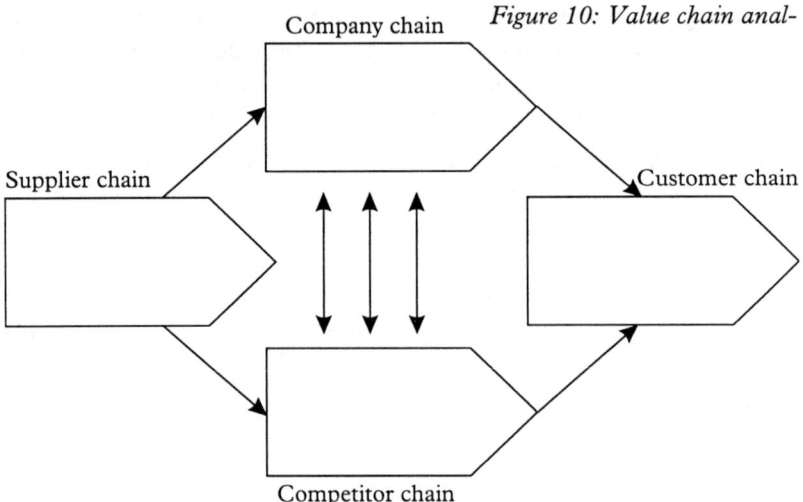

Figure 10: Value chain anal-

By including the vertical interfaces between the value chain of the focal company and its major suppliers and customers, a value chain system is established. One of the major strategic questions is how far into the customer's value chain a firm should integrate, and how far back into the supplier's value chain the firm should go. Again we are talking about dependence and close relationships.

The competitor's value chain should be included for comparative purposes so that benchmarking could be performed. For benchmarking to be meaningful, the comparative value chains should be detailed in terms of costs, quality and innovativeness of each value activity. Furthermore, the overall value chain configuration should be analyzed, searching for simplification and alternative and more efficient value chains to deliver the same products and services. Sometimes, benchmarking with completely different industries may provide fresh ideas for more innovative and cost-efficient solutions.

The experience in using value chain analysis in strategy development has again been very positive, especially in project-oriented industry, process industry and in technologically oriented industry. Service industries are sometimes more difficult to disaggregate into value chains, and sometimes the sequential nature of value chains has to be replaced by a more interactive value constellation (Normann & Ramirez, 1993). Pedagogically, value chains could preferably be drawn as a value tree with roots among suppliers and technological milieus and branches reaching the targeted customer segments. The appropriate cost structure for a value chain often requires modern value-based cost accounting, but approximations of relative costs will often be sufficient in most strategic analyses.

Strategic core analysis

Value chains disaggregate firms into value activities defined in terms of costs, quality, innovativeness and organization. What is still lacking are the resources and skills behind the value activities in the firm. The hole is filled in by what I call strategic core analysis (Reve, 1990). In strategic core analysis, each bundle of transactions which make up the value activities of a value chain is analyzed in terms of its criticality, its asset specificity, its replaceability and its value potential, and decisions are made on which activities should be governed internally, which should be left to strategic alliances, and which could most efficiently, and with little risk, be bought in the market.

The resulting value activities that emerge as most critical for the competitiveness of the firm constitute the strategic core of the firm. Strategic core activities should never be contracted out. Typically the strategic core of a successful company has a technological or conceptual component as well as a marketing component, and sometimes there are also some unique organizational or managerial qualities that make the firm run better than its competitors. The strategic core concept linked up with the value chain is illustrated in Figure 11.

Based on a sustainable strategic core, the firm can expand strategically along four paths: 1) downstream strategy, for example, linking more closely with customers, 2) upstream strategy, for example, linking closer with technological development, 3) horizontal strategy, for example,

Figure 11: Strategic core analysis

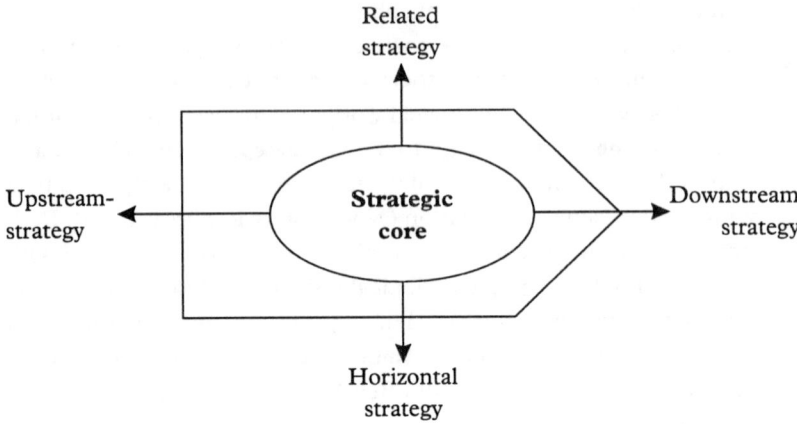

acquiring larger market shares, and 4) related strategy, for example, applying the strategic core in a new industry.

Commercially, the first two strategies often provide the largest strategic potential. Despite the large potential of following a vertical strategy, many corporations prefer a horizontal strategy, gaining higher market shares by mergers and acquisitions. This provides increased market power if the product can be differentiated, but only increased problems in many commodity-type industries. The more innovative strategic moves typically mean following a related strategy where existing core competence and market relationships are applied in a related industry. Shipyards moving into offshore fabrication, only then to move into project management, are but one example of a related strategy building on a common strategic core.

For many companies in the process of strategy development, strategic core analysis is often seen as the most innovative and useful part of the analytical exercise. This does not mean that the external analysis is of less value, but many companies already have a fairly good grip on their competitive situation. The same does not hold true for their understanding of their strategic core. Often the current core is compared with an ideal strategic core, and strategic moves have to be accompanied by the development of a new strategic core. Practical experience tells us that such moves have to be gradual and related if the firm is to succeed.

A weakness in strategic core analysis is the lack of exact methods to assess the critical nature of assets and competence. Often some abstraction is required to conceptualize what is the critical competence of the firm. An example was a manufacturer of fish powder machinery that termed its core competence, dehydration technology, and the firm found new applications in several other food-processing industries as well as in sewage treatment in the rapidly growing environmental industry.

What elements define the strategic core of a company? Considerable guidance is provided by the original writings of a leading Japanese professor of strategy, Hiroyuki Itami (1987). His most descriptive term is invisible assets, the competence and relationships which make the firm competitive. If these assets were obvious to everyone else, the strategic core could easily be imitated, and the relative competitive advantage would disappear. Many companies have taken this idea so literally that they have created a mystique about the inner qualities of the firm, for instance in terms of proprietary technology, key developmental skills or organizational culture. Microsoft is probably the most famous example.

Strategic core, as it is used in this paper, may have six components:

1. Critical resources
2. Unique technology
3. Core competence
4. Learning capabilities
5. Customer goodwill
6. Key relationships

The three first components of strategic core are those most often dealt with in the resource-based approaches to strategy (Wernerfelt, 1984; Prahalad & Hamel, 1990; Barney, 1991). The firm should control resources and capabilities that are valuable, rare, nonimitable and uniquely organized (Barney, 1991).

The fourth component is the learning capability of the firm. If the firm learns faster than other firms, it will maintain a relative competitive advantage. Other qualities of the firm could be fully visible. The firm will always learn and act faster if it is imitated. The problem is that there are organizational learning traps where errors also become part of the organizational repertoire.

The two last components are external relationships that the firm masters better than its competitors. The best example is the value of a well-established brand name such as Coca Cola or IKEA. Market relationships take time to develop, often requiring enormous market investments in intangibles. They are durable, and they rest on trust.

Similarly, firms could develop valuable reputations relative to suppliers and regulatory agencies. Integrity and being a good citizen may be of considerable strategic value in times of low confidence in business.

An integrated model of strategy development

This paper started with a definition of strategy as having two corresponding components: 1) external competitive positioning and 2) the internal resource base. Rather than conceiving these components in an intuitive sense, most firms need conceptual and analytical tools in their strategy development process. In the above sections a four-step methodology for strategic analysis was proposed, starting with 1) industry analysis (based on Porter's diamond model), 2) competitive analysis (based on Porter's five forces model), and continuing with 3) value chain analysis and 4) strategic core analysis. The analysis starts with macro variables (sometimes preceded by a scenario analysis), focusing on industrial clusters, markets and competition. The analysis ends with micro variables of the firm, focusing on value creation, organization, costs and competence.

Industry analysis and competitive analysis represent the external analysis, corresponding to what was earlier called opportunities and threats analysis. Value chain analysis and strategic core analysis represent the internal analysis, corresponding to what was earlier referred to as strengths and weaknesses analysis. The main difference in analytical approach is that the current analysis is theory-based, while traditional approaches were primarily checklists. In addition, the analytical approach presented here provides a coherent strategy language, including a number of simple pedagogical tools for communicating strategic analysis. The various analyses presented may be used with management teams to fuel strategy development processes. It provides the minimum amount of structure to strategy development processes to secure the required progress when working against deadlines. The success criteria are common language and communication.

What is integrative about the analytical approaches presented? The four analyses are hierarchically nested, rather like using Windows on your PC. The competitive arena box of the diamond model is opened and competitive analysis is applied at the next level of detail. The inner

Figure 12: An integrative model of strategy development

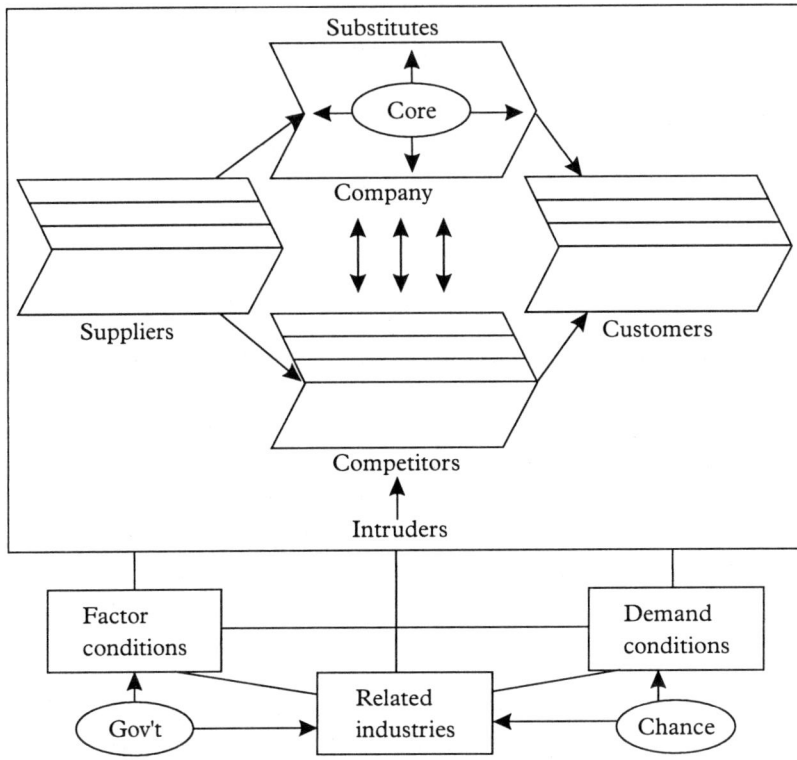

box of competitive analysis is opened up, and value chain analysis is introduced to disaggregate the firm into value-creating activities. Finally, the value creating activities of the firm are disaggregated into core skills and resources, which is the topic of strategic core analysis.

Figure 12 presents the final illustration of the integrated model of strategy development with the four analyses superimposed into one figure.

The hierarchical nesting can perhaps be better illustrated by computer graphics than by a simple paper copy.

Starting with the micro elements of core competence and core resources, these are combined into value-creating activities, supplemented with external skills and resources for then to make up the total value chain of the firm. The firm puts its efficient organizational boundaries around this constellation of skills and resources and forms the required internal and external contracts. Most importantly, the firm has to develop close relationships with customers, creating the required reputations as these relationships strengthen. Thus firms become organized bundles of core competence, resources and external relationships.

Firms meet in the marketplace, competing for demanding customers in the product market, for scarce competence and resources in the factor market, and for reputations and legitimacy in the institutional or political market. The outcome of these competitive games is to maximize or satisfy some objective function, typically profits for private firms.

Conclusion

What have been presented in this paper are actually the rudiments of a theory of the firm (Cyert & March 1963, Rumelt 1984, Reve 1990). The model assumes that the firm is boundedly rational and working under some type of competitive pressure. The model draws its concepts from microeconomics and organization theory, which are two of the main theoretical bases for the field of strategic management. Unlike more formalized models of the firm, the integrated strategy model presented here has been repeatedly applied in strategy development at the firm level with relatively promising results.

The next step is to take elements of the strategy model into more systematic empirical testing. Most importantly, the links between the four levels of analysis need to be empirically established. What type of value chain configuration is most efficient under given competitive conditions? What type of core competence is needed to deliver a certain value chain configuration? These and similar questions should be the target for future strategy research.

In the mean time we have to develop more precise theoretical concepts and better empirical operationalization. In particular, more work is needed to operationalize the concept of strategic core. The research agenda should also include the integration of competitive position approaches to strategy and internal resources approaches to strategy. In its extreme form, competitive position approaches treat the firm as a black box. Correspondingly, internal resource approaches to strategy are simply new arguments for the production-oriented firm, as if marketing orientation had never been developed. Again the conclusion must be to push for further integration of the two approaches to strategy, and this paper is a small contribution in that direction.

References

Ansoff, H.I. (1965): *Corporate Strategy*. London: Penguin.

Barney, J.B. (1991): Firm Resources and Sustained Competitive Advantage. *Journal of Management 17*: 99-120.

Caves, R. (1967): *American Industry: Structure, Conduct, Performance*. Englewood Cliffs, NJ: Prentice-Hall.

Chandler, A.D. Jr. (1990): *Scale and Scope: The Dynamics of Industrial Capitalism*. Cambridge, MA: Harvard University Press.

Cyert, R.M. & J.G. March (1963): *A Behavioral Theory of the Firm*. Englewood Cliffs, NJ: Prentice-Hall.

Itami, H. (1987): *Mobilizing Invisible Assets*. Cambridge, MA: Harvard University Press.

Kay, J. (1993): *Foundations of Corporate Success*. London: Oxford University Press.

Krugman, P.R. (1993): The Current Case for Industrial Policy. In D. Salvatore (ed.): *Protectionism and World Welfare*. Cambridge: Cambridge University Press, 160-179.

Macneil, I. (1980): *The New Social Contract: An Inquiry into Modern Contractual Relations*. New Haven, CT: Yale University Press.

Nelson, R.R. & S.G. Winter (1982): *An Evolutionary Theory of Economic Change*. Cambridge, MA: Harvard University Press.

Normann, R. & R. Ramirez (1993): From Value Chain to Value Constellation: Designing Interactive Strategy. *Harvard Business Review 72*: 65-77.

Porter, M.E. (1980): *Competitive Strategy*. New York: Free Press.

Porter, M.E. (1985): *Competitive Advantage*. New York: Free Press.

Porter, M.E. (1990): *The Competitive Advantage of Nations*. London: Macmillan.

Prahalad, C.K. & G. Hamel (1990): The Core Competence of the Corporation. *Harvard Business Review 68*: 79-91.

Reve, T. (1990): The Firm as a Nexus of Internal and External Contracts. In M. Aoki, B. Gustafsson & O.E. Williamson (eds.): *The Firm as a Nexus of Treaties*. London: Sage, 133-161.

Reve, T., T. Lensberg & K. Grønhaug (1992): *Et Konkurransedyktig Norge*. Oslo: Tano.

Reve, T. & L. Mathiesen (1994): European Industrial Competitiveness. *SNF-Report 35/94*. Bergen: Foundation for Research in Economics and Business Administration.

Rumelt, R. (1984): Toward a Strategic Theory of the Firm. In R. Lamb (ed.): *Competitive Strategic Management*. Englewood Cliffs, NJ: Prentice-Hall, 556-570.

Schumpeter, J.A. (1934): *The Theory of Economic Development*. Cambridge, MA: Harvard University Press.

Tirole, J. (1988): *Theory of Industrial Organization*. Cambridge, MA: MIT Press.

Wernerfelt, B. (1984): A Resource Based View of the Firm. *Strategic Management Journal 5*: 171-180.

Williamson, O.E. (1985): *The Economic Institutions of Capitalism*. New York: Free Press.

Strategic Change and Adaptation from a Resource Based Perspective

Joyce Falkenberg

The growth of firms needs to be viewed both as a process of exploiting existing capabilities and of developing new ones (Penrose, 1959; Teece, 1982). This resource-based perspective sheds new light on the understanding of organizational change and adaptation. In the recent past, the main focus of the change and adaptation literature has been on organizational responses to environmental changes. As the environment changed, organizations were expected to change and adapt their strategy. This perspective was implicit in Porter's 1980 definition of strategy formulation: «The essence of formulating competitive strategy is relating an organization to its environment» (Porter, 1980: 3). High performance was believed to be related to the dynamic, evolutionary nature of the fit between environment and organization (Romanelli & Tushman, 1988). However, research on organizational change and adaptation has led to contradictory findings; while some organizations have been able to adapt to environmental changes, other organizations were not able to adapt (Kelly & Amburgey, 1991), and some organizations, rather than reactively adapting to changes in their environment, were proactive in creating change in the environment (Wiersema & Bantel, 1993).

Based on the contradictory findings given above, the role of the environment as the determinant of organizational change and adaptation needs to be supplemented. Grant (1991) offers an explanation to the above finding that organizations do not adapt to environmental changes: «an externally focused orientation does not provide a secure foundation for formulating long-term strategy. When the external environment is in a state of flux, the firm's own resources and capabilities may be a much more stable basis on which to define its identity » (Grant 1991: 116). So although strategic change may be a result of environmental change, strategic change may emerge from within the organization as well. A more complete picture of strategy change could therefore be what Itami (1987) terms dynamic strategic fit: «the match over time between the factors that are external to a company and the internal factors and the content of strategy itself.» (Itami, 1987: 1).

The internal focus on resources is gaining attention. «Indeed, the core notion of strategy as a fit between the internal competencies of the firm and external opportunities incorporates a resource-based perspective» (Conner, 1991). This perspective focuses on an organization's internal resources as the source of sustainable competitive advantage. Hofer and Schendel (1978: 25) described competitive advantage as the «unique position an organization develops *vis-à-vis* its competitors through its patterns of resource deployments». The resource-based view of the firm focuses on two assumptions in analyzing sources of competitive advantage: 1) the model assumes that firms within an industry may be heterogeneous with respect to the strategic resources they control and 2) these resources may not be perfectly mobile across firms, thus heterogeneity can be long-lasting (Barney, 1991). The resources for a firm are limited with each firm having a unique collection of them. The resources accumulated determine the range of strategies the firm can take, and by implementing strategy the firm may accumulate more and different resources.

The resource-based perspective can be used to make a distinct contribution to the understanding of organizational change and adaptation, but explicit attention still needs to be paid to how resources can be used to maintain competitive advantage as the environment changes. The assumptions of the resource-based perspective, which lead to sustainable competitive advantage, are also the basis for the arguments for change or inertia in organizations. While growth involves a balance between exploiting the existing resources and the development of new ones (Penrose, 1959; Teece, Pisano & Shuen, 1990), the resource-based perspective suggests characteristics of resources which do not allow for changes. Because of these characteristics, competitive advantage may be lost due to changes in the environment; the advantages of the resources under present environmental conditions may result in resource inertia under future environmental conditions (Leonard-Barton, 1992).

Thompson, in his classic 1967 book, *Organizations in Action*, recognized the paradox of administration; the need for both stability and flexibility. Investigating the resource-based perspective to develop our understanding of organizational change and adaptation, these two aspects are clearly apparent. Resources within a firm can lead to organizational stability and even to rigidity; resources can also be used to give an organization flexibility. The resource-based perspective, with its focus on the characteristics and types of resources, will be used to gain additional insight into the understanding of organizational change and adaptation. This paper will build on the literature to develop an understanding of how resources and the relationship between resources and strategy can help increase our understanding of different major types of adaptation.

The prescriptions given about how the resource-based theory of the firm helps us better understand adaptation to environmental change has been handled only very generally in the literature. From a historical perspective, the work of Penrose (1959) sets the stage for the dynamic aspect of resource-based perspective in her explanation of the growth processes, and the limits to growth processes, of the firm. Following Penrose, much of the resource-based literature has implicitly or explicitly suggested a dynamic theory.

> In essence, the (strategy) concept is that a firm's competitive position is defined by a bundle of unique resources and relationships and that the task of general management is to adjust and renew these resources and relationships as time, competition and change erode their value. (Rumelt, 1984: 557-558)

Ulrich and Lake (1990) include the aspects of «to create» and «to adapt» in their definition of capabilities: »a business's ability to establish internal structures and processes that influence its members to create organization specific competencies and thus enable the business to adapt to changing customer and strategic needs». (p. 40) And Teece, Pisano and Shuen (1990) describe their approach to the resource-based view as a dynamic capabilities approach.

Although the dynamic aspect of the resource-based perspective has been made explicit, this approach needs to be made much more specific in stating how resources can influence the ability of an organization to adapt. In the following section, we review the literature on the characteristics of resources and the influence of these characteristics on the ability of an organization to change.

The next section of the paper discusses organizational change and adaptation and concludes with a classification of organizational change. While this classification helps us to understand the different types of organizational change, we must go beyond the classification to understand what lies behind the changes. Two important aspects will be taken up in this paper. The first concerns the relationship between strategy formulation or implementation; or as defined more precisely in this paper, the relationship between the strategy and the organizational resources. The second aspect concerns the characteristics of the resources that promote or delimit change. Finally, the paper will summarize the arguments in a framework which sets up the expected relationships for organizational change and adaptation from a resource-based perspective.

Organizational change and adaptation

Kelly and Amburgey (1991) outline the many ways that organizational change has been studied, including the need for change, how change occurs, the nature of change and how organizations change in anticipation to environmental threats and opportunities. The present paper focuses on how resources influence the process of change. Two types of organizational change have been found consistently in studying organizational adaptation. These two types have various terms associated with them: incremental convergence and radical reorientation (Tushman & Romanelli, 1985), or evolutionary vs. revolutionary (Greiner, 1972). Mezias and Glynn's (1993) review of the literature identified a third theme for managing organizational change, adding institutional to revolutionary and evolutionary approaches.

Van de Ven and Poole (1995), in classifying the literature on change and adaptation in terms of process, found support for yet another, additional approach. Based on an intensive literature review of alternative theories of change and development in the disciplines of biology, meteorology, geography, medicine, psychology, sociology, education, business and economics, they found four distinct families of process theories: life cycle theory, teleological theory, evolutionary theory and dialectic theory. Van de Ven & Poole argue for two levels of change, the organizational level and the population level, with life cycle theory and teleological theory at organizational levels, and evolutionary and dialectic theory at the population level. However, the present paper suggests that understanding of change and adaptation can be increased by assuming that all four theories can help explain change at the organizational level. For this there is support from, for example, Hrebiank & Joyce (1985), who suggest that environmental determinism (described here in terms of evolutionary theory) is also useful in thinking about organizational changes.

Life cycle theory assumes that change is a natural progression within an organization. The changes which occur are based on the history of the organization: «the developing entity has within it an underlying form, logic, program, or code which regulates the process of change and moves the entity from a given point of departure toward a subsequent end that is prefigured in the present state.» (Van de Ven & Poole, 1995: 575).

Evolutionary theory focuses on cumulative changes. While this theory is generally used to discuss cumulative changes in structural forms of populations of organizational entities (Hannan & Freeman, 1977; Aldrich, 1979), it also suggests an important way as to how individual organizations change. Change proceeds through variation, selection and retention. Here the opportunities for variation, the creation of novel forms, can emerge by blind or random change. Selection occurs through competition among the forms, with the environment selecting the forms that are best suited to the resource base, while retention involves the forces that perpetuate and maintain certain organization forms (Hannan & Freeman, 1977). Within organizations, evolutionary changes come about in the same way, but with the organization seeking variation, selection and retention (Hrebiniak & Joyce, 1985).

Teleological theory assumes that change is a result of planned action on the part of the organization to achieve a given goal: «the entity is purposeful and adaptive; by itself or in interaction with others, it constructs a envisioned end state, takes action to reach it, and monitors the progress.» (Van de Ven & Poole, 1995: 516). Important to the idea of the teleologic is equifinality, that there are several ways to achieve a given goal. Although the theory inherently affords creativity, there are limits to that creativity. «The organization's environment and its resources of knowledge, time, money, etc. constrain what it can accomplish» (Van de Ven & Poole, 1995: 516).

Dialectical theory assumes colliding events, forces and contradictory values which compete with each other for domination and control. This theory suggests that there are tensions between the periods of evolutionary and revolutionary forces which propel organizational growth. Stability is produced through «struggles and accommodations which maintain the status quo between oppositions. Change occurs when these opposing values, forces or events gain sufficient power to confront and engage the status quo.» (Van de Ven & Poole, 1995: 517).

While this classification is important as a basis for understanding different types of change, it does not help to explain why these changes occur. The purpose of the present paper is to explain how resources would influence these different categories of change; however, it is important to take an intermediate step. This intermediate step will focus on the relationship between strategy and resources as the driving force for change.

The interaction of resources and strategy

Within the resource-based perspective is a dynamic aspect which includes acquisition of new resources as well as the development and exploitation of existing resources (Wernerfelt, 1984). The focus on acquisition, development or exploitation suggests different relationships between strategy and resources. In the Western tradition, the prescription for strategy is first formulation and then implementation, with an important part of implementation being the acquisition of resources in order to implement the formulated strategy. This cycle has been found to be in sharp contrast to the Japanese description of much of their strategy in which resources were acquired and, based on the exploitation of these resources, a strategy was developed. See (Kagono, Nonaka, Sakakibara & Okumura (1985) for a comparison of the two perspectives.) These two different processes of strategic management, and the differences in characteristics of resources which are implicit in the perspectives, will be the basis of the discussion which follows.

These two different processes of strategic management imply very different roles of the interaction between strategy and resources. Itami and Numagami's (1992) build on this perspective, but focus particularly on the interaction between strategy and one resource, technology, which they justify as being the most fundamental of the core capabilities of a firm. They propose that there are at least three perspectives: 1) strategy capitalizes on resources, 2) strategy cultivates resources and 3) resources cultivate strategy. The following discussion builds on this literature with two important extensions; instead of focusing specifically on technology, it extends the interaction to a general discussion of resources, and a fourth perspective on the interaction between strategy and resources is proposed, this being a dynamic interaction between strategy and resources.

Interactions between strategy and resources can take the following perspectives:

1) between current strategy and current resources;
   strategy capitalizes on resources,

2) between future strategy and current resources;
   resources cultivate strategy,
3) between current strategy and new resources;
   strategy cultivates resources,
4) between future strategy and future resources;
   dynamic interaction between strategy and resources.

Strategy capitalizes on resources. The first interaction is based on the notion of contemporaneous match (Itami & Numagami, 1992). Current strategy takes advantage of current resources and is constrained by current resources. The focus is on the status quo, while recognizing that both strategy and resources change over time. While change occurs, current strategy does not affect future resources directly, nor do current resources affect current strategy explicitly (Itami & Numagami, 1992). This aspect adds a further explanation to the life cycle theory presented above.

Resources cultivate strategy. The Japanese style of strategy was described as one of accumulating resources which could then be used for different strategies. Resources can be accumulated in at least two different ways: one is a conscious effort to gather resources that might be useful in the future; the other is that resources which have been accumulated to allow for implementation of one strategy can be used for different strategies. The evolutionary theory described above is thus further explained.

Strategy cultivates resources. Strategy is formulated and resources are acquired to implement that strategy. This perspective is typical of the generalized belief of how companies in the United States first formulate, then implement, strategy. In the formulation of strategy, companies are able to suggest major changes in strategic direction, with the assumption that the necessary resources will be available to implement these strategies. This aspect, then, is a further description of the teleological theory.

Dynamic interaction between strategy and resources. New ways of competing, entrepreneurial vision, or innovation imply a dynamic interaction between strategy and resources. This view is supported by the existence (Van de Ven & Poole, 1995) of dialectical theory.

The focus here has been on the interaction between strategy and resources. By focusing on the process of change, that is, strategy leading change or resources leading change, implications are made as to the type of change from reproduction to creation (Van de Ven & Poole, 1995). While this focus has given further explanation to the different classifications of change, it is possible to extend the discussion by exploring the characteristics of resources. The next section focuses on the resource-based perspective, and, in particular, the characteristics of resources which can be important in change.

Resources as explanatory factors of change

Within the early literature on traditional strategic analysis, firm resources were defined as strengths that firms can use to conceive of and implement their strategies. (Learned, Christensen, Andrews & Guth, 1969). Daft (1983) further refined the definition of resources to include all assets, capabilities, organizational processes, firm attributes, information, knowledge, etc., controlled by a firm that enable the firm to conceive of and implement strategies that improve its efficiency and effectiveness. Wernerfelt (1984) categorized the resources: physical capital resources including the physical technology used in a firm, a firm's plant and equipment, its geographic location and its access to raw materials; human capital resources including the training, experience, judgment, intelligence, relationships and the insight of individual managers and workers in a firm; and organizational capital resources including the firm's formal reporting structure, its formal and informal planning, controlling and coordinating systems, as well as informal relations among groups within a firm and between a firm and those in its environment. Leonard-Barton (1992) added a fourth dimension to the above list; the values and norms associated with the various types of embodied and embedded knowledge and with the processes of knowledge creation and control.

Influenced by Penrose (1959), Amit & Shoemaker (1993) also differentiated between resources and capabilities, defining resources as «transferable input factors . . consist(ing) of proprietary know-how (for example, patents and trade secrets), financial or physical assets (for example, property, plant and equipment), human capital, government licenses, etc. Capabilities, in contrast, are tangible or intangible (invisible) assets that are firm-specific and are created over time through complex interactions among the firm's resources.» (Amit & Shoemaker,

1990: 4-5). While this differentiation is important in helping expand the concept of the different types of resources which are available to a firm, the present paper focuses on the characteristics of the resources (and capabilities) rather than on the different types.

Characteristics of resources

Not all resources are relevant as sources of sustaining competitive advantage; rather it is only those attributes of a firm's physical, human and organizational capital that enable a firm to conceive of and implement strategies that improve its efficiency and effectiveness which can be considered firm resources (Wernerfelt, 1984). It is these attributes or characteristics which will be the focus of this section, and important in the following discussion of change.

The work of Barney (1986, 1991) has been instrumental in determining when resources lead to sustainable advantage; companies must be heterogeneous with respect to the strategic resources they control, and the resources must be immobile across firms so that heterogeneity can be long lasting. Barney (1991) has recognized four attributes of resources as having the potential to be heterogeneous and immobile: 1) it must be valuable so as to exploit opportunities and/or neutralize threats in a firm's environment, 2) it must be rare among a firm's current and potential competition, 3) it must be imperfectly imitable, and 4) there cannot be strategically equivalent substitutes that are valuable, but neither rare nor imperfectly imitable. Valuable resources are those that enable a firm to conceive of or implement strategies that improve its efficiency and effectiveness. Rare resources give a competitive advantage to firms implementing value-creating strategies not simultaneously implemented by large numbers of other firms. Resources can be bundled to give value; some strategies require mixes of physical, human and organizational resources. Resources are a source of sustained competitive advantage only if the firms which do not posses the resources cannot obtain them, imitate them, or find substitutes for them.

These characteristics of resources which allow organizations to achieve sustainable competitive advantage also influence the adaptations an organization is able to make to changing environments. This aspect is discussed next.

Resource characteristics and change

Penrose (1959) noted that resources could be used in a variety of ways, so that the same resource used for different purposes, or in different ways and in combination with different types or amounts of services, provides a different service or set of services. This proposition needs further qualification. A more complete perspective is offered by Leonard-Barton (1992) who found that resources were sources of both change and rigidity in organizations. This section of the paper focuses on the characteristics of resources which allow them to be sources of sustainable competitive advantage, and then discusses how this promotes or prevents change and adaptation.

Fungible. A fungible resource is one which can be used in many different applications so that the type of strategic change is a function of the opportunities created by fungible resources. The use of a single resource in several businesses is the diversification pattern most often found (Andrews 1987). Schulze & Meyer (1991) discuss fungible in terms of capability mobility, the degree to which a capability can be used for different activities. However, fungible assets - product assets with little or no specificity - confront firms with a double-edged sword. While they can be applied with full discretion, they are seldom likely to produce sustainable competitive advantages (Russo, 1991).

Sticky. Teece, Pisano and Shuen (1990) claim that resource endowments are sticky over any strategically relevant time frame. This means that firms are stuck with what they have and must live with what they lack. Teece, Pisano and Shuen state three causes of stickiness: 1) capability development is viewed as an extremely complex process so that firms lack the organizational capacity to develop new capabilities quickly (Dierickx & Cool, 1989), 2) some assets are not tradable, for example, tacit know-how (Teece, 1982) and reputation (Dierickx & Cool, 1989), and 3) although assets can be purchased, firms gain little by doing so; purchasable resources are not sources of sustained competitive advantage.

Path dependence. Zucker (1977) describes core capabilities as being institutionalized; they are taken for granted within the corporation, based on an accumulation of decisions made over time and events in corporate history. In defining a firm's distinctive competence as the set of substantive rules and routines used by top management, managers' past decisions and decision rules are the basic genetics firms possess (Mahoney & Pandian, 1992). The core capabilities can often be traced back to the firm's first products. Core capabilities reflect accumulated behavior and beliefs based on early corporate successes (Leonard-Barton, 1992). Resources which lead to sustained competitive advantage for a firm are often a result of unique historical conditions, making it difficult for a firm which does not have a resource to obtain it. Therefore, the future strategy of a firm is determined by its history (Collis, 1991). Even the values within a company bear the imprint of the company founders and early leaders (Kimberly & Miles, 1980).

Causal ambiguity. Resources are imperfectly imitable because the ambiguity of what causes a resource or set of resources to lead to sustainable competitive advantage is uncertain, that is, causal ambiguity. Causal ambiguity exists when the link between the resources controlled by a firm and a firm's sustained competitive advantage is not understood or understood only very imperfectly. This actually keeps other firms from copying the resource, for example, by hiring managers who would not have knowledge of the linkage. As pointed out by Lippman and Rumelt (1982: 420), ambiguity may not only block imitation by rivals, but also may block factor mobility. While causal ambiguity can be a source of advantage *vis-à-vis* competitors, making a resource imperfectly imitable and thereby creating resource immobility, it can, for the same reason, result in institutionalism within the firm.

Reed and DeFillipi (1990) address three characteristics that individually or in combination can generate causal ambiguity: 1) tacitness, 2) complexity and 3) specificity. These will each be discussed separately. Tacitness refers to the implicit and noncodifiable accumulation of skills that results from learning by doing and is embodied within the skill component of competence. Organizational routines (Nelson & Winter, 1982) have a tacit dimension; these routines are often complex, not allowing for the knowledge embedded in these routines to be captured in codified form. But such tacit knowledge is «probably disorganized, informal and relatively inaccessible, making it potentially ill-suited for direct instruction». Crucial to the value of tacitness, then, is the inability of even a skilled performer to codify the decision rules and protocols.

Complexity results from having a large number of interdependent skills and assets. This actually keeps other firms from copying the resource, for example, by luring away managers who would not have knowledge of the linkage. Social complexity is a result of the interpersonal relations among managers in a firm, as well as, for example, the relation between the organization and its suppliers. While it is possible to specify how these socially complex resources add value to a firm, firms without attributes are not necessarily able to create them. For example, while technology may be imitable, the exploitation of this in a firm often requires the use of socially complex firm resources. Specificity refers to the transaction-specific skills and assets that are utilized in the production processes and provision of services for particular customers; the degree to which a resource meets the requirements for a particular activity (Reed & DeFillipi, 1990).

To summarize this discussion on causal ambiguity, if a firm understands the link between the resources it controls and its advantages, then other firms can learn about the link and acquire the necessary resources to implement the strategy. Although it may seem unlikely that a firm with a sustained competitive advantage will not understand the source of that advantage, given the very complex relationship between the firm resources and competitive advantage, such an incomplete understanding is not implausible. «Ambiguity may be so extreme that even managers within the firm do not understand the relationship between actions and outcomes» (Reed & DeFillipi, 1990). Lippman and Rumelt (1982) pointed out that ambiguity may not only block imitation by rivals, but may also block factor mobility.

The characteristics of resources which have been discussed here must be viewed in the dynamic aspect; as discussed above, these characteristics lead to both resource mobility (Schulze & Meyer, 1991) and to resource rigidity (Leonard-Barton, 1992). Fungible is the one characteristic which indicates that resources can be mobile. Yet as was stated above, fungible assets, although they can be applied with full discretion, are often not capable of leading to sustainable competitive advantage (Russo, 1991). The other characteristics suggest resource rigidity, that is, that organizations may not be able to adapt to changes in their environments.

In order to increase our understanding of organizational change and adaptation, however, we must look at these characteristics of resources in the light of the information on strategy.

The influence of resources on change: developing a framework

«The routine component of strategy formulation is the constant search for ways in which the firm's unique resources can be redeployed in changing circumstances» (Rumelt, 1984: 569). While Rumelt was clear in his expectations that resources could be used for change and adaptation, the discussion above suggests that both characteristics of resources, as well as differences in the interactions between strategy and resources, will lead to different expectations of organizational change and adaptation.

Table 1. A framework of the influence of resources on change processes

Change process	Interaction strategyresources	Type of strategic change expected	Characteristic of resource
Life cycle	Contemporaneous match	Reproduction	Path dependence
Evolutionary	Development	Cumulative	Stickiness
Teleological	Acquisition	Creation	Fungible
Dialectic	Exploitation	Innovation	Causal ambiguity

To further explain the classifications of change (Van de Ven & Poole, 1995), it is possible to look at both the relationship of resources and strategy, and also the characteristics of the resources (Table 1). Thus, this section proposes that an important explanatory factor in the process of change is the nature of the resource. That is, the characteristics of the resources for a creative change are different from those of a reproductive change.

Within the life cycle theory there is recognition that the organization must make adaptations to changes in the environment, but the changes are mediated by the imminent rules, logic, or programmes that exist within the organization (Van de Ven & Poole, 1995). A more complete understanding of the life cycle theory of change can be made by first incorporating an understanding of the relationship between strategy and resources. It can be assumed that the best description of that relationship is contemporaneous match (Itami & Numagami, 1992). When resources within the firm are path dependent, and the interaction between strategy and the resources is a focus on match, the adaptations the organization can make will be constrained. Here, the characteristic of path dependence is expected to be predominant. The path dependent aspect of resources suggests that these resources are institutionalized: that is, based on an accumulation of decisions made over time. The strategy changes, but it changes only in a life cycle aspect, a reproduction of the previous strategies.

Evolutionary theory focuses on cumulative changes; strategic changes are a result of the resources which exist in the firm. Although resources can be combined and recombined in a variety of ways (Barney, 1986), the resource characteristics of path dependence and stickiness suggest that the strategies are constrained by their history. Change proceeds through variation, selection and retention. Although the creation of novel forms exists, the constraint caused by the existing resources, plus the tendency for selection and retention, suggest that the changes will be sticky.

As stated above, teleological theory assumes that change is a result of planned action on the part of the organization to achieve a given goal. This implies that the firm will use the market for strategic resources (Barney, 1986). As discussed above, the value of the resources needed will vary from firm to firm; a firm which can obtain new resources in order to develop a strategy can pay more for those resources. However, while firms have the opportunity of creating completely new strategies, even in these cases their strategic choices can be constrained by the previous strategies, the values of the top management team, or cognition of environmental changes. Although these topics are beyond the scope of the present paper, it is important to recognize that choice may be constrained. It is also important to recognize that current strategic decisions for resource accumulation have long-term implications. Many resources which are acquired to implement a given strategy may allow for additional capacity in excess of what is needed for one strategy and thus can be used in another strategy (Penrose, 1959). This allows for change by diversification, but also allows for change by innovation, as described in the dialectic theory.

Organizations do change, often in creative, innovative ways. The interaction between resources and strategy, in which strategy and resources can change simultaneously, suggests new and creative changes, thus merging events (Van de Ven & Poole, 1995). The resource-based perspective helps us to understand these types of changes. Schumpeter recognized innovation in his discourse on the process of creative destruction (see Conner, 1991, for placement of Schumpeter's work in the context of the resource-based perspective). Schumpeterian competition involves carrying out new combinations of resources as well as organizational innovation (Mahoney & Pandian, 1992). Grant (1991) puts this in the perspective of the strategy-resource interaction: «The essential task, then, is to ensure that strategy constantly pushes slightly beyond the limits of the firm's capabilities at any point in time. This ensures not only the perfection of capabilities required by the current strategy, but also the development of capabilities required to meet the challenges of the future» (p. 132).

An important paradox is that it may be the characteristics of causal ambiguity which allow for these types of changes. Causal ambiguity, while keeping other organizations from copying, and a given organization from reproducing itself, can, because resources are tacit, complex and specific, and thus nonimitable, create innovation as they try to imitate. Simultaneously, resources can be exploited, leading to new combinations which then can lead to new strategies.

Conclusion

The resource-based perspective of the firm gives new insight into the understanding of organizational change and adaptation. This paper focused on the characteristics of the resources, and how these characteristics affect an organization's ability to change. The paper did not attempt to describe how different types of resources might be necessary to the change process, but this also is an area in which the resource-based perspective can contribute. This perspective is made explicit by Wiersema and Bantel (1993): «A shift in a firm's strategy, particularly at the corporate level where entirely new businesses might be entered and old businesses dropped, represents a change in the requisite managerial operating knowledge, experience, cognition, and perspectives». A different aspect is given by Teece, Pisano and Shuen (1990) who suggest that culture can be an important resource for change if the culture has the characteristic of being able to identify, support and reward learning.

The focus has been on the characteristics of individual resources with an implied domination of one characteristic. However, organizations contain bundles of resources, each of which can have different types of characteristics. While the proposed relationships (above) can be easily recognized in organizations, future research will have to deal with the complexities of many resources having many characteristics. For example, Itami (1987) defends the importance of invisible assets (the intangible assets such as a particular technology, accumulated consumer information, brand name, reputation, corporate culture) as being sources of competitive advantage because of their characteristics: hard to accumulate, capable of simultaneous multiple uses and both inputs and outputs of business activities.

While it is generally understood that a tight fit between the strategy, the required resources for that strategy and the current environment could result in organizational inertia, the different relationships of the environment, the strategy and the resources need to be attended to in an extension of the above framework. Here the focus was on change without specifying that different resources, or characteristics of resources, may be necessary to respond to different environmental changes.

When changes are uncertain or impossible to predict, it is necessary for management to build up resources that can be committed when unexpected changes occur (Itami, 1987). For example, Grant (1991) found evidence that companies whose strategies were based upon developing and exploiting clearly defined internal capabilities have been adept at adjusting to and exploiting external change. Barney (1986) proposes that environmental analysis cannot lead to competitive advantage because the information is available for all companies, so that even if a firm does not have this information themselves, the skill can be purchased. A different perspective is given by Grønhaug (Chapter 9 in this book). Grønhaug introduces the idea of expertise as a strategic resource; and certainly the expertise which he describes as being able to know the environment is an example of how the resource-based perspective can contribute to the environmental side of organizational change.

Organizations continue to change and adapt, or fail to change and adapt. By focusing on the resource-based perspective, this paper has offered additional insight into our understanding of both of these aspects of organizational change and adaptation.

References

Aldrich, H. (1979): *Organizations and Environments.* Englewood Cliffs, NJ: Prentice Hall.

Amit, R. & P.J. Shoemaker (1993): Strategic Assets and Organization Rents. *Strategic Management Journal 14*: 33-46.

Andrews, K.R. (1987): *The Concept of Corporate Strategy.* Homewood, IL: Irwin.

Barney, J. (1986): Strategic Factor Markets: Expectations, Luck, and Business Strategy. *Management Science 86*: 1231-1242.

Barney, J.B. (1991): Firm-Resources and Sustained Competitive Advantage. *Journal of Management 17*: 99-120.

Collis, D.J. (1991): A Resource-Based Analysis of Global Competition: The Case of the Ball-Bearing Industry. *Strategic Management Journal 12*: 49-68.

Conner, K.R. (1991): A Historical Comparison of Resource-Based Theory and Five Schools of Thought within Industrial Organization Economics: De We Have a New Theory of the Firm? *Journal of Management 17*: 155-171.

Daft, R. (1983): *Organization Theory and Design.* New York: West.

Dierickx, I. & K. Cool (1989): Asset Stock Accumulation and Sustainability of Competitive Advantage. *Management Science 35*: 1504-1511.

Grant, R.M. (1991): The Resource-Based Theory of Competitive Advantage: Implications for Strategy Formulation. *California Management Review 33*: 114-135.

Greiner, L. (1972): Evolution and Revolution as Organizations Grow. *Harvard Business Review 50(4): 37-46.*

Hannan, M. & J. Freeman (1977): The Population Ecology of Organizations. *American Journal of Sociology 82*: 929-964.

Hofer, C.W. & D. Schendel (1978): *Strategy Formulation: Analytical Concepts.* St. Paul, MN: West.

Hrebiniak, L.G. & W.F. Joyce (1985): Organizational Adaptation: Strategic Choice and Environmental Determinism. *Administrative Science Quarterly 30*: 336-349.

Itami, H. (in collaboration with T.W. Roehl) (1987): *Mobilizing Invisible Assets.* Cambridge, MA: Harvard University Press.

Itami, H. & T. Numagami (1992): Dynamic Interaction between Strategy and Technology. *Strategic Management Journal 13*: 119-135.

Kagono, T., I. Nonaka, K. Sakakibara & A. Okumura (1985): *Strategic vs. Evolutionary Management: A U.S.-Japan Comparison of Strategy and Organization*. Amsterdam: North Holland.

Kelly, D. & T.L. Amburgey (1991): Organizational Inertia and Momentum: A Dynamic Model of Strategic Change. *Academy of Management Journal 32*: 591-612.

Kimberly, J. & R. Miles (1980): *The Organizational Life Cycle*. San Francisco: Jossey-Bass.

Learned, E., C.R. Christensen, K.R. Andrews & W.D. Guth (1965): *Business Policy: Text and Cases*. Homewood, IL: Richard D. Irwin.

Leonard-Barton, D. (1992): Core Capabilities and Core Rigidities: A Paradox in Managing New Product Development. *Strategic Management Journal 13*: 111-126.

Lippman, S.A. & R.P. Rumelt (1982): Uncertain Imitability: An Analysis of Interfirm Differences in Efficiency under Competition. *Bell Journal of Economics 13*: 418-438.

Mahoney, J.T. & J.R. Pandian (1992): The Resource-Based View within the Conversation of Strategic Management. *Strategic Management Journal 13*: 363-380.

Mezias, S.J. & M.A. Glynn (1993): The Three Faces of Corporate Renewal: Institution, Revolution and Evolution. *Strategic Management Journal 14(2)*: 77-101.

Nelson, R. & S.G. Winter (1982): *An Evolutionary Theory of Economic Change*. Cambridge: Belknap Press.

Penrose, E. (1959): *The Theory of the Growth of the Firm*. Oxford: Blackwell.

Porter, M. (1980): *Competitive Strategy*. New York: Free Press.

Reed, R. & R.J. DeFillipi (1990): Causal Ambiguity, Barriers to Imitation, and Sustainable Competitive Advantage. *Academy of Management Review 15*: 88-102.

Romanelli, E. & M. Tushman (1988): Executive Leadership and Organizational Outcomes: An Evolutionary Perspective. In D. Hambrick (ed.): *The Executive Effect: Concepts and Methods for Studying Top Managers*. Greenwich, CT: JAI Press, 129-140.

Rumelt, R. (1984): Towards a Strategic Theory of the Firm. In R.B. Lamb (ed.): *Competitive Strategic Management*. Englewood Cliffs, NJ: Prentice-Hall, 556-570.

Russo, M. (1991): The Multidivisional Structure as an Enabling Device: A Longitudinal Study of Discretionary Cash as a Strategic Resource. *Academy of Management Journal 32*: 718-733.

Schulze, W. & G.D. Meyer (1991): The Relationship between Resources, Capabilities and Courses of Competitive Advantage as a Unifying Constructure in the Field of Business Strategy. Presented at the 1991 Academy of Management Meetings, Las Vegas. University of Colorado Working Paper 91-96.

Teece, D.J. (1982): An Economic Theory of Multiproduct Firms. *Journal of Economic Behavior and Organization 3*: 39-63.

Teece, D., G. Pisano & A. Shuen (1990): Firm Capabilities, Resources, and the Concept of Strategy. Working paper, EAP-38. Berkeley: University of California, Berkeley.

Thompson, J.D. (1967): *Organizations in Action*. New York: McGraw-Hill.

Tushman, M. & E. Romanelli (1985): Organizational Evolution: A Metamorphosis Model of Convergence and Reorientation. *Research in Organizational Behavior 7*: 171-222.

Van de Ven, A.H. & M.S. Poole (1995): Explaining Development and Change in Organizations. *Academy of Management Journal 20(3)*: 510-540.

Wernerfelt, B. (1984): A Resource-Based View of the Firm. *Strategic Management Journal 5*: 171-181.

Wiersema, M. & K.A. Bantel (1993): Top Management Team Turnover as an Adaptation Mechanism: The Role of the Environment. *Strategic Management Journal 14*: 485-504.

Core Competencies in a Network Organization

Randi Lunnan & Sven A. Haugland

The strategic management literature focuses on how firms can develop competitive advantage in order to be competitive in the marketplace. Two major perspectives that address the issue of competitive advantage from different angles are the positioning model (Porter, 1980; 1985) and the resource-based view of the firm (Penrose, 1959; Wernerfelt, 1984, Barney, 1991). In the positioning model, emphasis has primarily been on an analysis of the external environment, and competitive advantages are related to the firm's position in the environment. In this model, firms are treated as isolated actors competing against each other, and competitive advantages are related to a firm's ability to position itself in the marketplace. For example, a firm can develop a competitive advantage by producing at lower costs than its competitors, and creating some kind of barriers that prevent other firms from imitating the same actions (Porter, 1980; 1985).

Compared with the positioning model, the resource-based view of the firm relates competitive advantage to a firm's resources. According to Penrose (1959), a firm's unique character is based upon the firm's potential to produce different goods and services given its resources. Competitive advantage is then related to how a firm can combine its resources in ways that are different from its competitors.

However, both the positioning model and the resource-based perspective lack an understanding of the importance of linking internal and external factors. According to Kay (1993: vi), the match between a firm's capabilities and the challenges it faces in the environment is the most important issue for understanding corporate success and failure. A firm will establish relationships to actors in the environment; suppliers, customers and competitors, and these relationships are important building blocks for creating competitive advantage.

In this paper, we focus on how firms can develop competitive advantage by exploiting their distinct resources and competence, and by linking their competence to the development of relationships to actors in the environment. An example of the importance of relationships for developing competitive advantage are network organizations. In a network organization, individual firms combine their resources by cooperation, and develop competence across each individual organization. This organizational form is characterized by a high degree of flexibility, and is particularly well suited in rapidly changing environments.

The purpose of this paper is to address the importance of interorganizational relations in strategic management, and to discuss the link between a firm's competence and its relations to other organizations. By using a case study of a network organization in the Norwegian shipping industry, we will empirically explore the importance of interorganizational relations for a company's efforts to gain competitive advantage.

Theoretical background

Both the positioning model and the resource-based view of the firm relate competitive advantage to some kind of firm uniqueness. In the Porterian perspective, uniqueness is described in terms of the position in the marketplace, while the resource-based view proposes that uniqueness is based upon the firm's resources or combinations of resources. In contrast to these perspectives, Kay, in a recent book, links uniqueness to contracts and relationships.

> The uniqueness is a product of the firm's contracts and relationships. I see the firm as a set of relationships between its various stakeholders-employees, customers, investors, shareholders. The successful firm is one which creates a distinctive character in these relationships and which operates in an environment which maximizes the value of that distinctiveness. (Kay 1993: vii).

In this paper, we argue that there is a need for linking resources and relationships in order to understand how a firm can gain a competitive advantage. In particular, we argue that organizations develop relationships with other actors in order to extend the competence base (Nordhaug, 1993). Through exploitation of complementary resources, a company can gain a competitive advantage by cooperating with another company. We propose that firms can gain faster access to competitive advantage by developing competence in cooperation with other companies rather than by developing competence within the organization. Consequently, firms need to establish cooperative relationships, and the management of these relationships becomes a critical factor. From a managerial point of view, it is important to be aware of which types of competence should be located within the boundaries of the organization, and which should be developed in cooperation with other organizations. Further, a sound knowledge of the governance problems associated with cooperative strategies is required.

To address these questions in more detail, in the following we will discuss the concepts of resources and competence, describe what is meant by network organizations, and address the issue of how to govern interorganizational relations.

Resources and competence

In defining competitive advantage, researchers use such concepts as resources, competence, capabilities, assets and activities. However, there is no coherent understanding of how these concepts are defined and used, and what kind of relationships that exist between the concepts. According to Porter (1980, 1985) resources are perfectly mobile between firms, and competitive advantages are obtained by creating mobility barriers. Teece, Pisano & Shuen (1990) have a different point of view and argue that resources are not mobile and transferable. A company that is able to purchase resources and competence in the marketplace cannot obtain sustained competitive advantage. Based on the heterogeneity and immobility of firm resources, however, a firm can, by exploiting its distinct resources and competence, earn an excessive profit.

Amit & Schoemacher (1990) define a firm's resources as transferable input factors controlled by the firm, while competence is defined as: «... tangible or intangible assets that are firm specific and are created over time through complex interactions among the firm's resources». When resources are deployed and combined in ways that lower costs or improve product quality compared with competitors, the firm has gained a competitive advantage. Competitive advantages are often located in a few value activities referred to as strategic core activities. To explain a firm's advantages, we therefore need to analyze the competence embedded in the strategic core activities. This competence will be denoted core competence. Core competence provides enhanced productivity from firm resources and is based on developing, carrying, and exchanging information through the firm's human capital.

Why should competence be difficult to acquire and transfer between firms? Barney (1991) suggests three explanations: 1) The ability of a firm to obtain certain resources depends upon unique historical conditions, meaning that their ability to acquire and exploit resources depends on their place in time and space. 2) The link between the resources possessed by a firm and a firm's competitive advantage may be causally ambiguous. Other firms simply do not understand what resource to copy, and 3) each resource may be socially complex and not subject to direct management.

In addition, Teece, Pisano & Shuen (1990) point out the importance of learning processes in organizations. Learning processes are constrained and focused by such factors as history, technology, complementary assets, specific ways of doing things, etc. The mechanisms by which firms learn and accumulate skills and competence largely involve a tacit dimension that cannot easily be imitated.

Competence is thus rooted in the interaction of the firm's resources (Amit & Schoemacher, 1990). According to Hamel (1994), competence is: 1) an integration of skills, and 2) more than an asset. Furthermore, competence becomes a core competence 1) if it makes a disproportionate contribution to customer-perceived value, 2) if it is competitively unique, and 3) if it provides an entrance into new markets. A firm's competence comprises the mechanism that allows a firm to perform specific activities based upon its resources. If a company is able to perform these activities in a way superior to other companies, the company has gained a competitive advantage.

The literature assumes that competence is located within each individual organization. However, as we have pointed out, a network organization performs activities based on resources from more than one individual company. Based on resources from different companies, the network performs specific activities. The competence that is required for conducting these activities cannot thus be located within each member organization but belongs to the network as a kind of collective entity. The competence exists across organizational boundaries. If the network is able to perform the activities better than other organizations or networks, the network has gained a competitive advantage, but this competitive advantage cannot be transferred directly to each individual organization.

Developing competence across organizational boundaries requires interaction and governance. In combining resources from many different companies, the network needs to coordinate the actions of the individual organizations. These governance mechanisms are important for the network in the process of combining resources from the member companies in such a way that it performs activities better than its competitors and develops a competitive advantage. Before describing how competence can be organized in a network, we will define in more detail a network organization and discuss issues related to the governance of interorganizational relations.

Network organizations

A network organization is characterized by cooperation and interdependence among individual companies in producing a product or a service. Each individual company will specialize in one or several tasks within the production of a product or a service, and through cooperation the network, as a set of organizations, produces the complete product. Network organizations have gained increased interest over the past years, and rapid technological development is one important factor explaining the use of network organizations (Powell, 1987; Johnston & Lawrence, 1988). Network organizations are characterized by a high degree of flexibility and are particularly well suited to operate in rapidly changing environments.

In this paper, we take the view that one organization, the focal organization, is in charge of the network. This organization possesses the knowledge of how to organize and govern the network in order to make it as efficient as possible (Miles & Snow, 1986). A focal organization, specializing in one or several tasks, needs to develop competence in cooperation with other organizations to deliver the product or service required. Having decided on which types of competence are to be located within its boundaries, the focal organization must decide which are to be developed in cooperation with other organizations and organize and govern its relationships with the cooperating organizations.

The governance of interorganizational relations

In a network organization, the development of competence takes place between organizations. The governance of interorganizational relations within the network is thus of importance for this development to take place. We will, therefore, briefly discuss some important issues related to the governance of interorganizational relations.

In the literature on interorganizational relations, a central problem is to understand the variety of different ways in which such relations are organized and governed. In recent research on interorganizational relations, transaction cost economics (Williamson, 1985) has been a frequently used theoretical framework (Dwyer & Oh, 1988; Heide & John 1988, 1990, Noordewier, John & Nevin 1990). According to this framework, the transaction is the basic unit of analysis, and properties of the transaction are the principal variables underlying the emergence of different governance mechanisms. These governance mechanisms may range from market to internal organization, with bilateral governance or hybrid modes being the intermediary forms (Williamson 1991). The different intermediary forms are considered to fall between markets and hierarchies, defined as ideal types (Bradach & Eccles 1989). Important transactional properties are asset specificity, uncertainty and frequency.

Different governance mechanisms thus result from transactions that differ with respect to asset specificity, uncertainty and frequency. In particular, the theory predicts that as asset specificity increases, market mechanisms are gradually replaced by organizational mechanisms based on authority. With reference to a specific transaction with certain characteristics, it is possible to determine what will be the most efficient governance structure.

Although Williamson (1985) posits that transactions within the boundaries of a firm are governed by authority, researchers have observed the use of authority in market transactions and the use of market incentives within organizations (Stinchcombe 1985, Eccles 1981) indicating that authority and market incentives are combined. Bradach & Eccles (1989) have further extended this argument and proposed that price, authority and trust are three independent governance mechanisms. Price reflects the use of market mechanisms, while authority means the reliance on organizational mechanisms such as rules and procedures. Trust, however, implies monitoring transactions by social norms and the development of personal relationships. These governance mechanisms can be used in different combinations, forming a governance vector with three elements. In the following, we will briefly describe what characterizes price, authority and trust as governance mechanisms.

Price. Market incentives are effective when there are many alternative buyers and sellers and the product is a standard commodity. Through supply and demand, the right price is established, and nobody is cheated. For transactions governed by price, the negotiations are between faceless actors; the identity of the parties is of limited interest. The focus is on establishing legally binding contract procedures in order to secure contract fulfillment, and to avoid hostile actions.

Authority. Developing formal rules and procedures controlling work activities are commonly used within organizations, but can also be used in order to govern interorganizational relations. Stinchcombe (1985) mentions five elements of authority often used as governance elements between independent actors. One party has the right to: 1) set the agenda, 2) control and motivate, 3) develop rules and procedures, 4) specify conflict-solving procedures, and 5) decide what are reasonable costs when no market price exists.

Trust. Trust as a concept has lately received considerable attention. However, many different definitions of the concept exist, and the concept has been used in a variety of units and levels of analysis. At least three major approaches to trust can be found. Trust can be treated as: 1) a property of individuals, as 2) a property of interpersonal relationships, or as 3) a kind of social organization (Lewis & Weigert 1985, Shapiro 1987). The two first approaches are psychological, while trust as a kind of social organization, views trust as a property of collective units. Trust describes the relations among groups of people. According to Lewis & Weigert, «trust exists in a social system insofar as the members of that system act according to and are secure in the expected futures constituted by the presence of each other or their symbolic representations» (1985: 968).

Collective units can be at different levels of analysis, and trust-based social organization can take various forms depending on the specific collective units in question. We are studying business firms and relations among business firms. How can we describe trust-based social organization or trust as a governance mechanism between business firms?

One way of describing trust-based governance is to study the degree of mutual expectations between the actors involved. Mutual expectations serve the role of securing that each business partner will fulfill their obligations and not undertake any action harmful to other partners. By trusting each other, sharing the same expectations, each partner will act as if they had a legally binding contract, thus reducing the need for other governance mechanisms (Luhmann 1979). As Van Wijk (1984) explains: «As long as the actor's initiatives are based on their mutual expectations, coordination is ensured even though specific outcomes are not known ahead of time». Similar arguments are also found in Dore (1983), Lorents (1988), Gerlach (1987), Johnston & Lawrence (1988).

By trusting partners, that is, expecting them to perform their work optimally and not cheat given the opportunity, the need for other control mechanisms can be reduced. There is less need to control employees or another firm's managers if you trust them. Transactions can be carried out without detailed contract documents or formalized work procedures, and both parties anticipate that problems can be solved jointly when they appear. Jarillo (1988) claims that transaction costs can be reduced when trust is present, because problems created by uncertainty and opportunistic behavior will be rather limited.

Although the governance framework presented here primarily focuses on governance problems associated with transactions and exchange relations, the framework can be used for describing the governance problems we are addressing here. In the following section, we will link the idea of developing competence across organizational boundaries to the specific governance problems that need to be handled.

Organizing competence in a network

A basic assumption in this paper is that companies can develop competitive advantage by cooperating with other companies. By pooling resources, companies can, for example, get faster access to the market, and thus be ahead of competitors. In rapidly changing environments, it is critical for organizations at any time to possess the required competence to be competitive. Network organizations, as opposed to individual organizations developing all necessary types of competence within the organization, can develop new types of competence by drawing upon the network members' resources, and by changing the composition of the network. Competitive advantage based upon cooperation therefore requires that the companies: 1) develop competence across organizational borders, and 2) develop governance mechanisms to secure an efficient handling of these relationships. This is illustrated in Figure 1.

However, a firm developing competence in cooperation with other firms faces the risk of being exploited. A cooperating organization can act opportunistically, and take advantage of skills developed in the network. By terminating a relationship, a cooperating organization can continue the operations independently, and leave the cooperating organization with a loss. The risk of being exposed to opportunistic behavior is a key element in transaction cost economics (Williamson, 1985).

Figure 1: Network competencies and governence

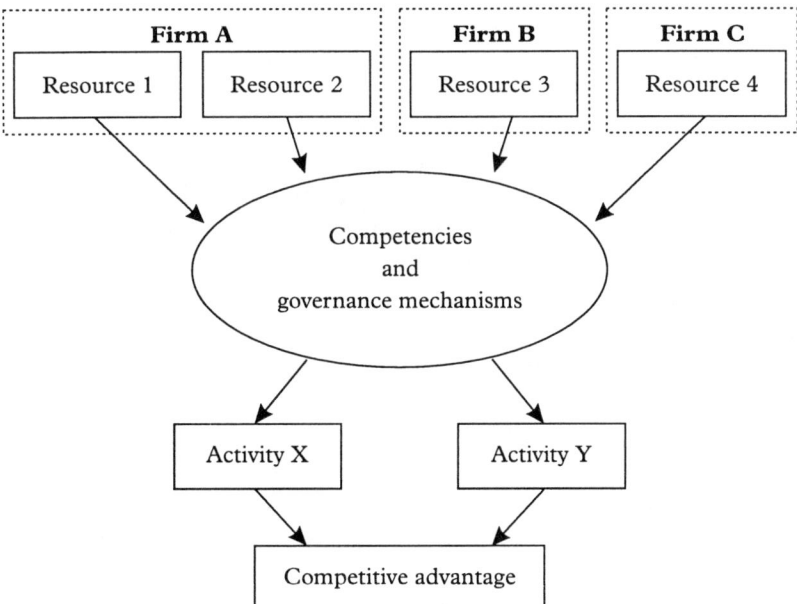

Here, opportunistic behavior is related to asset specificity. If an organization terminates a relationship, the cooperating organization will be exposed to a loss because of specific investments made in order to perform specific transactions. A specific governance solution is based on the need to protect these specific investments. In situations characterized by a high degree of asset specificity, market governance will be replaced by hierarchical governance.

In contrast to transaction cost economics, we will, however, argue that the risk of being exploited is related to specific types of competence developed in cooperation with other organizations, and that organizations develop specific governance solutions in order to protect this competence. We also propose that for a specific governance solution, market mechanisms (price), hierarchical mechanisms (authority), and social mechanisms (trust) can be combined.

In arguing that the governance of relationships is related to the specific types of competence developed, we take the view in particular that the governance of interorganizational relations is related to the strategic core of the cooperating organizations (Haugland 1994). Strategic core can be defined as: «... assets of high specificity which are necessary to attain the firm's strategic goals ... The strategic core is the *raison d'être* of the firm, defining its economic rationale within an industry» (Reve 1990: 139). The strategic core reflects the core skills of a firm.

To relate the governance of cooperative relationships to strategic core, we will consider especially the following two issues as important: 1) how closely related are those skills developed to the strategic cores of the organizations, and 2) have the cooperating organizations similar or quite different strategic cores? If an organization develops competence in cooperation with another organization, and this is closely related to its strategic core, we would expect a close relationship to be established. If the competence, however, is peripheral to the strategic core, a more distant relationship would be expected. In addition, the question of similar or different strategic cores is also important. Since we are concerned with developing competence in cooperation with another organization, the ability of each organization to make use of it independently depends upon the similarity of the strategic cores. If two cooperating organizations have different strategic cores, it is less likely that each individual organization will be able to make individual use of the competence.

If a company develops competence closely related to its strategic core in cooperation with another company, and the strategic cores of the two companies are similar, we will expect a governance solution indicating a close relationship, protecting the parties from being exploited by opportunistic behavior. A close relationship means that the actors establish interorganizational linkages, and consequently the relationship cannot be described as an arm's length competitive relationship. By using authority and/or trust in addition to price, the parties will develop overlapping boundaries enabling them to develop competence across organizational boundaries and protect them from being exploited.

Since we are at an early stage of research in using these constructs, we will not develop specific hypotheses related to our discussion. We will only show the relevance of this perspective by presenting the results of an explorative case study. Before doing so, we will briefly describe the empirical setting and the data collection procedure.

Empirical setting and data collection

An explorative case study of the Norwegian shipping company Laboremus was conducted. Shipping as an industry is highly international, and various forms of alliances and cooperation take place between companies. Traditionally, Norwegian shipping companies have been integrated, performing all necessary value-adding activities, but in recent years more and more shipping companies take the form of network organizations.

Laboremus

Laboremus was founded in 1910, but its history as a modern, industrial shipping company started in 1986 with major investment in small gas tankers. In this market, Laboremus, together with its alliance partners, Norwegian Gas Carriers (NGC) and the Dutch UNIGAS, became one of the world's leading participants. Controlling a large, modern fleet and establishing a broad network of contacts, the company was able to avoid many off-hire days. This is vital to profitability in industrial shipping. Purchases and sales of tankers gave additional profits and increased the company's ability to expand and invest. Despite its success in the gas market, Laboremus wanted to reduce the risk of operating in only one market and expanded into the transportation of refined oil products. However, their main market remained gas transportation, with major products being ethylene, propylene and butadiene. In 1989, the Laboremus corporation had an annual turnover of NOK 1.242 billion, of which NOK 0.807 billion came from the focal company Laboremus, at that time with 17 employees.

For the purpose of this paper, we will concentrate on the most important value-creating activities Laboremus needed to control in order to be a complete industrial shipping company. A simplified value chain is depicted in Figure 2.

Shipping industrial cargo from one port to another involves a series of activities and operations. First, the shipping company must have the necessary ships at its disposal. Laboremus managed a number of both gas and oil tankers. Most of these tankers were jointly owned with other investors or leased. Secondly, a ship needs cargo. As pointed out above, Laboremus operated in two different markets; the gas market and the market for refined oil products. Procurement of cargo was handled by two companies; NGC and Nortank. NGC handled gas cargoes, while Nortank handled refined oil products. These companies are called operation companies. Thirdly, a ship needs crew members, supplies of food, insurance etc. These services were provided by several ship management companies. However, in most instances, the Kosmos Ship

Figure 2: Value chain

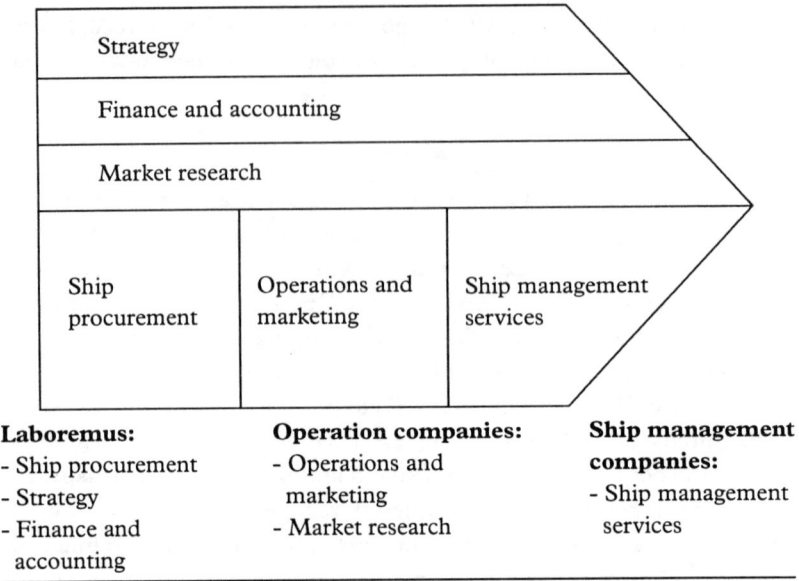

Laboremus:
- Ship procurement
- Strategy
- Finance and
  accounting

Operation companies:
- Operations and
  marketing
- Market research

Ship management companies:
- Ship management
  services

Management company was used. Finance and accounting are also vital in shipping. Due to the liberal Norwegian shipping taxation policy, ships can be considered as investment objects. Therefore these functions had a major impact on profitability, and were performed by Laboremus.

Laboremus deliberately chose to have a small administrative staff and limit the number of operations performed in-house. Ship procurement, finance and accounting, along with strategy and network management were handled in-house. All vital decisions related to these activities were made by two top managers. These top managers were also responsible for analyzing market trends in cooperation with consultants and the operation companies.

As already pointed out above, Laboremus cooperated with two operation companies and owned shares in both companies. At the time of our study, Laboremus controlled all the NGC shares and 40% of the Nortank shares. With regard to the ship management companies, Laboremus cooperated with several companies. However, Kosmos Ship Management, the most frequently used company, was controlled by the same investment group.

Data collection

Our primary objective in this study was to analyze how Laboremus developed competence in cooperation with partners and to study how Laboremus governed the relations with the partners, especially the operation and management companies. We are in particular interested in revealing the core competence of Laboremus, and analyzing how price, authority and trust were used as governance mechanisms. Many of the concepts we are using are not well defined, and few studies using the concepts have been reported. Due to these difficulties, several measurement methods were used. We observed behavior in meetings between the partners: how did they meet, talk and respond? How did they address each other, and how did they speak of the other company when its representatives were not present? We also observed physical factors such as location of offices: how far apart were the companies? Was it easy to reach the business partner? How did they communicate?

Further, we interviewed the top managers in Laboremus, the two operation companies and Kosmos Ship Management, both personally and by telephone. Some managers were interviewed more than once. The interviews were unstructured, and each interview lasted from 1-4 hours and was tape-recorded. Furthermore, we had access to annual reports, reports from external consultants, memos and notes, contract documents, and analyses performed both by Laboremus and their partners.

In Table 1, we report the major indicators used for measuring core competence, price, authority and trust.

Table 1. Major indicators used for measuring core competence, price, authority and trust

Types of core competence were defined from such statements as:
- «Our strength is ...«
- «Our main competence is concentrated around ...«
- «The core of our business ...«

The following indicators were used for price governance:
- stressing the importance of finding the cheapest alternative
- emphasized detailed contracts and on alternative partners
- relationships characterized by no or little personal contact

The following indicators were used for authority governance:
- stressing formalization and centralization in the relationship
- putting importance on ownership
- statements stressing dominance, control, orders
- legalizing direct interference

The following indicators were used for trust governance:
- common expectations
- implicit rules and norms concerning relational behavior
- development of a common view in relations
- relational investments, long-term view and priority-setting
- partner care and concern
- frequent meetings and talks

Laboremus as a network organization

Performing only a few value activities in-house, and placing complementary activities with external companies, Laboremus can be described as a network organization. With only seventeen full-time employees, Laboremus was only a fraction of the size of similar, integrated companies in terms of number of employees. To the customer, however, Laboremus sold an integrated shipping product. The customer conceived the shipping network as one entity, not as a collection of several companies.

In analyzing Laboremus, we will concentrate on the relationships between Laboremus and the operation and management companies. These relationships illustrate two different resources Laboremus needed in order to offer an integrated shipping product. Furthermore, the two relations were governed differently, contrasting governance solutions used in developing competence closely related to strategic core, and developing competence more peripheral to strategic core.

A key characteristic of Laboremus was the ability to combine resources from several companies into one integrated shipping product. Further, Laboremus possessed thorough knowledge on shipping. The company was not only able to perform activities in the gas and refined oil products market, but the company had experience and ideas about opportunities and activities in various shipping markets. Laboremus' strategy was built around this ability to organize and perform shipping activities in nearly all types of shipping markets. The competitive advantages of the company were thus based upon the competence of combining specific resources from several shipping companies, and the competence of moving from one shipping market to another; this can be viewed as the strategic core of Laboremus.

Laboremus cooperated with two operation companies: NGC in the gas market and Nortank in the refined oil products market. The operation companies handled all relations with customers, brokers and agents. Access to market information, new needs and market signals were available first to the operation companies. Early access to this information was vital to Laboremus in several ways. In order to possess an optimal number of different ships, Laboremus depended upon quick and accurate market information to decide on the timing for purchases and sales of tankers. NGC's skills in operations were important for avoiding off-hire days in the gas market. However, NGC's ability to keep the fleet occupied successfully depended upon an optimal number of different ships. The two firms controlled closely interrelated resources, and by cooperation, the firms developed competence across firm boundaries that enabled them to perform activities in the market better than their competitors.

Laboremus owned NGC and Nortank shares, suggesting authority elements. Company decisions were influenced by the views of Laboremus. However, both Laboremus and their partners strongly argued that there was no need to control the partner. Laboremus further pointed to the importance of developing common views and mutual expectations, to ensure that both companies were satisfied with decisions and actions. Trust between the parties was often mentioned. Authority elements were certainly visible, but the most important governance mechanism seemed to be trust. Trust was especially important in the gas market. Terms like gentleman's agreement and evergreen contract were often used in this market. A gentleman's agreement refers to contracts settled informally and off the record between business acquaintances, while an evergreen contract refers to contract renewals without new bidding processes.

As pointed out above, Laboremus cooperated with several ship management companies. Ship management services were offered by a large number of companies, and in most instances standard prices were offered. We were able to study the standard contracts used in such transactions. Management services represent important resources in shipping. Such resources are vital for producing an integrated shipping product. However, a weaker link existed between the resources of Laboremus and the resources of the management companies compared with the link between Laboremus and the operation companies. The competence developed in cooperation with the management companies was therefore less important by comparison with that developed in cooperation with the management companies.

Since management services are standard and offered by a large number of companies, Laboremus was able to choose the cheapest supplier. Several companies were hired at the same time, allowing Laboremus to control product quality. Price was a dominant governance element, and the same companies were used regularly. A contract was not broken until the company had demonstrated higher prices or worse quality. In fact, the same shipping management companies had been used for years, even if several others existed in the market. To some extent, common expectations between Laboremus and these companies had been developed concerning crew and customer relationships. Along with the re-hiring aspect, this may lead to arguments about a trust element in these relationships. However, price was the dominant governance element, but to some extent combined with trust.

Flexibility was vital to the success of Laboremus. Traditionally, Norwegian shipping companies have ordered new vessels from shipyards all over the world and sailed the ships for a very long period of time. However, for Laboremus a ship was viewed as a commodity to be bought and sold. Laboremus purchased and sold the same ships several times. Further, since the competence of Laboremus and that of the operation companies was so strongly interrelated, why did Laboremus not internalize these activities? When Laboremus entered the refined oil products market, the company was unable to use NGC. The operating activities in the gas market are completely different from the operating activities in the refined oil products market. If Laboremus had performed these activities in-house, the company would have faced problems if they decided to leave this market. However, through ownership interests in both companies, Laboremus obtained some authority and control, while flexibility still remained.

Discussion

In the previous section we analyzed Laboremus as a network organization. We pointed out that the relationships between Laboremus and the operation companies were governed differently from the relationships between Laboremus and the management companies. Close relationships were established with the operation companies, and trust was the dominant governance element combined with some degree of authority.

More distant relationships existed between Laboremus and the management companies, and here price was the dominant governance element combined with some degree of trust.

The competence developed between Laboremus and the operation companies had a large impact on the profitability of Laboremus. The operation activities were closely related to the strategic core of Laboremus, and Laboremus was vulnerable to changes in these relationships. If these relationships had been terminated, Laboremus would have faced major risks. It is also interesting to note how authority and trust were combined. Although, NGC was completely owned and Nortank part owned by Laboremus, trust dominated the day-to-day governance of these relationships.

With regard to the management companies, Laboremus did not develop competence in cooperation with these companies to the same extent. The services performed by these companies can more or less be viewed as purchases of standard services. Alternative sources existed, and termination of these relationships was not critical for Laboremus. Consequently, more distant relationships were developed. However, adding trust to a price-dominated governance of these relationships is interesting.

In this article we have argued that the governance of interorganizational relationships is related to the question of developing competence in cooperation with other organizations. Few studies have been conducted using this perspective, and many of the constructs are not well defined. Our explorative case study indicates that this perspective may contribute to our understanding of the importance of interorganizational relations for creating competitive advantages. This initial study therefore suggests that more research is needed to understand how organizations can develop competence across organizational boundaries by establishing cooperative relationships.

References

Amit, R. & P.J. Schoemacher (1990): *Key Success Factors: Their Foundation and Application.* Unpublished Working Paper, University of British Colombia, and University of Chicago.

Barney, J. (1991): Firm Resources and Sustained Competitive Advantage. *Journal of Management 17*: 99-120.

Bradach, J. L. & R.G. Eccles (1989): Price, Authority and Trust: From Ideal Types to Plural Forms. *Annual Review of Sociology 15*: 97-118.

Dore, R. (1983): Goodwill and the Spirit of Market Capitalism. *British Journal of Sociology 34*: 459-482.

Dwyer, R. & S. Oh (1988): A Transaction Cost Perspective on Vertical Contractual Structure and Interchannel Competitive Strategies. *Journal of Marketing 52*: 21-34.

Eccles, R. (1981): The Quasifirm in the Construction Industry. *Journal of Economic Behavior and Organization 2*: 335-357.

Gerlach, M. (1987): Business Alliances and the Strategy of the Japanese Firm. *California Management Review 30*: 126-142.

Hamel, G. (1994): The Concept of Core Competence. In G. Hamel & A. Heene (eds.): *Competence-Based Competition.* Chichester: Wiley.

Haugland, S.A. (1994): *Strategiske allianser: En empirisk studie av nasjonale og internasjonale samarbeidsrelasjoner.* SNF-Report no. 15/94, Foundation for Research in Economics and Business Administration. Bergen: Norwegian School of Economics and Business Administration.

Heide, J.B. & G. John (1988): The Role of Dependence Balancing in Safeguarding Transaction-Specific Assets in Conventional Channels. *Journal of Marketing 52*: 20-35.

Heide, J.B. & G. John (1990): Alliances in Industrial Purchasing: The Determinants of Joint Action in Buyer-Supplier Relationships. *Journal of Marketing Research 27*: 24-36.

Jarillo, J.C. (1988): On Strategic Networks. *Strategic Management Journal 9*: 31-41.

Johnston, R. & P.R. Lawrence (1988): Beyond Vertical Integration? The Rise of the Value-Adding Partnership. *Harvard Business Review 66(4):* 94-101.

Kay, J. (1993): *Foundations of Corporate Success.* Oxford: Oxford University Press.

Lewis, J.D. & A. Weigert (1985): Trust as a Social Reality. *Social Forces 63*: 967-985.

Lorents, E. (1988): Neither Friends nor Strangers: Informal Networks of Subcontracting in French Industry. In D. Gambetta (ed.): *Trust: Making and Breaking Cooperative Relations*. Oxford: Blackwell.

Luhmann, N. (1979): *Trust and Power*. New York: Wiley and Sons.

Miles, R. & C.C. Snow (1986): Organizations: New Concepts for New Forms. *California Management Review 28*: 62-73.

Noordewier, T., G. John & J.R. Nevin (1990): Performance Outcomes of Purchasing Arrangements in Industrial Buyer-Vendor Relationships. *Journal of Marketing 54*: 80-93.

Nordhaug, O. (1993): *Human Capital in Organizations: Competence, Training, and Learning*. Oslo: Scandinavian University Press.

Penrose, E.T. (1959): *The Theory of the Growth of the Firm*. Oxford: Basil Blackwell.

Porter, M. (1980): *Competitive Strategy*. New York: The Free Press.

Porter, M. (1985): *Competitive Advantage*. New York: The Free Press.

Powell, W.W. (1987): Hybrid Organizational Arrangements: New Forms or Transitional Development? *California Management Review 30*: 67-87.

Reve, T. (1990): The Firm as a Nexus of Internal and External Contracts. In M. Aoki, B. Gustafsson & O.E. Williamson (eds.): *The Firms as a Nexus of Treaties*. London: Sage, 133-161.

Shapiro, S. (1987): The Social Control of Impersonal Trust. *American Journal of Sociology 93*: 625-658.

Stinchcombe, A.L. (1985): Contracts as Hierarchical Documents. In A. Stinchcombe & C. Heimer (eds.): *Organization Theory and Project Management*. Bergen: Norwegian University Press.

Teece, D., Pisano, G. & Shuen, A. (1990): Firm Capabilities, Resources and the Concept of Strategy. Working Paper, EAP-38. Berkeley: University of California, Berkeley.

Van Wijk, C. (1984): The Role of Trust and Shared Understanding in Loan Decisions. Unpublished Ph.D. dissertation, University of Columbia.

Wernerfelt, B. (1984): A Resource-Based View of the Firm. *Strategic Management Journal 5*: 171-180.

Williamson, O.E. (1985): *The Economic Institutions of Capitalism*. New York: The Free Press.

Williamson, O.E. (1991): Comparative Economic Organization: The Analysis of Discrete Structural Alternatives. *Administrative Science Quarterly 35*: 269-296.

Rethinking the Metaphore of Strategic Management

Bente Løwendahl & Øivind Revang

In post-modern society, knowledge and technology have become the dominant social forces shaping society (Hage & Powers, 1992: 8). The creation of new knowledge and the speed of its diffusion, between both humans as well as technology, are the driving forces behind what has been called a process of «complexification» (Hage & Powers, 1992). In post-industrial organizations, work tasks are defined in terms of information-gathering, problem-solving, the production of creative ideas, and the ability to respond flexibly to new situations or adjust flexibly when interacting with others.

Despite the challenges resulting from such societal processes, however, the majority of the writers on strategic management still presume a model based on the belief that «organizations succeed when they operate in states of stability and harmony to adapt intentionally to their environments» (Stacey, 1993: xix). This model is based on an open system perspective (Burns & Stalker, 1961; Blau & Scott, 1963; Lawrence & Lorsch, 1967) combined with the norm of technical-economic rationality (Thompson, 1967). Theories emphasize the «running (of) the organizational «machine» in as surprise free a way as possible» (Stacey, 1993: xix), and the design of these «machines» and the choice of strategies such that surprises may be avoided and efficiency enhanced (Mintzberg, 1979, 1983; Nadler & Tushman, 1992). This conventional way of thinking is no longer sufficient when we face the post-industrial society (Bell, 1973), both because hidden or forgotten assumptions are challenged, and the explanations and understanding it produces are losing relevance. This article confronts the conventional way of thinking about strategy and suggests some directions for further research needed to upgrade our knowledge about, and explanations of, strategic issues to a version more associated with the new realities facing many organizations and managers today.

In this paper we look into a number of challenges resulting from the processes leading to increasing complexification and argue that we need a qualitative shift in strategic management thinking if we are to be able to generate meaningful models and theories for such modern organizations. Neither the top management-designed strategies (however complex) nor the bottom-up emergent strategies of the type «let all the flowers bloom» are likely to offer the necessary insights into strategic management of such complexity. An illustration of the challenge is provided by Philip Purcell, CEO of Dean Witter.

> Things move too fast. We've had three different key products in four years, so what is strategy? You simply get great people and back them. And even they can't tell you what they'll be doing next year. (Philip Purcell as cited in Eccles & Crane, 1988: 123)

The first section of this article discusses in further detail the processes leading to increasing complexification, with a particular emphasis on increasing knowledge and improving competence at all levels of society as a driving force. The following section highlights organizational and strategic challenges resulting from a high degree of complexification, and argues that traditional models assuming an all-knowing strategic apex, and increased efficiency and effectiveness through design, control, formalization and other rationalization processes, are inadequate. Finally, the third section discusses the implications for an expanded strategic management research agenda.

Complexification, turning organizations post-modern

Production is the key axial process of modern societies. The way it is organized might be held to determine, or at least to have serious consequences for, political, cultural and other developments (Crook, Pakuliski & Waters, 1992: 167). The dominant principle for organizational design through the 20th century in the Western Hemisphere has been Taylorism or Fordism and the Weberian bureaucracy; or organizational species like professional bureaucracies and divisionalized companies whose strongest heritage lies in these principles. The result is hierarchically designed organizations dividing hand and brain (Braverman, 1974; Mumphy & Putnam, 1992), where a specialized work force needs managerial layers to control and coordinate it. The common way of organizing production in modern society then resulted in relatively clear roles and relationships between those who occupied them. This organizing principle goes together with the distinction between owners (capitalists) and employees, who have to sell their work capabilities to earn their pay. Drucker, one of the early users of the term post-modern in 1957 (See Toulmin, 1990: 6) writes today about the post-capitalist society (Drucker 1993), illustrating that the change in society is taking place both in the way we organize and in ownership of the means of production.

The dominant process occurring in modern society has been rationalization (Hage & Powers, 1992), the attempt to streamline and simplify through codification of rules, mechanization of work, simplification of tasks (including deskilling) and routinization of work flow (Hage & Powers, 1992). Rationalization then means the recognition of better ways of arranging work. The knowledge explaining and guiding modern behavior has a positivistic foundation. The approach, including the search for objective knowledge using rational methods often based on quantitative techniques, has dominated the field of knowledge production; a search for general analytical principles in the attempts of mapping reality (Knights, 1992; Mumphy & Putnam, 1992). This thinking also guides managerial behavior. Whenever a new topic or issue comes up, the way to handle it becomes: isolate it and break it down into manageable entities and standard procedures or activities.

In post-modern society, knowledge and technology have become the dominant social forces shaping society, and transforming social roles at the level of individual people (Hage & Powers, 1992: 8). The result is a need for more flexible social institutions, complex selves and creative minds. A distinctive characteristic of our time is that practitioners of every occupation with a significant knowledge base must keep learning. Rather than rationalization, which results in deskilling, the opposite process comes into play; namely, role occupants must acquire more knowledge so that they can recognize and respond adequately to individualized circumstances. Each discovery represents an expansion in required knowledge, and therefore greater options and more complexity (Hage & Powers, 1992: 52).

The two processes, rationalization and complexification, are driving the principles of organization and strategy toward opposite poles of a continuum; universalism and particularism. Universalism requires that one treats all objects in a particular class in the same way. Particularism, in contrast, requires that a person treats objects «in accordance

with their standing in some particular relationship to him or his collectivity» (Parsons & Shils, 1951). Two different principles of knowledge
production are dominant at the different ends of the universalism-
particularism continuum, constituting the ground for methods of research and principles for researchers.

First, generalization – making forests out of trees – dominates the universal end, being usually performed by gathering data and finding the
general patterns in them, often guided by the rational assumptions embedded in «quantitative scientific methods». When we apply the results of
analyses based on the ideas of generalization on reality – an activity often
called implementation, which is not well understood and is often a minor
field compared with strategic analysis in textbooks on strategy (Pfeffer,
1992) – it is assumed that analysis, decision-making and implementation
can be divided into different sequences, performed by different persons
and executed at different times (Mintzberg, 1990). An illustration of the
problematic distance between such assumptions and reality is provided
by Knights in his example of the bank managers trying to force-fit Porter's
frameworks (Porter, 1980, 1985) to their strategy processes (Knights,
1992: 524-525). Another illustration is offered by Morgan (1993), who
describes strategic termites, people who do not follow predetermined detailed plans (results of analyses); people who are both incremental and
opportunistic in their approach to change (Morgan, 1993).

Second, at the other end of the continuum, the principle of interpretation is dominant. Particularism in post-modern conditions requires
that interpretation becomes a two-way process – viewing both trees and
forest at the same time, and not taking for granted that the latter is the
sum of the parts of which it is constituted. Forests are forests, but no
two are the same. Interpreting here requires an understanding of both
the situation at hand and theoretical knowledge; the individual, whether
researcher, consultant or strategist, has to be reflective in order to be
able to merge theory and practice into the required unique solutions for
each particular case (Schön, 1983). Such work can be said to be interpretive interactionism (Denzin, 1989), rather than data-gathering.
More effort is expended in the construction of meaning into the situation - often from more than one point of view (Thomas & Pruett, 1993)
– than in presenting it. Each situation here has to be handled as one
unique event and/or process. Analysis, decision-making and implementation are all aspects of the same process, intimately intertwined, ap-
pearing at the same time. Post-modern interpretation thus turns the assumptions about analytical, bias-free, objective analyses upside down.

For the affirmative post-modernist, reality is political, subjective, controversial, mere personal interpretation (Rosenau, 1992).

The impact of complexification on occupational roles is therefore the opposite to that of rationalization. Complexification is driven by the accumulation of additional knowledge and the addition of more demanding activities (Hage & Powers, 1992). This process is not well understood, but three components may shed light on the process (Hage & Powers, 1992):

- Knowledge is accumulated, resulting in an expansion of the professional, technical and managerial sectors of the labor force.

- Organizations specialize in order to deal with niche markets that develop as our knowledge base increases. The growing number of small specialized firms, the vertical cutback in the value chain of large corporations, joint ventures, network constellations and profit centers within large organizational entities are illustrations of this.

- Greater periods of time are spent acquiring specialized occupational training. The sophistication of the production process is rapidly decreasing the demand for unskilled workers. The speed of progress in knowledge areas increases demand for constantly upgrading human competence and skills.

If we transfer this understanding to challenges in the field of strategic management, we can see that the enhanced importance of «human capital» and information systems as the knowledge base in organizations, more concern about what customers really need and want, and empowerment become the new instruments for coordination and control (Clegg, 1990: 203), thus leading to fewer managerial layers. Knowledge workers need to be challenged to achieve. They prefer that demands be made on them by knowledge rather than bosses, and they prefer performance-oriented organizations to authority-oriented ones (Sadler, 1988), or task-driven to authority-driven ones (Beer, Eisenstat & Spector, 1990). Specialization and accumulation of knowledge also lead to a variety of organizational forms, the one ideal type inherited from modernity being accompanied by the many different ideal types of post-modernity (Clegg, 1990; Handy, 1990; Mitroff, 1987). Post-modern organizations are in irreversible change, not turning back to a homeostatic balance, retaining their basic forms or pathways (Bergquist,

1993). Thus, complexification is transferring the field of strategic management from searching for general solutions to understanding and accepting that different solutions can work equally well. Managerial roles and strategic behavior are transferred beyond rational management (Quinn, 1990) to a new logic that challenges the established order in the field of thinking and acting in organizations (Mitroff, 1987; Galbraith, Lawler & Associates 1993).

Our general view is that, while organizations still have an increased need for particular solutions (unique solutions constructed for the focal organization), mainstream research within the field of strategy is searching for, and responding with, universal principles (Daft & Buenger, 1990). In many cases, meaning and knowledge are constructed within the world of theories (or metatheories), rather than by interpreting what's going on. We may be at risk of distancing the empirical world ever increasingly from our scientific image of it.

Three processes challenging our conventional wisdom

From visible assets and invisible customers to invisible assets and visible customers

Going from modern to post-modern conditions calls for an important transformation in the traditional thinking around resources and the transformation of resources within firms. The most important assets in modern production were land and capital in the form of machinery, raw materials and cash. The balance sheet of the company is still visualizing their value. The products were sold. The main objective for the sales personnel was «to get rid of the products that were produced», an activity that later is expanded to marketing, with new concepts such as segments, promotion and market research, market position and market share. The market was not just a place where products were sold: it comprised different segments of customers with different needs and wants; yet as individuals, the customers were relatively anonymous or invisible as part of a segment the company could aim at. In the field of strategy, the focus was on companies jockeying for position in these segments, trying to position themselves relative to their competitors (Porter, 1980). Success was not just measured in sales volume, but as market shares in different geographical as well as demographic segments.

The turn to post-modern conditions, where knowledge and skills play a more important role, is changing some of the basic premises on which our strategic theories and models were developed. First, the assets that become more important and critical for survival and success are invisible (Itami, 1987); knowledge, skills and learning are not reported in numbers as assets on the balance sheets. Their growing importance leads to a search for new managerial tools and techniques, and expressions like lifelong learning, the learning company (Senge, 1990) and competence configuration become increasingly popular. Second, many firms are customizing both their production and product development. Customers are treated like individuals, not as objects belonging to a constructed segment or class of customer, which leads to a closer connection between organizations both through formal arrangements, monitoring techniques like customer satisfaction indexes, benchmarking and individualization of production and products (Schonberger, 1990; Whiteley, 1991; Quinn Mills, 1991; Dimancescu, 1992; Pine, 1993).

The following example illustrates this fundamental shift: in the early months of 1990, Scandinavian Airlines System (SAS) introduced a marketing campaign in the largest Scandinavian newspapers. On a double page set-up, with a color picture showing a crowd of thousands of people, we could read. «In the '80s we saw a customer in each individual, in the '90s we see an individual in each customer.« Such a change, from viewing customers in the market as different segments to seeing them as individuals or subjects, calls for dramatic changes in marketing techniques and methods, as well as in company-based information systems; and, at the very foundation, a change in the meaning of concepts used. The serious problems this company has faced during the 1990s can be interpreted as a lack of transformation of organizing principles, thinking and knowledge in the entire organization. The consequences of the transformation in market view were out of range considering their organizational capabilities and resources. In many respects, this illustration from SAS may serve as an example of the difficulties involved when organizational change processes require substantial shifts in the mindsets of organizational members.

Pine (1993) addresses the change from customers as markets to customers as individuals as a change from mass production to mass customization. Ohmae (1990) is advocating field work, with participation and interpretation to discover subjective needs and translate these to products and services, as the new way of doing market research, and gives us examples of how such a change calls for qualitative market research using methods from anthropology. Traditional market research, relying on quantitative number crunching, is based on an ideal of objectivity. Turning to individualization calls for changing the philosophy on which thinking and acting are constituted. The old positivistic approach dominating modern times (Toulmin, 1990) is not compatible with post-modern conditions (Rosenau, 1992).

From vertical to horizontal organizations

The increased visibility of customers as subjects changes our perspective on production and challenges our traditional thinking on how organizations allocate resources to achieve superiority. Customized production starts and ends with the customer. The organization has to activate the appropriate processes rapidly in order to fulfill customer needs. Traditional functional organizational structures are, in such a view, just a way of grouping resources for internal accounting. A view of organizations as latent processes that are activated on request changes our organizational perspective from vertical (top-down or bottom-up) to horizontal (Ostroff & Smith, 1992). Post-modern conditions mean that empowered individuals, with subjective tastes, wants and needs, play a more important part than in modernity. Companies have to develop close ties with subjective individuals in their roles as organizational members or as customers in order to develop in an appropriate direction. The traditional top-down or bottom-up approaches, which in their broadest sense both represent inside-out perspectives, have to be expanded to an outside-in perspective. How our customers look at us, what they think and how they act, become more important than how the organization members look upon themselves and their customers (Crozier, 1989). As a consequence, we also see that markets and hierarchies are being supplanted by network structures (Miles & Snow, 1984; Thorelli, 1986; Miles, 1989: Ghoshal & Bartlett, 1990; Rockart & Short, 1989, 1991).

Design of structures and systems must then be understood as the means of encouraging and facilitating action, not as ends in themselves. The stable organizing element is not found in the structure of the organization, but in the structure of the evoked processes; that is, how firms systematize, activate and allocate adequate competence as resources to fulfill requests from individual customers. When structures depend on action required to satisfy the needs and wants requested by the individual customer, the strategy-structure continuum becomes a meaningless relation as a general dimension for determining the fit between an organization and the environment. Instead, this general principle can be seen as deconstructed into a two-way fit in separate relationships. The general assumption about an organization as an entity coordinating its separate parts must then be expanded or reframed to cover the coordination of different and loosely coupled relationship processes, which become the important parts in horizontal organizations. Strategic partnerships and relations are not hierarchies, nor are they markets. They are networks. And networks are rapidly becoming the most important organizational form in post-industrial society (Ghoshal & Bartlett, 1990). Thus, relationship-based resource allocation as well as relationship effectiveness and efficiency will have a growing importance for most firms.

From one ideal type of organizing to many

The traditional view of organization and strategy is to see the organization as a mechanism that turns resources into products; and strategy as the instrument for positioning the focal organization in the industry and marketplace. In many sectors today, companies can access the same assets, machinery, engineers, knowledge and capital. Increasingly, assets are becoming parts of the environment and not under company control. It can then be hard to develop unique assets as a competitive weapon. Instead there is an increased focus on the human capital as a firm-specific resource base. A firm that can use assets that are available to their competitors as well in an inimitable way, because of their unique invisible assets, may achieve sustainable competitive advantage.

In modern mass production, there seems to be a strong tendency to standardize products and components, resulting in low switching costs for customers. In post-industrial competition, however, the difference between organizations no longer resides in strategies in the market on either side of the input-output continuum controlled by an ideal type of hierarchical machine, but rather in the uniqueness of how they organize customers and assets and the way they are continuously improving these relationships. Systematizing learning from experience and transferring externalized learning to others become important processes in strategies for improvement (Revang, 1993). Organizational life becomes more an issue of helping your friends (named individuals) – customers or partners and organizational members – than an issue of behaving universalistically (Heimer, 1992).

The resources that make a difference then are no longer objective entities such as raw materials, technology or financial assets, but individual subjects such as personalized customers and subjective knowledge-bearers; and sense-making beings like engineers, managers and craftspeople as well as unique arrangements for deploying and cultivating them. Taking subjectivity seriously means that each organization has to generate its own principles or genetic code, and not replicating or adjusting to one single ideal type. «The true post-industrial mind must have the capacity to imagine scenarios that have not occurred, to envision new ways in which relationships and patterns of social organization can be restructured» (Hage & Powers, 1992: 70).

Strategic management in post-industrial organizations

The above discussion illustrates the extent to which the increasing complexification of organizations leads to challenges to organizational theory and practice alike. What, then, can be said about the role of strategic management; what might be the advice to the strategic manager of the post-modern organization? In the following section, we challenge a number of the traditional strategic management perspectives, highlighting the extent to which these perspectives implicitly require an increasingly rational (and utopian) top manager or a top management team. In the following section, we suggest some potentially fruitful avenues to follow if we are to be able to deal with this increasing complexity as researchers or as practitioners.

Strategic management – Homo economicus disguised?

The traditional response to the challenges of increasing complexity (due to increased knowledge and specialization) in organizations has been to improve efficiency through rationalization (Hage & Powers, 1992), breaking down or simplifying the complex issues to manageable entities. Organizations are designed and strategies chosen such that complexity is reduced, uncertainty is minimized and core operations are buffered against unavoidable uncertainty (to the extent possible) (Thompson, 1967). Rationalization is a process that leads to specialization and deskilling, important components on which to build and legitimate a managerial hierarchy with a strategic apex at the very top, thus dividing doing and thinking.

Practitioners and researchers alike, however, are talking about increasing demands for flexibility, responsiveness to changing customer requirements, and rapid response to new challenges (Miles & Snow, 1986; Kanter, 1989; Quinn, 1992; Davidow & Malone, 1992; Pine, 1993; Hastings, 1993). As more firms connect to other economic entities through alliances, participation in networks, licensing and other formal arrangements, they establish ties, although development over time may change the role of the relationship as well as its content. Whereas the hierarchical, rationalized organization may be highly efficient in terms of reproducing itself, in particular where only minor incremental changes are required, the model may not be adequate for modern postindustrial firms. Such firms seem to be increasingly characterized by dispersed critical competence, loosely coupled internal units with tight couplings to external actors through long-term relationships, and increasing complexity in terms of both the content and the types and numbers of interactions within the firm, as well as between the firm and its environment. Although it may be tempting to resort to the traditional design and rationalization solution yet one more time, its simplicity is likely to be deceptive. Our society is not unitary, but pluralistic; and our organizations today are incompatible with the idea of something being normal (Drucker, 1993: 46).

The strategist. Much has been said in organization theory, strategic management and even economics, regarding the ideal case, the hypothetical rational person used for modeling purposes in classical economics. Since Simon (1945) established the concept of bounded rationality, hardly any strategy researcher dares advocate a close link between a rational person and reality. Yet in strategic management theory, the ultimate strategist still seems to be a member of the *Homo economicus* species. As organizations become more and more complex, the strategist is required to deal with ever increasing complexity both in terms of handling vast amounts of information and synthesizing information of multiple kinds into clear decisions and actions which fit neatly together. In modern texts, decisions and actions should converge into a pattern even at the symbolic level, setting the direction for the organization through an overall strategic intent (Hamel & Prahalad, 1989). But in order to do this, the strategist seems to be both omniscient and able to predict the future.

Modern strategy texts frequently start with a caveat stating that the text is anchored in a rationalist paradigm, although we know that this is not an accurate picture of reality (See e.g. Grant, 1991). The inaccuracy of separating formulation and implementation is discussed, yet the text still advocates the importance of well-informed top managers who actually do analyze, formulate, and implement (or plan, allocate, organize, control, and direct). Despite the recognition that the micro-level processes do not add up to the whole of the complex reality, the fundamental belief is that dealing with the bits and pieces in an additive manner will improve performance. The paradigm of bounded rationality increases the faith in the strategic apex, where the planner/designer of the processes resides, whereas the doers are found at lower levels of the patriarchy (Mumby & Putnam, 1992). The ultimate strategist is supported by increasingly sophisticated tools that aid in analysis, information-processing, and even decision-making. Yet the «man on the top» (or sometimes «men» in modern texts) is/are still left alone with the responsibility and the role expectations that seem to fit better with a belief in *Homo economicus* than with an understanding of the human limitations of knowledge, as well as the unknowable nature of future strategic direction in a post industrial environment.

The chess player. In many strategy texts (e.g. Chandler, 1962; Porter, 1986), the model presumes a CEO who allocates resources and configures the resources of the firm in order to best match the demands of the environment (Stinchcombe, 1990). Resources, including «human resources», are allocated to their best possible use, if necessary through sophisticated calculations based on complex models for operations planning. People are moved in the organization and allocated like chess pieces moved on a board. The examples are numerous, in particular in United States-based corporations, illustrating how people are even moved to overseas positions at short notice and at the company's discretion, regardless of personal and family considerations. Again, this thinking illustrates a situation where power and authority, even over careers, resides at the strategic apex; a power vested in the top manager by the owners of the firm.

However, in post-industrial organizations the chess pieces move of their own free will, and frequently the chess pieces have a better overview of the most likely responses of the other chess pieces around them than the player who has to deal with the complexity of all the other chess pieces simultaneously. They also have the power and the authority as they control both the client-relevant information, their personalized relationship with customers, and the key value-creating asset (that is, problem-solving capabilities). Even the best chess players are caught by surprise by unexpected moves; imagine what would happen if the pieces started moving on their own at times, yet at other times following orders from above. The ultimate strategist would then have to know not only how to move the pieces in a stable world, and *vis-à-vis* the other player, but also the intent and abilities of each of the pieces on both sides. Would not such a player have to be even more rational than *Homo economicus?* Yet in the strategy literature, he is not uncommon. In the post-industrial competitive environment, the game of chess is no longer an appropriate metaphor; without the obedience of the chess pieces, chess is impossible!

The architect. The strategist as an architect is another frequently used (implicit) metaphor (e.g. Howard, 1992), not unlike that of the chess player. When the CEO is unable to plan the strategy, he or she is expected to design the systems, the processes, and the organizational structures that will promote the appropriate decentralized decisions and actions. Strategy may be allowed to emerge bottom-up, but the top manager controls the direction of this emergent strategy through the design of the framework within which these strategies may emerge. The ultimate architect in a post-industrial organization must be able to design not only the appropriate organization best suited for both efficiency and effectiveness, but also the meta-system so that the «self-organizing organization» (Eccles & Crane, 1988) organizes itself in the right way. Such a design requires knowledge not only of how to design organizations, but what the environment will demand and what the people in the organization know. It requires knowledge of how a meta-organization may be planned and a meta-strategy designed in such a way that the evolving pattern is guided in the appropriate direction. Can any manager know enough to plan such structures? Are they not merely another *Homo economicus* in disguise?

The cheerleader. Finally, there is the strategic manager who manages by «leading others to lead themselves» (Manz & Sims, 1989); the manager who mobilizes the culture, helps it to evolve in the right direction, manages through symbolic actions and «value-driven leadership» (Badaracco & Ellsworth, 1989), and thus is able to make the employees want to move in the same direction. These managers are not omniscient in the information-based cognitive view of the manager; they are twice born and have developed the appropriate characteristics based on both in born talents and responses to challenges experienced over time (Zaleznik, 1977). Yet again, managers must know (intuitively or by calculation) what this direction is. Are they yet again omniscient? Is this just another theory X in disguise? As Alvesson & Willmott (1992: 458) point out, it is easy to understand how some of the prescriptive advice to managers may be interpreted as manipulative when it suggests designing cultures that will improve efficiency and increase the motivation of employees towards the goals of the owners. Is there always someone at the top who knows better and has a better view of both the internal and the external perspective? Is *Homo economicus* simply dead, but unwilling to lie down?

Which apex when the pyramid is upside down?

Not only does the complexification process lead to impossible challenges for a model requiring a top manager who knows and understands the unknowable, but, as discussed above, the organizational characteristics also change as the result of this process. Power and authority no longer reside with the owners of capital, but rather with the owners of the new critical resources for value creation: competence, customer information and established relationships to key people within the firm as well as outside. In addition, as the result of the trend towards more universally applicable competence and quicker changes in firm-specific outputs, employees become increasingly mobile across employers. The strategic apex no longer exists, neither as a center of information nor as a center of power and authority. In fact, the whole concept of a pyramid, with the most powerful actor at its top, no longer fits in with the reality of post-industrial organizations. Where is the strategic apex of an organization where the pyramid is turned upside down (Carlzon, 1985)?

Organizing principles for people and roles: not tasks, authorities, and formal relationships

> If America is to win in the new global competition, we need to begin telling one another a new story in which companies compete by drawing upon the talents and creativity of all their employees, not just a few maverick inventors and dynamic CEOs. (Robert Reich, 1987)

Not only is the role of the top manager and the position at a strategic apex being challenged, but the relationships between people in these post-industrial organizations also (need to) change in response to increasing complexification. The result is likely to be an organization with empowered or «emancipated» employees (Alvesson & Willmott, 1992), where employees at all levels take responsibility in a broader sense than the authority and responsibility traditionally allocated to each position in a line-staff hierarchy. Temporary hierarchies result (Marshall, 1989, cited in Mumby & Putnam, 1992) as people occupy multiple roles, and their responsibilities and authorities shift, depending on which role is activated and which relationships are engaged in at each point in time. Employees are seen as subjects, rather than objects (or chess pieces), and their own judgments guide their actions *vis-à-vis* the people they deal with in their internal as well as external relationships. Multiple roles and temporary hierarchies do not necessarily lead to an erosion of authority and responsibility, nor to the impossibility of the dual authority matrix structure. On the contrary, post-industrial people balance this increased complexity through increased investments in relationships to fewer people holding a larger number of roles (Hage & Powers, 1992), as illustrated by the established practices of many professional service firms (Løwendahl, 1996).

The challenge will be to balance this empowerment with strategic direction, and the solution will no longer be increased rationalization through formalization. The issue is not one of either reducing complexity or increasing the capacity to handle complexity (paraphrasing Galbraith, 1973 on information-processing). In post-industrial society, the organization will have to manage the complexity and live with paradoxes. Reducing complexity means organizing away the challenges that stem from multiple roles and competence, and those arising from the demands of diverse customers influencing the organization outside-in. That would mean organizing away the very characteristics of the environment to which the post-industrial organization is required to adapt, at the risk of buffering itself from the entire market, rigidifying itself to such an extent that it will become an extinct species similar to the dinosaurs of ancient times.

Luckily, it is not at all clear that an empowered group of people taking responsibility for a broader set of roles and responsibilities will necessarily turn into an inefficient ad hocracy (Mintzberg, 1983) or, even worse, an organized anarchy (Cohen & March, 1974). Perhaps the need for the controlling apex and the supervising *Homo economicus* is a myth, and modern post-industrial people have outgrown the need for the paternalistic strategist at the top. Unfortunately, our language, models and metaphors in strategic management are not yet fit for these new ways of organizing, and we risk being trapped in our old conceptual schemes. Traditional talk about organizational and strategic principles then easily becomes hypocrisy (Brunsson, 1989). This challenge is discussed at greater length in the following section.

Implications for research

Fix the language

Confucius, upon being asked what he would do if appointed to rule a country, replied, «The first thing I would do is to 'fix the language'» (Pfeffer, 1992: 283). In our view, the field of strategic management, our concepts, models and thinking schemes, are based on modernist, structuralist and positivistic assumptions (Daft & Buenger, 1990). By using them, we force these assumptions on our reality, for in the cases where meaning is created by wandering around at the theoretical level, reality drifts away. To grasp post-modern strategies we have to take Confucius' advice seriously; we have to fix the language we use. If not, we will be stuck with words that do not work. Examples of such words that do not work are numerous in the (strategic) management literature. Words such as those included in the acronym POSDCORB (Gulick, 1930, cited in Mintzberg, 1973) are typical of the positivist language of traditional management texts: planning, organizing, staffing, directing, coordinating, reporting, budgeting. Recent strategy texts add other words to the vocabulary; choosing, designing, controlling, motivating, rewarding, analyzing, allocating, configuring, implementing, managing, developing, positioning – to mention a few of the most common concepts used in the strategy rhetoric. These terms are deeply rooted in the rational, positivist, paradigm of the vanishing modern times, and hence not equally helpful for our thinking about strategic management in a post-industrial world.[1]

In its traditional meaning, rhetoric refers to the formal field of study that examines how language is used to shape the way people think and act, a field that needs to be properly understood as one of the central concerns of effective management (Eccles & Nohria, 1992: 9). Imagine management or management research without a language; the very idea may strike us as totally absurd. In the world of organizations, language

---

1. For a detailed discussion of these issues, see Mumby and Putnam (1992) and Knights (1992). The latter also includes a discussion of the self-fulfilling character of many of our strategic management concepts, as they are taken to represent reality and used in the creation of new meaning by the people in power in organizations.

is everywhere, shaping the way we think and act. How will we be able to observe phenomena for which we do not have concepts to use as labels? Karl Weick (1969) writes «How can I know what I see until I hear what I say». We can push this even further by saying «How can I know what I see when it is dependent on the language in which I think?» Sandelands and Drazin (1989) argue that the problems of organization theory are essentially problems in the use of words. Language thus is constructing social life, and thereby affecting (strategic) behavior and relations (Shotter, 1993).

One recent, and potentially fruitful, theory development in strategic management may be the resource-based theory (Barney, 1991; Conner, 1991; Itami, 1987; Rumelt, 1984; Teece, Pisano & Shuen, 1989; Wernerfelt, 1984). The incorporation of «invisible assets» (Itami, 1987) and the explicit attention to the competence of members of the organization offer substantial potential for future research. However, even within this new strategic management direction, we face the danger of being trapped in our old paradigmatic language of positive science (Daft & Buenger, 1990), and some of the writers within this new area seem to have in mind the same old strategist or *Homo economicus* in disguise. In traditional neoclassical economic theory, resources can be measured and evaluated as substitutable input factors. Humans in modern times could easily be seen as a muscle-power resource; humans in post-modern organizations have to be seen as sense-making beings, who carry subjective knowledge, language, interpretation and creativity in their bodies. Such abilities are not substitutable in the same sense as the resource humans as workers, and often one human can not be substituted for another because the mental capabilities are not compatible. Hence the associations we sense from the term resource-based theory may easily become a return journey to modern times. Researchers may end up hiding themselves in Plato's cave, chatting around the fire, and analyzing the dancing shadows on the wall with concepts inherited from earlier generations in their tribe, and progressing by constructing quantitative models for explaining and predicting the behavior of the shadows. At the same time the world in flux outside is developing, showing less and less similarities with the gray two-dimensional images dancing on the cave wall.

Pfeffer (1992) writes that we perceive things according to how they are described in conversation and debate, and that facts can be produced to justify almost any decision. For many writers, the concern about decisions, control and leadership is replaced by symbolic action dressed up in language, ceremonies and settings (Pfeffer, 1992), or rhetoric, action and identity (Eccles & Nohria, 1992), or imagination improving our abilities to see and understand situations in new ways (Morgan, 1986; 1993). According to Mumby and Putnam (1992: 481):

> Scholars need to abandon their efforts to construct a final organizational vocabulary based on the belief that truth is «out there» waiting to be discovered. The final truth of organizations is not out there. Rather, it is constantly unfolding in the discourse constructed by theorists and researchers to make sense of and explain organizations.

Some concepts that may work better in a post-industrial context are: activating latent processes, facilitating action, enabling the organic organizational growth, interpreting, intuiting, experimenting (small scale), «imaginization» (Morgan, 1993), doing, testing and trying. Further research and work on the development of new and more appropriate concepts is clearly needed.

Abandon quantitative techniques (measurements), at least for a while

For many decades quantitative techniques have dominated the field of management education. In so doing, they have constituted a way of thinking around, structuring and analyzing managerial issues. Their advocates are not only responsible for the correct application of techniques they have imported from elsewhere, they are responsible for the techniques themselves. Whenever they face issues they do not understand, they try to translate them into their own language, which is rather abstract, and where the notions of truth, rationality, science, and objectivity have become bound up together. Objective truth, truth as correspondence, is what we arrive at by using such techniques, of which natural science provides the paradigm. And we think of scientific rationality as a matter of following procedures laid down in advance. Taking rationality in this way gives their advocates a special position. For the social sciences and humanities – the important knowledge bases for reflexive, interpretive interaction – cannot offer such procedures. Since such techniques are constituted on assumptions that are being eroded, or at least their domain of relevance is shrinking with the movement towards a post-industrial society, we have to reconsider their use and position.

That their use may lead to ineffectiveness, of activity being a waste of resources by preoccupying intellects with a potential to be creative, and the loss of the sense and interpretation of reality, etc., is not a major issue per se. Free people should choose for themselves what is important to them; the prime issue is that such techniques prevent the creativity that is called for in a post-industrial world from being internalized into management research.

Intellectual advocates of quantitative techniques define errors in a specific way. They define them not according to the standards and procedures of the form of life in which they occur, but by comparison with a society-independent «reality», «rationality» or «truth». Using these measures they have condemned entire cultures as being based on illusion and prejudice (Feyerabend, 1987). To facilitate «fixing the language» through creative thinking, and the generation of new perspectives, conceptual frameworks, images and creative concepts to describe and interpret the subjective, complex, reality, we ought probably to abandon the use of such techniques. We should do so at least for a while, until we have rediscovered their assumptions, reframed their field of usefulness and downgraded them to a level where they no longer have superiority, but must compete with different alternative ways of grasping reality. «You don't understand a phenomenon if you don't understand it in more than one way», has to be (re)introduced into the specialized field of quantitative management research.

It is a paradox that the attempt to be scientific in the field of strategic management actually leads to less knowledge (Daft & Buenger, 1990). The adoption of normal scientific (Kuhn, 1962) thinking produces inflexibility, bureaucratization of techniques, and methodological pretension. The desire to be scientific in strategic management has meant that most often only quantitative variables are measured (Daft & Buenger, 1990), leaving us without robust theories to probe into deeper aspects of the phenomenon at hand. The more the field of strategic management embraces a single assumption set, and the louder the insistence on rigid, quantitative procedures, the more likely it is that studies will fail to produce breakthroughs (Daft & Buenger, 1990). And in the present situation it is breakthroughs into alternative ways of understanding that we really need.

Farewell to reason

Feyerabend (1987: 281) argues that successful research does not obey general standards; it relies on one thing one time for one trick, another time on another, and the moves that advance it are not always known to the movers. He shows that scientific progress often has been undertaken by rebels disobeying what has been taken for the accepted common sense in the field, by people searching for new explanations and new discoveries. In the field of management, Kreiner (1989) makes the observation that the vast attention paid to autobiographies of well-known industrialists such as Iacocca (1984) indicates the representations of organizations that society is willing to accept as truthful do not have to be connected to any scientific method. What Feyerabend writes about the history of scientific development can today be found in some contributions to the field of strategic management. In giving advice to managers, Mitroff (1987: 40) writes that we must be prepared to challenge all constraints, distrust simplicity, question the boundaries of a problem and challenge as many assumptions as possible. A similar position is taken by Peters in his *Liberation Management* (Peters, 1992) and Drucker in writing about the new world of organizations (Drucker, 1989; Drucker, 1992). Stacey (1992) advocates a similar approach: the use of categories of strategic behavior to prompt questions, and raises issues about the specific actions they should take in a particular company, instead of reasoning in terms of direct cause and effect. Handy (1989) focuses on the same topics, labeling them as re-framing, re-inventing, upside-down thinking, and shamrock organizations, and designating our post-modern times as the «Age of Unreason», a time when conventional thinking and training is not producing appropriate solutions.

Thus, both the researcher in the field of strategic management and the manager should not just challenge existing «truths», but try to escape from the trap of rationalization embedded in analytical cause and effect reasoning. In its most stark sense, post-modernism stands for the death of reason (Power; 1990), and the understanding of organizations and management becomes a process of organizing understanding (Jeffcutt, 1993). Just by doing so we can expect a new, adequate and meaningful understanding of new and old strategic issues that can help us and our organizations on our journey out of the psychic prison inside Plato's cave into the (great) wide-open future we are creating as we move along.

Conclusion

Strategy and organization theory have traditionally been searching for principles that are essentially universal in nature, based on the process of rationalization. A post-modern research program in strategy must emphasize both the relative nature of managerial principles and their limitations. In this paper we have raised a number of issues that must be dealt with at the boundaries of strategic management if we are to be able to develop theories and meaningful concepts for post-industrial management. Not only do we need to challenge our established paradigms, but we even need to rethink the boundaries of our own ways of thinking.

If managers have to think unconventionally to secure the survival of their organizations, if people are becoming more educated and are filling more complex jobs, if scientific progress is not linear and rational, and if societies are going through a fundamental transformation, why should research in strategic management remain stuck in the groove of the most certain way of becoming obsolete, namely rationalization?

What students learn in school seems difficult to unlearn, and studying techniques as if they were subjects constitutes a belief that there are right and wrong answers. «Life appears as a series of eureka problems, so called because once you are shown the correct approach or answer, it is immediately self-evident that the answer is, in fact, correct» (Pfeffer, 1992: 18). Today we socialize our students to think and see right and wrong solutions, by applying standardized techniques. In doing so we do not prepare them well for post-modern conditions. Even the so widely applied case-method of teaching students has typically been employed to teach students how to find the one right answer to the one most important problem, rather than how to grapple with a complex context and deal with multiple perspectives simultaneously (Mintzberg, 1990).

Similarly, we may have to rethink the traditional «division of labor» of academics, consultants, and business ACB – where knowledge is produced by academics, distributed by consultants and applied by business managers. In post-modern research, a close and interactive relationship between science and its application is required where managers learn from academics and academics learn from managers. If trial and error procedures are required in order to solve unique problems, academics need to be immersed in the processes. *Ex cathedra* theorizing is less and less likely to produce solutions to the ever-changing problems of real life managers. And, after all, was it not the purpose of strategic management to be problem driven, applied, and helpful to business?

We have a long way to go, and perhaps we as researchers also need to develop alternative modes of knowledge generation such as those advocated by March (1971) in terms of foolishness and play. Perhaps we need to bring together the cognitive and rational parts of reasoning and the more intuitive, creative parts of our sense-making capacities, as was advocated by Bateson (1979) in his discussion of «mind *and* nature» rather than «mind *versus* nature"?

This is a tall order, as we are all educated in a paradigm advocating the supremacy of the cognitive, the rational, the positivist, the controlled and planned. As indicated in this chapter, a research agenda challenging the present boundaries of strategic thinking will need to develop in a number of different directions and from multiple perspectives. We do not foresee any new one best paradigm; on the contrary, the multidisciplinary nature of the strategy research agenda needs to be even further encouraged. And we need to support creative and unusual approaches, and encourage multiple viewpoints in parallel in order to develop new and more appropriate concepts, models and even ways of thinking about strategic management. As Hage and Powers (1992) put it, in post-industrial society we need individuals with «complex selves and creative minds». Are we as researchers – predominantly trained and socialized in a positivist tradition – ready to take on the challenges of post-industrial life and post-industrial research? Are we ready to change and expand our research agendas sufficiently so that we will be able to provide relevant research results for post-industrial managers? In all probability, we will need to radically rethink the boundaries of strategic management in order to avoid the danger of obsolescence.

References

Alvesson, M. & H. Willmott (1992): On the Idea of Emancipation in Management and Organization Studies. *Academy of Management Review 17*: 432-464.

Badaracco, J.L. & R.R. Ellsworth (1989): *Leadership and the Quest for Integrity*. Boston, MA: Harvard Business School Press.

Barney, J.B. (1991): Firm Resources and Sustained Competitive Advantage. *Journal of Management 17*: 99-120.

Bateson, G. (1979): *Mind and Nature; A Necessary Unity*. New York: Bantam.

Beer, M., R.A. Eisenstat & B. Spector (1990): *The Critical Path to Corporate Renewal*. Boston: Harvard Business School Press.

Bell, D. (1973): *The Coming of the Post-Industrial Society*. New York: Basic Books.

Bergquist, W. (1993): *The Postmodern Organization? Mastering the Art of Irreversible Change*. San Francisco: Jossey-Bass Publishers.

Blau, P M. & S.W. Scott (1963): *Formal Organizations: A Comparative Approach*. London: Routledge & Kengan Paul.

Braverman, H. (1974): *Labor and Monopoly Capitalism*. New York: Monthly Review Press.

Brunsson, N. (1989): *The Organization of Hypocrisy. Talk, Decisions and Actions in Organizations*. New York: John Wiley.

Burns, T. & G.M. Stalker (1961): *The Management of Innovation*. London: Tavistock.

Carlzon, J. (1985): *Riv Pyramidene*. Oslo: Gyldendal.

Chandler (1962): *Strategy and Structure*. MIT Press. Cambridge, MA.

Clegg (1990): Modern Organisations. *Organisation Sudies in the Postmodern World*. London: Sage.

Cohen, M.D. & J.G. March. (1974): *Leadership and Ambiguity*. New York: McGraw-Hill.

Conner, K.R. (1991): A Historical Comparison of Resource Based Theory and Five Schools of Thought within Industrial Organization Economics: Do We Have a New Theory of the Firm? *Journal of Management 17*: 121-154.

Crook, S., Pakuliski, J. & Waters, M. (1992): *Postmodernization – Changes in Advanced Society*. London: Sage.

Crozier, M. (1989): *L'entreprise a l'ecoute*. Paris: Intereditions.

Daft, R.L. & Buenger, V. (1990): Hitching a Ride on a Fast Train to Nowhere? The Past and Future of Strategic Management Research. In J.W. Fredrickson (ed.): *Perspectives on Strategic Management*. New York: Harper & Row, 81-103.

Davidow, W.H. & Malone, M.S. (1992): *The Virtual Corporation-Structuring and Restructuring the Corporation for the 21st Century*. New York: Edward Burlingame Books/HarperBusiness.

Denzin, N.K. (1989): *Interpretive Interactionism*. London: Sage.

Dimancescu, D. (1992): *The Seamless Enterprise – Making Cross Functional Management Work*. New York: Harper Business.

Drucker, P. (1989): *The New Realities*. Oxford: Heinemann Professional Publishing Ltd.

Drucker, P. (1992): The New Society of Organizations. *Harvard Business Review sept.-oct.*: 95-104.

Drucker, P. (1993): *Post-Capitalist Society*. Oxford: Butterworth Heinemann.

Eccles, R.G. & D.B. Crane (1988): *Doing Deals – Investment Banks at Work*. Boston: Harvard Business School.

Eccles, R.G. & N. Nohria (1992): *Beyond the Hype – Rediscovering the Essence of Management*. Boston, MA: Harvard Business School Press.

Feyerabend, P. (1987): *Farewell to Reason*. New York: Verto.

Galbraith, J.R. (1973): *Designing Complex Organizations*. New York: Addison-Wesley.

Galbraith, J.R., Lawler, E.E., III & Associates (1993): *Organizing for the Future – The New Logic for Managing Complex Organizations*. San Francisco: Jossey-Bass Publishers.

Ghoshal, S. & C.A. Bartlett (1990): The Multinational Corporation as an International Network. *Academy of Management Review 15*: 603-625.

Grant, R.M. (1991): *Contemporary Strategy Analysis. Concepts, Techniques, Applications*. Oxford: Blackwell.

Hage, J. & C.H. Powers (1992): *Post-Industrial Lives-Roles and Relationships in the 21st Century*. London: Sage Publications.

Hamel, G. & C.K. Prahalad (1989): Strategic Intent. *Harvard Business Review 67*: 63-76.

Handy, C. (1989): *The Age of Unreason*. London: Arrow Books Ltd.

Hastings, C. (1993): *The New Organization – Growing the Culture of Organizational Networking*. London: McGraw-Hill.

Heimer, C.A. (1992): Doing Your Job and Helping Your Friends: Universalistic Norms about Obligations to Particular Others in Networks. In N. Nohria & R.G. Eccels (eds.): *Networks and Organizations: Structure, Form and Action*. Boston, MA: Harvard Business School Press, 143-164.

Howard, R. (1992): The CEO as Organizational Architect: An interview with Xerox's Paul Allaire. *Harvard Business Review sept.-oct.*: 107-121.

Iacocca, L. (1984): *Iacocca: An Autobiography*. New York: Bantam Books.

Itami, H. (1987): *Mobilizing Invisible Assets*. Cambridge, MA: Harvard University Press.

Jeffcutt, P. (1993): From Interpretation to Representation. In J. Hassard & M. Parker (eds.): *Postmodernism and Organizations*. London: Sage Publications, 25-48.

Kanter, R.M. (1989): *When Giants Learn to Dance*. London: Simon & Schuster.

Knights, D. (1992): Changing Spaces: The Disruptive Impact of a New Epistemological Location for the Study of Management. *Academy of Management Review 17*: 514-536.

Kreiner, K. (1989): *The Postmodern Epoch of Organization Theory*. Paper presented at the Post Modern Management Conference, Barcelona.

Kuhn, T.S. (1962): *The Structure of Scientific Revolution*. Chicago: University of Chicago Press.

Lawrence, P.R. & J.W. Lorsch (1967): *Organization and Environment*. Homewood, IL: Richard D. Irwin.

Løwendahl, B.R. (1996): *Strategic Management of Professional Service Firms*. Copenhagen: Copenhagen Business School Press. Forthcoming.

Manz, C.C. & H.P. Sims (1989): *Superleadership; Leading Others to Lead Themselves*. Englewood Cliffs, NJ: Prentice Hall.

March, J.G. (1971): The Technology of Foolishness. *Civiløkonomen 18*: Reprinted in J.G. March: Decisions and Organizations, New York: Blackwell, 1988, 253-265.

Miles, R.E. (1989): Adapting to Technology and Competition: A new Industrial Relation System for the 21st Century. *California Management Journal 31*: 9-27.

Miles, R.H. & C.C. Snow (1984): Fit, Failure and the Hall of Fame. *California Management Review 26*: 10-28.

Miles, R.E. & C.C. Snow (1986): Network Organizations: New Concepts for New Forms. *California Management Review 28*: 62-73.

Mintzberg, H. (1973): *The Nature of Managerial Work*. New York: Harper & Row.

Mintzberg, H. (1979): *The Structuring of Organizations*. Englewood Cliffs, NJ: Prentice-Hall International Editions.

Mintzberg, H. (1983): *Structure in Fives: Designing Effective Organizations*. Englewood Cliffs, NJ: Prentice-Hall International Editions.

Mintzberg, H. (1990): Strategy Formation: Schools of Thought. In J.W. Fredrickson (ed.): *Perspectives on Strategic Management*. New York: Harper & Row, 105-237.

Mitroff, I.I. (1987): *Business NOT as Usual – Rethinking Our Individual Corporate and Industrial Strategies for Global Competition*. San Francisco: Jossey-Bass Publishers.

Morgan, G. (1986): *Images of Organization*. Beverly Hills, CA: Sage Publications.

Morgan, G. (1993): *Imaginization – The Art of Creative Management*. London: Sage Publications.

Mumphy, D.K. & L.L. Putnam (1992): The Politics of Emotion: A Feminist Reading of Bounded Rationality. *Academy of Management Review 17*: 465-486.

Nadler, D. & M.L. Tushman (1992): Designing Organizations That Have Good Fit: A Framework for Understanding New Architectures. In D. Nadler, M.S. Gestrain & R.B. Shaw (eds.): *Organizational Architecture*. San Francisco: Jossey-Bass, 39-59.

Ohmae, K. (1990): *The Borderless World – Power and Strategy in the Interlinked Economy*. New York: Harper Business.

Ostroff, F. & F. Smith (1992): The Horizontal Organization. *The McKinsey Quarterly 1*: 148-168.

Parsons, T. & E.A. Shils (1951): Categories of the Orientation and Organization of Action. In T. Parsons & E.A. Shils (eds.): *Toward a General Theory of Action*. New York: Harper & Row, 53-109.

Peters, T. (1992): *Liberation Management – Necessary Disorganization for the Nanosecond Nineties*. London: Macmillan.

Pfeffer, J. (1992): *Managing with Power – Politics and Influence in Organizations*. Boston, MA: Harvard Business School Press.

Pine II, J.B. (1993): *Mass Customization – The New Frontier in Business Competition*. Boston, MA: Harvard Business School Press.

Porter, M.E. (1980): *Competitive Strategy – Techniques for Analyzing Industries and Competitors*. New York: The Free Press.

Porter, M.E. (1985): *Competitive Advantage – Creating and Sustaining Superior Performance*. New York: The Free Press.

Porter, M.E. (1986): Competition in Global Industries: A Conceptual Framework. In M.E. Porter (ed.): *Competition in Global Industries*. Boston, MA: Harvard Business School Press, 15-60.

Power, M. (1990): Modernism, Postmodernism and Organization. In J. Hassard & D. Pym (eds.): *The Theory and Philosophy of Organizations – Critical Issues and New Perspectives*. London: Routledge, 109-124.

Quinn, R.E. (1990): *Beyond Rational Management – Mastering the Paradoxes and Competing Demands of High Performance*. San Francisco: Jossey-Bass.

Quinn, J.B. (1992): *Intelligent Enterprise*. New York: The Free Press.

Quinn Mills, D. (1991): *Rebirth of the Corporation*. New York: John Wiley & Sons, Inc.

Reich, R.B. (1987): The Team as Hero. *Harvard Business Review 65(3):* 77-83.

Revang, Ø. (1993): Knowledge, Skill and Information – Some Consequences for Management and Organization Design. In J. Olaisen (ed.): *Information Management*. Oslo: Scandinavian University Press, 329-343.

Rockart, J.F. & J.E. Short (1989): IT in the 1990s: Managing Organizational Interdependence. *Sloan Management Review* Winter: 7-17.

Rockart, J.F. & J.E. Short (1991): The Networked Organization and the Management of Interdependence. In M.S.S. Morton (ed.): *The Corporation of the 1990s*. New York: Oxford University Press, 189-219.

Rosenau, P.M. (1992): *Post-Modernism and the Social Sciences; Insights, Inroads, and Intrusions*. Princeton, NJ: Princeton University Press.

Rumelt, R.P. (1984): Towards a Strategic Theory of the Firm. In B. Lamb (ed.): *Competitive Strategic Management*. Englewood Cliffs, NJ: Prentice Hall, 556-570.

Sadler, P. (1988): *Managerial Leadership in the Post-Industrial Society*. Aldershot: Gower Publishing Company.

Sandelands, L. & R. Drazin (1989): On the Language of Organization Theory. *Organization Studies 10*: 457-478.

Schonberger, R.J. (1990): *Building a Chain of Customers*. New York: The Free Press.

Schön, D.A. (1983): *The Reflective Practitioner*. New York: Basic Books.

Senge, P.M. (1990): *The Fifth Discipline – The Art & Practice of the Learning Organization*. New York: Doubleday/Currency.

Shotter, J. (1993): *Conversational Realities – Constructing Life through Language*. London: Sage.

Simon, H. (1945): *Administrative Behavior*. New York: Free Press, (3rd edn 1976).

Stacey, R.D. (1992): *Managing Chaos*. London: Kogean Page.

Stacey, R D. (1993): *Strategic Management and Organizational Dynamics*. London: Pitman Publishing.

Stinchcombe, A. (1990): *Information and Organizations*. Berkeley: University of California Press.

Teece, D.J., G. Pisano & A. Shuen (1989): Firm Capabilities, Resources, and the Concept of Strategy. Working paper. Berkeley: University of California at Berkeley.

Thomas, H. & M. Pruett (1993): Introduction to the Special Issue: Perspectives on Theory Building in Strategic Management. *Journal of Management Studies 30*: 3-10.

Thompson, J.D. (1967): *Organizations in Action*. New York: McGraw-Hill.

Thorelli, H.B. (1986): Networks, Between Markets and Hierarchies. *Strategic Management Journal 7*: 37-51.

Toulmin, S. (1990): *Cosmopolis: The Hidden Agenda of Modernity*. New York: The Free Press.

Weick, K.E. (1969): *The Social Psychology of Organizing*. New York: Random House.

Wernerfelt, B. (1984): A Resource Based View of the Firm. *Strategic Management Journal 5*: 171-180.

Whiteley, R.C. (1991): *The Customer Driven Company*. Kent: Century Business.

Zaleznik, A. (1977): Managers and Leaders: Are They Different? *Harvard Business Review* May-June: 67-88.

Section Three

Applying the
Resource Based Perspective

In this section, we focus on application of the resource based perspective. In the first article Nordhaug makes the important link between organizational competencies, defined as the knowledge and skills in the organization, and individual competencies. In making this link, Nordhaug builds on the conceptual perspectives of skills, knowledge, memory and distinctive competencies to develop an integrated framework.

To increase our understanding of how the resource based perspective can lead to sustained competitive advantage, it is possible to focus on a specific strategic asset. In his paper, Grønhaug focuses on expert knowledge as a specific asset. Expertise is defined as superb special skills and knowledge. It is a key element of core competence as a prerequisite for capability based strategies. The article describes expert knowledge and then focuses on how, why and under what conditions expert knowledge may lead to competitive advantages.

Information systems cannot be viewed as a strategic resource because the technology behind information systems is non-proprietary and imitable. However, Anne Mette Fuglseth and Kjell Grønhaug argue that how these systems are used can lead to their being a strategic resource. As an example they use the case of credit evaluations of a major Norwegian bank.

Institutional markets emerge as disparate organizations become more similar to one another, resulting in actions being constrained in their ability to change. Given this homogenization of firms, the resource based perspective offers 'a way out'. Martin Gjelsvik's article investigates how firms may succeed in creating sustainable competitive advantages even within institutional environments. He uses the example of Norwegian savings banks.

Collective Competences

Odd Nordhaug

During the last decade, there has been an increasing tendency within the administrative sciences to emphasize the significance of intangible resources in the form of knowledge and skills in organizations. The question of how to conceptualize the substance and impact of such resources has been approached from widely dissimilar angles within different bodies of literature. In many ways this is a strength since the various traditions together have created a rich arsenal of concepts, perspectives and, to a modest degree, theoretical propositions. At the same time, it reflects the typical situation of an emerging field of inquiry characterized by a myriad of concepts and perspectives created for largely dissimilar purposes, and by the absence of a shared theoretical foundation.

Consequently, there is an apparent need to establish a common conceptual ground for the study of competence in organizations, including links between the micro, meso, and macro levels of analysis. The point of departure in this paper is that the establishment of an integrated perspective, upon which there can be widespread consensus in the research community, stands out as a major research challenge.

In the following, four dissimilar conceptual perspectives developed within different lines of research are presented and discussed with emphasis on their key constructs, main focus, conceptualization of generation processes and the levels of analysis included. The perspectives are labeled according to their basic theoretical construct and include organizational skills, organizational knowledge, organizational memory and distinctive competence.

Following the review and comparison of the four conceptual perspectives, an integrated framework for the study of competence in the form of knowledge and skills resources in organizations is outlined. The framework includes both the micro and the macro level and, moreover, suggests how the meso level of teams is crucial in linking the two other levels together.

Background

The study of competence and aggregates of competence in organizations is at an early stage, and the existing literature is both scant and fragmented. There is hence a need to develop basic concepts and theory on the nature of competence and its significance for the functioning of organizations. The relationship between human resources in the form of knowledge and skills and organizational performance has not been much studied in depth, although concepts such as key competence, distinctive competence, strategic skills, and core competence have been introduced to indicate that human resources play a crucial role for such performance (Selznick, 1957; Winter, 1987; Naugle & Davies; 1987; Prahalad & Hamel, 1990; Nordhaug & Grønhaug, 1994). However, the ways in which competence, defined as the knowledge and skills in the organization, influences organizational behavior and performance have not been systematically investigated. The relatively modest amount of research conducted in this area has, to a considerable degree, concentrated on the macro level of firms by focusing on key or core organizational competence. The core competence of a firm has largely been taken as given, and few attempts have been made to link employee and organizational competence. This is parallel to the situation in the strategy literature, where the links between individual beliefs and cognitive structures, organization-wide beliefs and assumptions and political processes have typically been ignored, creating gaps in the research relating the interaction between individual-level understanding and organizational action. As noted by Lyles and Schwenk (1991: 156), some researchers recognize that organizations have knowledge structures as do individuals, whereas others discuss the cognition of key individuals without taking into account the ways in which these are influenced by organizational events and without discussing the degree to which understandings are shared by other members of the organization.

Within the organizational theory literature, proponents of the so-called new institutionalism contend that there are strong pressures and incentives for organizations to conform with and copy the organizational design, practices and procedures of other organizations within the same sector or organizational field (for an overview, see Powell & DiMaggio, 1991). Hence, it is argued that organizations operating within the same field tend to become more similar over time with regard to many essential dimensions. Yet, in contrast to the organizational population ecologists, new institutionalists reject the claim that organizations mimicking other organizations usually have no significant competitive advantage. On the contrary, they maintain that reliance on established and legitimated procedures increases organizational legitimacy and survival characteristics (DiMaggio & Powell, 1991: 75).

Concurrently, within recent industrial organization economics and strategy literature, many authors argue that the competitive advantages of firms have largely shifted from being founded on technological resources to being based on competence resources in the form of knowledge and skills carried by employees, collective or supra-individual competence structures, and the integration of such structures and technology. A core argument is that lasting technological leverage on competitors has been increasingly difficult to develop and protect, among other things due to the soaring pace of technological innovation and the diffusion of innovation. As argued by Quinn, Door and Paquette (1991: 305), physical facilities, including seemingly superior products, seldom guarantee a sustainable competitive edge: «They are too easily bypassed, reverse engineered, cloned, or slightly surpassed. Instead, a maintainable advantage usually derives from outstanding depth in selected human skills, logistic capabilities, knowledge bases, or other service strengths that competitors cannot reproduce and that lead to greater demonstrable value for the customer». In the same vein, Ulrich and Lake (1990: 57-53), when discussing achievement of competitive advantage through goods or services that cannot be easily replicated by competitors, maintain that among the potential sources of uniqueness, organizational capability is the most difficult one to copy. Financial capability may be duplicated if competitors are equally good at reducing costs or gaining access to capital. Strategic capability is often copied because new products are analyzed, and technological capability also easily loses its uniqueness over time as competitors may acquire or develop equivalent equipment. Imitating organizational capability, however, is much more difficult and complex: «It requires not only changing one's method of managing costs and capital, modifying products, or purchasing technologies but also implementing pervasive new ways of thinking among all employees».

Yet another fundamental point is the fact that the use of both competence and all other resources is always preceded by, and emerges as a consequence of, human action; that is, the application of individual competence. This view is supported by Schultz (1981: 74), who argues that various forms of capital differ significantly in their attributes. He furthermore notes that human beings are productive agents with the attributes of human capital, and that they are also the optimizing agents. Therefore, fundamentally, it is their preferences that matter in the use that is made of the various forms of capital.

A largely separate research tradition has concentrated on the study of organizational learning (for an overview, see Huber, 1991). However, this research has been predominantly process-oriented and has not to any considerable degree raised the issue of the existing competence base that all learning must ultimately build on, and which in itself consequently frames and sets limits for the organizational learning that can possibly take place. Accordingly, Kogut and Zander (1991: 384) note that it is curious that the considerable attention given to how organizations learn has obscured the implication that organizations know something: «In fact, the knowledge of the firm, as opposed to learning, is relatively observable; operating rules, manufacturing technologies, and customer data banks are tangible representations of this knowledge. But the danger of this simple characterization is that everything that describes a firm becomes an aspect of its knowledge. While this is true by definition, the theoretical challenge is to understand the knowledge base of a firm as leading to a set of capabilities which enhance the chances for growth and survival». It is also pointed out that learning has little significance in the absence of a theory of organizational knowledge, since creating new knowledge does not occur in abstraction from current abilities, but rather appears as the products of a firm's combinative capabilities to generate new applications from existing knowledge (Kogut & Zander, 1992: 391). This is basically an extension of Schumpeter's (1934) analysis of innovations as combined results of existing knowledge and incremental learning partly building on this knowledge, and it is largely this logic that underlies the conception of path dependence as a description of the historical embeddedness of organizations, which often creates strong inertia.

In summary, most of the research on organizational learning has concentrated solely on dynamic aspects of competence in organizations and largely neglects the importance of static aspects such as the nature of the knowledge and skills controlled by the organization. Hence, there is a strong need to incorporate this into organizational learning theory, among other things in order to include the knowledge base upon which new learning, which often takes the form of an extension of the former base, is added.

If we accept both the proposition in new institutionalist organizational theory that, in the course of time, organizational design tends to be similar in competing organizations, and the proposition in the industrial organization economics and strategic management literature that the significance of technology for competitive advantage has diminished, it seems potentially fruitful to look to the individual and aggregate competence of individuals in organizations, including synergies, when differences in organizational performance are to be explained. Whether such differences can be attributed to competence resources, and the way in which these are configured and utilized, remains an empirical question. However, there is good reason to assume that competence is at least an important co-determinant of variation in organizational performance. Given this assumption, a paramount immediate research challenge is to generate a widely shared conceptual and theoretical ground that can form a foundation for replicable empirical research. A step in this direction is presented in the last section of this paper.

As a concluding introductory remark, the point of departure is the conception that sustainable competitive advantage primarily has to be built on other resources than the purely technological and financial ones, and I argue that, among the former resources, individual as well as organizational types of competence are the most crucial. The focus will be on perspectives that embrace efforts to conceptualize collective knowledge and skill resources in organizations, as well as how these resources are constituted. Hence, interest lies in the issue of how collective organizational competence is defined and conceived of as a social phenomenon. In the following, the main perspectives on collective competence in the literature are reviewed and discussed. Thereafter, on this basis, an attempt is made to outline an integrated analytical framework suitable for the study of collective competence in organizations.

Organizational skills

The notion of organizational skills reflects a belief that organizations can do something on their own, that is, do something the sum of individuals involved in the organization could not accomplish without the existence of organizational structures and other coordination mechanisms. These are a sort of supra-individual skills that must somehow be constituted by an aggregate of individual skills plus synergies derived from the structuring and coordination of human action within the organization.

Early research within this perspective focused on the institutionalization of work-related behavior through the establishment of organizational routines and procedures, epitomized by the concept of standard operation procedure (March & Simon, 1958; Cyert & March, 1963). Later, this line of research has been followed up by institutional economists concentrating on the coordination of tasks. Nelson & Winter (1982: 63) argue that the notion of a collection of describable tasks falls far short of characterizing what the firm as a functioning entity knows and conclude that what the firm knows includes the system of coordinating relations among the tasks, the relations that combine the tasks into a productive performance. Furthermore, they define organizational skills as routines made up of efficiently integrated sub-routines that can be further divided into smaller routines. A basic point in their perspective is that organizational routines are usually accomplished without conscious awareness, in the sense that they do not require the attention of top management. It is thus implied that the execution of many tasks is decentralized so that the higher echelons in the organizational hierarchy are relieved of a wide range of decisions (Galbraith, 1973), and the authors compare this with the ability of skilled individuals to perform without attending to details. Implicit in their arguments is also a conception that improvisation, in order to handle novel situations, requires centralized action simply because no established organizational routines cover such situations adequately.

Although Nelson and Winter place the main focus on routines at the organizational macro level, they also discuss how these routines are constituted by sub-routines and the competence of members in the sense that the specific features accounting for the ability of a given organization to accomplish particular things are reflected primarily in the collection of individual members' repertoires. At the same time, some degree of centralized control of the system is required, since organizations are poor at improvising coordinated responses to novel situations: «... an individual lacking skills appropriate to the situation may respond awkwardly, but an organization lacking appropriate routines may not respond at all» (Nelson & Winter, 1982: 125).

Acknowledging the significance of individual-level skills as building stones in the foundation for organizational capabilities, Stinchcombe (1990) compares such skills with computer programmes, and notes that individuals too possess skills which are routinized in the sense that higher faculties are not activated when these skills are applied. This is close to the concept of tacit knowledge as developed by Polanyi (1964) and later utilized by numerous researchers. In regard to dynamic aspects, Stinchcombe views change in routines, and the speed at which they are executed, as major sources of competitive advantage or other types of organizational success, and emphasizes the need for organizational arrangements that can serve to acquire the information required to drive these change processes.

In summary, the literature on organizational skills has been preoccupied with the emergence and maintenance of systems in the form of institutionalized rules, routines and standardized procedures that ensure stability in operational activities and increased independence of single individuals. Both the micro and the macro level are included in the analysis, since links are established between individual action and competence on the one hand and organizational mechanisms or skills on the other.

Organizational knowledge

Whereas the literature on organizational skills has been preoccupied with studying standardized routines and procedures, the literature on organizational knowledge has focused on the existence and structuring of cognitive elements both in the form of factual information and values, norms and habits. This literature has been heavily inspired by the sociology of knowledge and ethno-methodologically oriented micro sociology; and much in the same way as for organizational skills, the notion of institutionalization or structuring of human action into standardized practices is a cornerstone in theory building. As noted by Cicourel (1981: 66-67), routine practices within bureaucratic organizations are fairly explicit procedures that have been adopted or have emerged. These practices and procedures are regarded as culturally organized knowledge structures that exist outside the heads of members of the culture, that is, in the environment. A vital point in this reasoning is that the interaction of members of a group is needed for the practices and procedures to achieve structural status.

Supporting the view of Argyris and Schön (1978) that organizations are basically cognitive enterprises which learn and generate knowledge, Lyles and Schwenk (1992: 157) argue that organizational knowledge structures serve to define relationships, behavior and actions for the individuals involved. Providing no direct definition of the concept of knowledge structure, they delimit themselves to stating that it deals with goals, cause-and-effect beliefs and other cognitive elements. The knowledge structure is conceived of as being more directly linked to organizational strategy, and more subject to change than the constructs of organizational climate or culture, «neither of which changes readily or provides specific strategies for action for an organization». Furthermore, knowledge structures are considered to be different from personal schemes, as they are socially constructed and rely on consensus or agreement (Lyles & Schwenk, 1992: 157).

In the literature on organizational knowledge, an important distinction is drawn between core and peripheral knowledge. The basic criteria defining either of the two categories are the degree of consensus, the substantive content, and who the transmitter of the communication is. Core knowledge represents knowledge that is widely shared and agreed upon, particularly knowledge related to organizational mission, goals and beliefs. A parallel can be drawn to the notion of paradigms in the philosophy of science (Kuhn, 1962). Core knowledge is viewed as enabling organizational members to understand the purpose and mission of the organization, and providing a guide to expectations about organizational behavior in competitive situations. Yet another parallel is drawn to the concept of metascript (Abelson, 1981): «... it is abstract and lacks detail but still provides a guide to the firm's business situations. It has widespread agreement and acceptance among the managers. ... this core set provides the initial knowledge structure through which the organizational members compare themselves to other organizations: it provides a basis for that comparison by providing knowledge about acceptable behavior or actions for the firm» (Lyles & Schwenk, 1992: 160/162). Finally, it is assumed that the core knowledge is limited to knowledge communicated and sponsored by the top management of the organization.

Whereas core knowledge embraces information about the basic mission and goals of the organization, the peripheral knowledge is conceptualized as including information on sub-goals and the various means mobilized to promote those goals. The notion of relatedness is introduced to account for the degree of interlinkage between the two types of knowledge, and the core knowledge structures are conceived of as far more stable than the peripheral ones: «Thus the core set are usually unquestioned, embedded knowledge elements that remain unchallenged unless a major strategic event occurs. The peripheral set, on the other hand, is the area in which organizational debate and alternative viewpoints emerge. The more tightly coupled the core set and the peripheral set, the more difficult it will be for the firm to make changes in its knowledge structure» (Lyles & Schwenk, 1992: 169). However, although it is contended that core knowledge structures rarely change, it seems that the relationships represented in the knowledge structure do become more complex over time as additional elements are incorporated (Narayanan & Fahey, 1982).

One important similarity between the perspectives focusing on organizational skills and organizational knowledge structures, respectively, is a conception that both of these constructs exhibit a hierarchical composition. As previously pointed out, Nelson & Winter view organizational routines as composed of smaller sub-routines on several lower levels. Likewise, as proposed by Anderson (1983: 76), and later adopted by Lyles & Schwenk (1991), «large knowledge structures must be encoded hierarchically, with smaller cognitive units embedded in larger ones». A similar point is made by Kogut & Zander (1992: 390) when they argue that a firm's functional knowledge is nested within a higher-order set of recipes which act as organizing principles and conceive of complex organizations as communities within which varieties of functional expertise can be communicated and combined by a common language and organizing principles. According to these authors, what permits the nesting of a firm's knowledge is the possibility of separating the expertise needed to generate the technology and the ability to use it. On the other hand, this separation, when done, may in many cases increase the probability of imitation as important knowledge becomes widely diffused in the organization.

In dynamic terms, the notion of transmission is essential to theories on knowledge dissemination. Within the sociology of knowledge and social anthropology, transmission of knowledge about cultural elements between generations has occupied a central place. Transmission is commonly defined as the process by which cultural understanding are communicated to a succession of actors. A distinction can be drawn between two types of transmission; a branching manner in which each successive actor communicates the meaning to multiple actors, and a purely sequential one producing a chain of actors, each of whom communicates the meaning only to the next actor on the chain: «In any case, whether transmission occurs within a single 'generation' or between 'generations', it proceeds from actor to actor independent of any of the earlier transmitting actors» (Zucker, 1991: 387).

Kogut & Zander (1992: 387) express a need to move beyond the classification of information and know-how and to consider why knowledge is not easily transmitted and replicated. Their argument might be extended to include the need to focus on knowledge that is easily transmitted, especially since organizations frequently want to protect the knowledge carried by their employees from being spread to individuals in competing organizations. Nevertheless, organizations often find them-selves in a difficult dilemma in this respect: caught between the need to facilitate intraorganizational transfer of knowledge and skills and the need to inhibit knowledge and skills from being transferred to other or-ganizations. Hence, efforts to make knowledge easily transmittable in-ternally may often imply that it is also more easily transferred out of the organization.

Organizational memory

The existence of collective knowledge structures that are socially con-structed was already noted by classical sociologists. Emile Durkheim (1895/1938) pointed at «collective ways of acting or thinking (that) have a reality outside of the individuals who, at every moment of time, con-form to it.» Fleck (1938) maintained that cognition is largely the result of social activities, «... since the existing stock of knowledge exceeds the range available to any one individual». Halbwachs (1950/1980: 51) used the term collective memory to depict information about the past shared by individuals, a concept that has later been picked up by other scholars (Schumann & Scott, 1989).

Durkheim and his students were among the first in the social sciences to argue that groups of individuals can possess knowledge in a way tran-scending the cognitive facilities of any single individual. This is made possible through the process of sharing. Hence, the retention of organi-zational memory is not conceived of merely as an individual-level phe-nomenon, but can apply to a supra-individual collectivity as well through a process of sharing (Walsh & Ungson, 1991: 68). An identical logic was formulated by Nelson and Winter (1982) who contended that viewing organizational memory as reducible to individual member memories implies overlooking or undervaluing the interlinkage of indi-vidual memories by shared experiences in the past, «experiences that have established the extremely detailed and specific communication system that underlies routine performance» (Nelson & Winter, 1982: 105).

According to Walsh and Ungson (1991), organizational memory can be defined as stored information about the history of the organization that can be brought to bear on present decisions. The memory has a du-al location by being represented jointly by individual recollections and socially shared interpretations. A slightly different, albeit clearly related, approach is offered by Simon (1991: 129) who, with reference to recent research in cognitive psychology on human expertise, notes that expertise is always based on extensive knowledge, and that this knowledge is stored in the form of an indexed encyclopedia, in technical terms referred to as a production system. He goes on to state that the memories of an organization can be represented as a vast collection of such production systems: «This representation becomes much more than a metaphor as we see more and more examples of human expertise captured in automated expert systems. One motive for such automation, but certainly not the only one, is that it makes organizational memory less vulnerable to turnover.» In general, turnover of personnel is viewed as a jeopardy to long-term organizational memory, since much of the memory of organizations is stored in human heads, and only a little of it in procedures put down on paper (Simon, 1991: 128). This point is also made by Huber (1991: 195), who contends that the problem of poor organizational memory is more complex than considerations of the deficiencies of humans, as repositories of organizational knowledge, might suggest. In addition to personnel turnover, organizational memory may be hurt by non-anticipation of future needs for certain information, which causes information not to be stored or to be stored in ways that make it difficult to retrieve. Moreover, employees requiring certain information are frequently unaware of the existence and location of information possessed or stored by other employees (Huber, 1991: 195).

In regard to the dynamics of organizational knowledge, an essential point is that organizational memory and learning processes not only record history but also shape its future course. Moreover, the direction of that future course depends greatly on the processes by which memory is maintained (Huber, 1991: 192-193). Besides, success often inhibits experimentation and innovation, thus leading to competence traps. This means that conditions under which efficient performance is achieved, despite using an inferior procedure or technology, leads an organization to accumulate additional experience, and thus renders knowledge of more favorable procedures or technologies too limited to make their use worthwhile (Levitt & March, 1988; Huber, 1991).

Distinctive types of competence

Parts of the literature on strategy and organization theory focus on the competence in firms that serves to distinguish them from competing firms. Researchers have concentrated on knowledge and skill resources that vary systematically in nature between organizations, and great

emphasis has been put on how such resources can be nurtured and protected from being copied or acquired by other organizations.

According to Conner (1991: 122), a historical review of strategy research indicates that a resource-based perspective has been central in
the field for a long time, particularly contributions that link special types
of competence in deploying and combining human, physical and reputational capital with strategy (Barnard, 1938; Selznick, 1957; Chandler,
1962; Ansoff, 1965; Andrews, 1971; Rumelt, 1974; Wernerfelt, 1984;
Teece, Pisano & Shuen, 1990; Collis, 1991; Leonard-Barton, 1992;
Grønhaug & Nordhaug, 1992). The basic logic of the resource-based
perspective is that the firm's unique capabilities in terms of technical
know-how and managerial ability are important sources of heterogeneity that may create sustained competitive advantage, and that distinctive
competence and superior organizational routines in one or more of the
firm's value-chain functions may enable the firm to generate rents from
a resource advantage (Mahoney & Pandian, 1992: 365; Hitt & Ireland,
1985). Furthermore, it is important to note that it is not only the quality
and composition of resources *per se* that matter but also the way in which
they are being utilized. As noted by Penrose (1959: 54), firms may
achieve rents not because they possess better resources, but because
their distinctive types of competence allow them to make better use of
their resources (Penrose, 1959: 54; Mahoney & Pandian, 1992).

Recently, new conceptual developments have emerged that revolve
around the notion of core competence in firms. Naugle and Davies
(1987) preferred the term strategic skill pools, whereas the breakthrough of the concept of core competence can be dated to the contribution of Prahalad and Hamel (1990). This perspective has probably
had its greatest influence through the related prescriptive statements
about firms' outsourcing of activities. One illustration is provided by
Quinn, Doorley and Paquette (1991) arguing that, due to new technologies, firms can divide up their value chains, handle the key strategic elements internally, outsource others advantageously, and still coordinate
all essential activities more effectively to meet customers' needs: «Under
these circumstances, moving to a less-integrated but more focused organization is not just feasible but imperative for competitive success.
Companies that understand this new approach, Honda, Apple, and
Merck among them, build their strategies not around products but
around deep knowledge of a few highly developed core service skills ...
The company strips itself down to the essentials necessary to deliver to
customers the greatest possible value from its core skills, and outsources

as much of the rest as possible» (Quinn, Doorley & Paquette, 1991: 301). This reasoning can be criticized from two main angles: for neglecting the significance of control over the production process, which may be hard to maintain through outsourcing, and for ignoring the substantial transaction costs of setting up the numerous contractual arrangements needed, costs that may outweigh possible gains in production costs.

A common characteristic of most conceptualizations of distinctive or core competence is their diffusiveness. Frequently, labels such as core competence are used as a type of post hoc explanation of performance differences that are not regarded as following from differences in easily measurable factors such as hard economic data. In the same way as organizational culture has been applied in attempts to account for unexplained differentials in the performance of firms, the quality of core competence often serves as a virtually all-encompassing variable apparently believed by many to explain most of the residual variance. Several serious analytical problems associated with the manner in which the term is used are thus indicated. It has not been thoroughly conceptualized, but rather rested on fairly shaky tentative arguments. For example, Prahalad & Hamel provide two widely dissimilar definitions of core competence. In the first, they are viewed as «... the collective learning in the organization, especially how to coordinate diverse production skills and integrate multiple streams of technologies». This is exemplified by Sony's capacity to miniaturize, Philips' optical-media expertise, and Casio's capacity to harmonize know-how in miniaturization, microprocessor design, material science and ultra-thin precision casing (Prahalad & Hamel, 1990: 281). In the second definition, core competence is said to comprise «communication, involvement and a deep commitment to working across organizational boundaries» (Prahalad & Hamel, 1990: 283). In contrast to the first definition, it is difficult to see how this very general definition includes factors that hold the key to separating one firm from another since many of them are characterized by communication, involvement and commitment to cooperation across organizational borders. We are hence left with two totally different theoretical constructs which, if operationalized, would result in completely dissimilar variables. Moreover, given that core competence is considered to be resources, that is, input into some resource transformation process, how is it that they, in some formulations, are aligned with performance? At this point, the risk is obvious of constructing tautologies by confounding core competence and the activities or fields in which the firm and its employees are successful by external standards. As noted by Løwendahl and Nordhaug (1993), although it is interesting to learn *ex post* that selected companies have succeeded because *ex ante* they possessed certain types of core competence that other firms did not possess, when it is concluded that a firm has succeeded because it did well what it was able to do well, the territory of tautology has been entered.

The crucial issue of how core competence is anchored in competence at the micro level of employees and work groups is left virtually unaddressed in the strategic management literature. Consequently, it is difficult to imagine how a structuralist perspective, which is not based on the micro elements of which core competence is composed, can serve as guidance for managerial action as to developing the core competence required to create sustained competitive advantage. It is impossible to figure out how core competence can be generated and maintained if, concurrently, one does not know the main building blocks.

There is thus a need to single out and endeavor to isolate empirically the individual knowledge and skills, group-related competence and synergies that contribute to the constitution of core competence on the organizational level in firms. Only then will it be feasible to derive practical implications; for example, as to which individual types of competence are particularly valuable to a company, and thus ought to be protected more strongly than other types of competence.

An additional shortcoming of the conceptualization of core competence is the fact that, contrary to the conceptualization of core knowledge structures previously discussed, peripheral competence is not taken into consideration to any notable degree. As long as core competence is implicitly defined relative to other types of competence, an exhaustive definition would have to include these, or at least allow them to serve as a point of reference when core competence is to be more thoroughly conceptualized.

Discussion

Four largely disparate conceptual perspectives of competence resources in organizations have been presented; the purpose is now to compare them by identifying their respective idiosyncrasies and similarities with respect to central dimensions. These dimensions encompass the key concept and its constituent elements, the main focus, the most central theoretical sources, and the levels of analysis included. The comparison is presented in Table 1.

Table 1. Four perspectives

Theoretical construct	Main elements	Generation process	Primary sources	Levels of analysis
Organizational skills	Rules, routines, procedures	Institutionalizat ion of individual knowledge and skills	Evolutionary economics, organization theory	Micro and macro
Organizational knowledge	Knowledge structures	Transmission of knowledge between generations, structuring of knowledge	Sociology of knowledge, philosophy of science	Micro and macro
Organizational memory	Repositories of information about the history of the organization	Sharing and social construction of knowledge	Evolutionary economics, cognitive psychology	Micro and macro
Distinctive types of competence	Unique combinative capabilities	Random evolution or planned development of key knowledge and skills	Organization theory, industrial organization economics, research on corporate strategy	Macro

As shown in Table 1, there are substantial differences between the perspectives, with the exception of organizational knowledge and organizational memory, which share essential properties and could be treated as elements within one fairly distinct perspective. Whereas the latter is related to information or knowledge about the history of the organization and is viewed as generated and maintained through the sharing of socially constructed knowledge, the organizational knowledge perspective is clearly more comprehensive, covering not only history-related information but all kinds of knowledge shared in the organization. Consequently, organizational memory can be regarded as a subcategory of organizational knowledge.

The generation processes outlined, which are inherent in the four perspectives, vary considerably. Once again, the smallest difference is between organizational knowledge and organizational memory, both emphasizing the social construction and diffusion of knowledge as well as the significance of successive or intergenerational transfer between individuals. Since both individual actors and knowledge structures are included, the perspective encompasses both the micro and the macro level of analysis.

Proponents of the organizational skills perspective have been preoccupied with how individual knowledge and skills become frozen or institutionalized into extra-individual skills in the form of standard operational procedures, rules and routines which may allow for more efficient operation, and frequently ensure decreased organizational dependence on specific single individuals carrying the competence that have been built into organizational skills. In the same manner as for the knowledge perspective, the literature on collective skills embraces the micro and the macro level in organizations.

The literature on distinctive competence, while being relatively broad and multifaceted, focuses on unique combinative capabilities made up of technology and competence on the organizational macro level, the main emphasis being put on the latter. Parts of the literature concentrate on the more or less random evolution of strategic organizational competence (for example, 3M's random invention of Post-It™ pads on the basis of sticky tape), whereas other parts are characterized by a prescriptive position oriented towards the need for firms to systematically plan, nurture and develop distinctive competence to stay competitive. Unlike the three perspectives already mentioned, almost without exception, the distinctive competence framework only encompasses the organizational macro level and is thus a predominantly structuralist perspective.

Together, the conceptual perspectives represent a rich potential for the further theoretical study of human capital in organizations and for empirical research attempting to lay bare the significance of such capital for organizational performance and survival. Yet, the disparities between them indicate that they are likely to develop in largely different ways and directions. Consequently, at this stage, the vital issue of possible integration intended to build a unified perspective is clearly accentuated, and in the following section an organizational competence perspective is delineated.

An integrated perspective

The organizational competence perspective, as originally formulated by Løwendahl & Nordhaug (1993) and further expanded on in the following presentation, is associated with the skills perspective, the knowledge perspective and the distinctive competence perspective previously discussed. However, whereas the latter focuses on isolating the types of competence that generate specific competitive advantages, the organizational competence framework is characterized by a broader approach including the whole range of knowledge and skill resources present in organizations.

While the micro level of analysis is missing in most of the works departing from the core competence concept, in the organizational competence perspective attempts are made to explicate competence on the levels of individuals, teams and organizations, and, moreover, to bridge these levels. It therefore seeks to be more holistic, and goes further than concentrating solely on factors that are directly advantageous with regard to competitiveness in product markets.

Within the organizational competence perspective, competence carried by individuals is conceptualized as a combination of three different elements; knowledge, skills and aptitudes (Nordhaug, 1993). Whereas personal knowledge may be improved by studying, skills are typically learned through practice, and frequently with the assistance of an instructor or a mentor in an apprenticeship-type of relationship. Knowledge is inherently information-based, while skills are always based upon some type of explicit or tacit knowledge, and often a combination of the two (Nordhaug, 1994; Winter, 1985; Polanyi, 1964). Finally, aptitudes contribute to an individual's competence in a given area, both directly in terms of how competent the person is and indirectly by influencing how easily the individual acquires new knowledge or skills. Per definition, being congenital, aptitudes are not transferable to others and hence cannot be learned. However, aptitudes may be latent and hence represent a hidden competence potential that may at some point of time be activated.

Moving up one level, the aggregate of types of competence plus competence synergies available to an organization is conceived of as its competence base. The base is conceptualized as including both individual and collective types of competence and can be extended by the application of externally available competence (Nordhaug, 1993: ch. 4). In addition to the individual and collective competence that is manifest in the organization, the base comprises latent competence that represents an untapped potential for the organization.

Shifting the focus to the organizational macro level, one suggestion is that, also at this level, competence comprises three constituent elements (Løwendahl, 1992; Løwendahl & Nordhaug, 1993). First, firms possess large amounts of knowledge such as databases containing information about customers and competitors and knowledge carried by employees. Second, organizational competence also embraces the organizational skills in the form of rules, routines and standard operating procedures. Third, the competence of organizations encompasses an element analogous to aptitudes on the individual level that is often broadly referred to as culture. An example is Løwendahl & Nordhaug (1993), who note that organizations differ substantially in terms of their capacity to learn, to correct their course of action, to change and to facilitate innovation. These differences extend beyond discrepancies in their capacity as defined solely by knowledge resources, organizational routines and skills. The authors go on to suggest that, on the organizational level, corporate culture represents an analytical parallel to individual aptitudes. (In a similar manner, (Hall 1992: 136) defines competence as including the know-how of employees (as well as suppliers and advisers) and the collective aptitudes which add up to organizational culture.)

In the same way as human beings are born with a set of specific aptitudes, firms are born with a certain culture that can later be developed in different directions, but which normally also sets limits for the development of the organization. An illustration is provided by the challenges facing recently established firms that are in the process of developing beyond the entrepreneurial stage, and, consequently, need to change their leadership style and culture to become compatible with a more stable, operationally oriented stage of development.

An important point in the organizational competence line of thought is that collective competence emerges also on the meso level in organizations, primarily in work teams. Consequently, it is fruitful to talk about a hierarchy of types of competence, where the aggregated individual types of competence constitute a foundation, and supra-individual types of competence on the team level and the organizational level are created through the interactions of individuals. Collective competence hence cannot be fully appropriated to individuals and, concurrently, skills and synergies developed in a specific group context can only be sustained through continued interaction between the individuals involved.

Figure 1 draws together the three levels and, moreover, depicts a conception of the aggregation and transformation of individual competence into team competence, and, furthermore, the aggregation and transformation of these into organizational competence.

The three single elements of individual competence, that is, knowledge, skills and aptitudes, are here seen as being partly aggregated and

Figure 1: Three-level competence framework

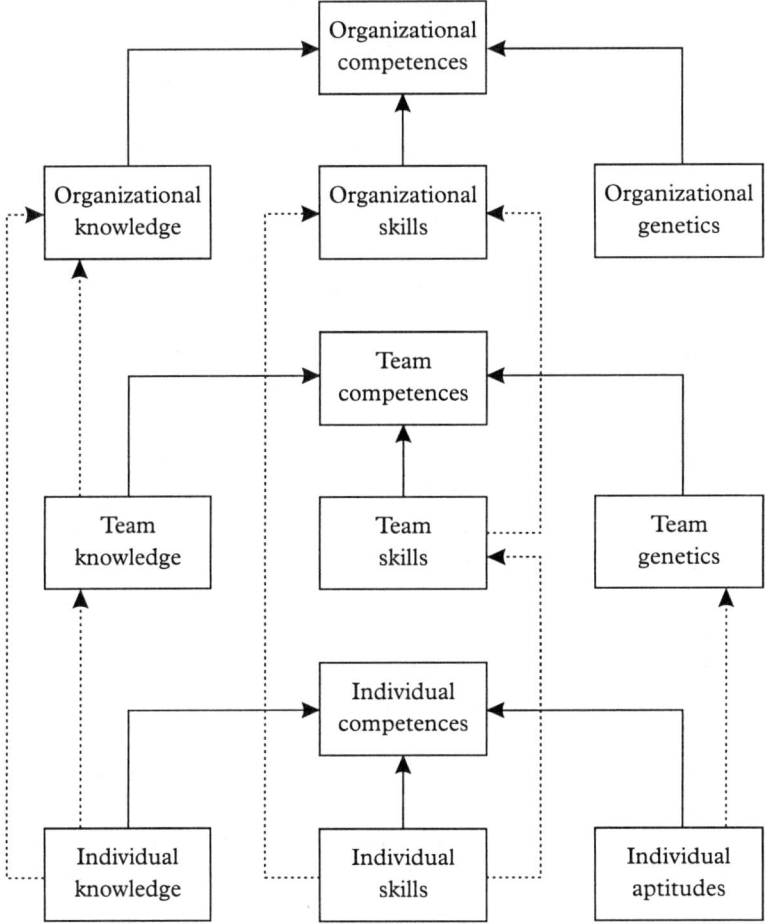

partly transformed into similar, although clearly not homomorphic, properties on the level of work teams. In order to avoid any anthropomorphic fallacy, the similarity should not be taken too literally. Yet, there is reason to argue that teams, like human beings, collectively possess certain amounts of knowledge and also exhibit a range of supraindividual skills that can create group performance. It also seems reasonable to assert that these repositories of knowledge and skills are in part made up of the contributing knowledge and skills of the individual members, and in addition by interaction effects that may create synergies with regard to competence and performance. This is what is meant by the notion of the transformation process (Nordhaug, 1990, 1991). The link between aptitudes on the individual level and the notion of team genetics on the group level is far more problematic than the two former links. It makes sense to say that the character and the limits of team members' aptitudes, that is, their congenital talents, also have an impact on the group level, and, furthermore, that they are likely to form a structural condition for the opportunities and limits of the team in relation to attainable performance levels.

On the third level of analysis, distinctions are drawn between organizational knowledge, organizational skills and organizational genetics, which together are seen as constituting organizational competence. The two former elements are conceived of as being constituted partly by aggregated individual competence elements and partly by aggregated team-embedded competence elements that are inappropriable to single individuals. The third part of organizational competence, organizational genetics, is defined as historically given and, in contrast to organizational skills and knowledge, not as being partly constituted by lower-level competence elements. In the same manner as for team genetics, the term organizational genetics reflects a conception that all organizations contain opportunities and limitations defined at the time of their conception and foundation that are largely independent of the organization's subsequent development of knowledge and skills (Stinchcombe, 1965; Huber, 1992).

The inherent limitations determined by organizational genetics are illustrated by Powell (1991: 192), who notes that organizational procedures and forms may persevere because of path-dependent processes of development in which initial choices preclude future options, including those that would have been more effective in the long run. A parallel can also be drawn to Stinchcombe's (1965) classical work on founding processes in organizations and the concept of imprinting, implying that basic structural properties are determined through these processes, vary according to the time of foundation, and have a tendency to persist over time. Moreover, this reasoning parallels the resource-based view in the strategy literature, in which the firm's distinctive competence is frequently defined by the set of substantive rules and routines used by top management. As noted by Mahoney and Pandian (1992: 370), managers' past decisions and decision rules are the basic genetics firms possess, and sustainable advantage is thus a history-dependent or path-dependent process (Arthur, 1988; Barney, 1991). In conclusion, organizational genetics reflect historically determined organizational properties that became institutionally embedded during the conception and the foundation of the organization.

The competence of individuals, in addition to being transmitted through cooperation in teams, may also inherently represent an integral part of the organizational competence. First, they always represent a potential to the organization, despite the ways in which they are contemporaneously configured in teams and organizational subunits. That is, if all teams were dissolved and the employees were still present, the organization would not have lost all its competence resources but only those embedded within social linkages inherent in the teams. Second, for various reasons, not all individual competence is mediated through cooperative efforts in teams. In many organizations, a substantial share of the work activities do not revolve around work groups, at least not if these are strictly defined as formal groups. Nevertheless, very few individuals are able to perform work without having to interact with others, so that, in most cases, considerable interactive elements are involved in individual applications of competence. It may, therefore, be more fruitful to speak about individual competence being partly embedded in social relations, of which the formal work team is one of several categories. Moreover, it is reasonable to look beyond formal work groups and emphasize that teams in this context also clearly comprise informal clusters of employees within which work activities are carried out.

In summary, within the organizational competence perspective, the organization's ability to achieve high performance in the short term depends on its current competence base, as well as the competence configuration and synergies yielded. Furthermore, in a long-term perspective, the performance of the firm is also conditioned by its degree of success in updating and expanding the competence base: that is, how it manages the competence flow within the organization and between the organization and its environment.

Conclusion

In order to fruitfully develop the study of competence in organizations, there is a need to track down the analysis of collective competence to the micro-level and, moreover, to examine the relationships between the individual level, the team level and the organizational level. It has been argued in this article that the concept of the competence base represents a useful tool in this respect. However, collective competence embraces more than the mere aggregates of knowledge, skills and aptitudes possessed by employees. There are, for example at the level of work groups, synergies that may be investigated. Moreover, the configuration and co-ordination of individual and group competence are decisive for the extent to which, as well as the ways in which, core competence is actually constituted. It is not simply sufficient to possess a number of useful types of competence: these must also be clustered and interlinked in such a manner that synergies and integration effects are created leading to the generation of collective competence.

Since the study of individual and collective competence in organizations remains at an early stage, and the literature is both scant and fragmented, there is an apparent need to develop and refine basic concepts and theoretical propositions on the nature of competence and its impact on important aspects of organizational behavior. For example, the relationship between competence and organizational performance has not been much investigated, albeit such concepts as core competence, distinctive competence and strategic skills are indicative of a drive to move in this direction. Moreover, the relatively modest amount of research carried out in this area has, to a substantial degree, focused on the macro level of firms. Collective competence, whether labeled core competence or distinctive competence, has largely been taken as a given entity, and few attempts have been made to interlink employee competence, team competence and organizational competence. It is important to realize that, although other resources also contribute to creating organizational competence, individuals and work teams (including management teams) remain the basic carriers of the competence of the firm. Given the perspective that organizational competence is, in part, constituted by individual knowledge, skills and aptitudes, as well as team knowledge, skills, and team genetics, there is a clear need for future research in this area to study closely the relationship between the micro, meso, and macro levels.

References

Abelson, R.P. (1981): Psychological Status of the Script Concept. *American Psychologist 36*: 715-729.

Anderson, J. (1983): *The Architecture of Cognition.* Cambridge, MA: Harvard University Press.

Andrews, K. (1971): *The Concept of Corporate Strategy.* Homewood, IL: Dow Jones-Irwin.

Ansoff, H.I. (1965): *Corporate Strategy: An Analytical Approach to Business Policy for Growth and Expansion.* New York: McGraw-Hill.

Argyris, C. & D. Schön (1978): *Organizational Learning: A Theory of Action Perspective.* Reading, MA: Addison-Wesley.

Arthur, W.B. (1988): Self-Reinforcing Mechanisms in Economics. In P.W. Anderson, K.J. Arrow & D. Pines (eds.): *The Economy as an Evolving Complex System.* Redwood City, CA: Addison-Wesley.

Barnard, C.I. (1938): *Functions of the Executive.* Cambridge, MA: Harvard University Press.

Barney, J.B. (1991): Firm Resources and Sustained Competitive Advantage. *Journal of Management 17*: 99-120.

Chandler, A.D. (1962): *Strategy and Structure: Chapters in the History of the American Industrial Enterprise.* Cambridge, MA: MIT Press.

Cicourel, A.V. (1981): Notes on the Integration of Micro- and Macro-Levels of Analysis. In K. Knorr-Cetina & A.V. Cicourel (eds.): *Advances in Social Theory and Methodology. Toward an Integration of Micro- and Macro-Sociologies.* Boston: Routledge & Kegan Paul.

Collis, D.J. (1991): A Resource-Based Analysis of Global Competition: The Case of the Bearings Industry. *Strategic Management Journal 12*: 49-68.

Conner, K.R. (1991): A Historical Comparison of Resource-Based Theory and Five Schools of Thought within Industrial Organization Economics: Do We Have a New Theory of the Firm? *Journal of Management 17*: 121-154.

Cyert, R.M. & J.G. March (1963): *A Behavioral Theory of the Firm.* Englewood Cliffs, NJ: Prentice-Hall.

DiMaggio, P.J. & W.W. Powell (1991): Institutional Isomorphism and Collective Rationality. In W.W. Powell & P. DiMaggio (eds.): *The New Institutionalism in Organizational Analysis.* Chicago: University of Chicago Press.

Durkheim, E. (1938) (1895): *The Rules of Sociological Method.* New York: The Free Press.

Fleck, L. (1938): *Genesis and Development of a Scientific Fact*. Chicago: University of Chicago Press.

Galbraith, J. (1973): *Designing Complex Organizations*. Reading, MA: Addison-Wesley.

Grønhaug, K. & O. Nordhaug (1992): Strategy and Competence in Firms. *European Management Journal 4*: 438-444.

Halbwachs, M. (1980) (1950): *The Collective Memory*. New York: Harper.

Hall, R. (1992): The Strategic Analysis of Intangible Resources. *Strategic Management Journal 13*: 135-144.

Hitt, M.A. & R.D. Ireland (1985): Corporate Distinctive Competence, Strategy, Industry and Performance. *Strategic Management Journal 6*: 273-293.

Huber, G.P. (1991): Organizational Learning: The Contributing Processes and the Literature. *Organization Science 2*: 88-115.

Kogut, B. & U. Zander (1992): Knowledge of the Firm, Combinative Capabilities, and the Replication of Technology. *Organization Science 3*: 383-397.

Kuhn, T.S. (1962): *The Structure of Scientific Revolutions*. Chicago: University of Chicago Press.

Leonard-Barton, D. (1992): Core Capabilities and Core Rigidities: A Paradox in Managing New Product Development. *Strategic Management Journal 13*: 111-125.

Levitt, B. & J.G. March (1988): Organizational Learning. *Annual Review of Sociology 14*: 319-340.

Løwendahl, B. (1992): *Global Strategies for Professional Business Service Firms*. Ph.D. dissertation. Philadelphia: Wharton School, University of Pennsylvania.

Løwendahl, B. & O. Nordhaug (1993): *Competencies in Firms: A Theoretical Framework*. Working paper. Bergen/Oslo: Norwegian School of Economics and Business Administration/Norwegian School of Management.

Lyles, M.A. & C.R. Schwenk (1992): Top Management, Strategy and Organizational Knowledge Structures. *Journal of Management Studies 29*: 155-174.

Mahoney, J.T. & J.R. Pandian (1992): The Resource-Based View within the Conversation of Strategic Management. *Strategic Management Journal 13*: 363-380.

March, J.G. & H.A. Simon (1958): *Organizations*. New York: Wiley.

Narayanan, V. & L. Fahey (1982): The Micro-Politics of Strategy Formulation. *Academy of Management Review 7*: 25-34.

Naugle, D.G. & G.A. Davies (1987): Strategic-Skill Pools and Competitive Advantage. *Business Horizon 30*: 35-42.

Nelson, R.R. & S.G. Winter (1982): *An Evolutionary Theory of Economic Change*. Cambridge, MA: Harvard University Press.

Nordhaug, O. (1990): Organizational Effects of Training: Aggregation and Transformation. *Scandinavian Journal of Management* 7: 111-122.

Nordhaug, O. (1991): Human Resource Provision and Transformation: The Role of Training and Development. *Human Resource Management Journal 1*: 17-26.

Nordhaug, O. (1994): *Human Capital in Organizations*. New York: Oxford University Press. (2nd Edition).

Nordhaug, O. & K. Grønhaug (1994): Competencies as Resources in Firms. *International Journal of Human Resource Management 5:* 89-106.

Penrose, E.T. (1959): *The Theory of the Growth of the Firm*. New York: Wiley.

Polanyi, M. (1964): *The Tacit Dimension*. Garden City, NY: Doubleday Anchor.

Powell, W.W. (1991): Expanding the Scope of Institutional Analysis. In W.W. Powell & P. DiMaggio (eds.): *The New Institutionalism in Organizational Analysis*. Chicago: University of Chicago Press.

Powell, W.W. & P. DiMaggio (eds.) (1991): The New Institutionalism in Organizational Analysis. Chicago: University of Chicago Press.

Prahalad, C.K. & G. Hamel (1990): The Core Competence of the Corporation. *Harvard Business Review may-june:* 79-91.

Quinn, J.B., T.L. Doorley & P.C. Paquette (1991): Beyond Products: Service-Based Strategy. In C.A. Montgomery & M.E. Porter (eds.): *Strategy. Seeking and Securing Competitive Advantage*. Cambridge, MA: Harvard Business School Press.

Rumelt, R.P. (1974): *Strategy, Structure and Economic Performance*. Cambridge, MA: Harvard University Press.

Schultz, T.W. (1981): *Investing in People. The Economics of Population Quality*. Berkeley, CA: University of California Press.

Schumann, H. & J. Scott (1989): Generations and Collective Memories. *American Sociological Review 54*: 359-381.

Schumpeter, J. (1934): *The Theory of Economic Development*. Cambridge, MA: Harvard University Press.

Selznick, P. (1957): *Leadership in Administration*. New York: Harper & Row.

Simon, H.A. (1991): Bounded Rationality and Organizational Learning. *Organization Science 2*: 125-134.

Stinchcombe, A.L. (1965): Social Structure and Organizations. In J.G. March (ed.): *Handbook of Organizations*. Chicago: Rand McNally.

Stinchcombe, A.L. (1990). *Information and Organizations*. Berkeley, CA: University of California Press.

Teece, D.J., G. Pisano & A. Shuen (1990): *Firm Capabilities, Resources and the Concept of Strategy*. Economic Analysis and Policy Working Paper EAP-38. Berkeley, CA: Center for Research in Management, University of California.

Ulrich, D. & D. Lake (1990): *Organizational Capability*. New York: Wiley.

Walsh, J.P. & G.R. Ungson (1991): Organizational Memory. *Academy of Management Review 16*: 57-91.

Wernerfelt, B. (1984): A Resource-Based View of the Firm. *Strategic Management Journal 5*: 171-180.

Winter, S.G. (1987): Knowledge and Skills as Strategic Assets. In D.J. Teece (ed.): *The Competitive Challenge*. Cambridge, MA: Ballinger.

Zucker, L.G. (1991): Institutionalization and Cultural Persistence. In W.W. Powell & P. DiMaggio (eds.): *The New Institutionalism in Organizational Analysis*. Chicago: University of Chicago Press.

Expert Knowledge
as a Strategic Asset

Kjell Grønhaug

This paper argues, in line with the resource-based view of the firm (Wernerfelt 1984), that expertise can be considered an important strategic asset, allowing for excess profit and sustainable competitive advantages. By strategic we here mean that this asset is (can be) important for the organization by influencing its performance; that it (the asset) to some degree is (can be) unique to the firm, and that expert knowledge is sticky and difficult to imitate, allowing for sustainable competitive advantages (Barney, 1991; Grant, 1991).

Expertise can be thought of as superb «special skills and knowledge» (Random House Dictionary). In this paper the emphasis will be on the knowledge aspects of expertise, and less on meteoric skills (Shanteau, 1992). The reason for this distinction is the importance of expert knowledge and understanding for updating and renewal. Information (knowledge) is a prerequisite in purposeful, strategic tasks, for example, in order to exploit opportunities and adjust the organization and its activities to its ever-changing environments, which is the heart of strategic thinking (Porter, 1980).

Expert knowledge should also be considered as a key element of organizational core competence (Prahalad & Hamel, 1990), or capabilities as emphasized in the resource-based perspective on strategy (Teece, Pisano & Shuen, 1990). Without superior knowledge (and information-processing capacity) it will be impossible to develop and benefit from such competence or capabilities. This paper thus focuses on a critical resource which is a prerequisite for competence or capability-based strategies. Compared with the literature on competence or capability-based strategies, however, this paper represents a new approach by specifically focusing on the expert knowledge of individuals and organizations and addressing the research questions of how, why and under what conditions expert knowledge may yield competitive advantages. Also, in contrast to the vast literature on expertise (Chi, Glaser & Farr, 1988; Lord

& Maher, 1990), this paper adds to present knowledge. In using research findings from the nature of expertise as the point of departure, the paper focuses on elements of expert knowledge unique to the organization, which may yield sustainable competitive advantages.

There is a vast and fast-growing literature on expertise. Most of this literature focuses on the individual expert, acquisition of expertise, information-processing and decision-making (Chi, Glaser & Farr, 1988). In this paper, characteristics of expertise at the individual level serve as a point of departure. If, however, expertise was a purely individual phenomenon, it would be inappropriate to consider expertise as a sticky, organization-specific asset, as the expert could be attracted and hired by a competing firm, which would make sustainable competitive advantages impossible. In this paper the individual experts are considered in their organizational context, focusing on how experts involved in specific tasks in that context will (can) develop organization-specific expertise which is difficult to imitate, thus making sustainable competitive advantages possible.

The paper proceeds as follows: first, characteristics of expertise and its acquisition are briefly described. This description emphasizes the knowledge bases of expertise (that is, procedural and declarative), and the tacit and domain-specific aspects of expert knowledge. Parts of the declarative knowledge are related to the organizational context, and therefore explain uniqueness of organizational expertise. The uniqueness and tacit aspects of the organizational expertise make it a strategic asset. The paper then discusses how expertise can be a source of competitive advantage and how it can be a competitive advantage in its own right through signaling effects. The next section examines the mechanisms which explain the dynamics of expert knowledge, and thus why this resource (expert knowledge) may yield sustainable competitive advantages. Included in this section is a discussion of factors that may inhibit expertise dynamics and lead to the deterioration of this resource as a strategic asset. Paradoxically, the same mechanisms that can explain expertise dynamics may partially explain expertise deterioration as well. Finally, some theoretical and managerial implications are highlighted.

Expert: characteristics and acquisition

This section describes the basic characteristics of expertise and its acquisition. As noted above, the primary literature on the nature of expertise has been individualistic. In addition to recognizing that the individual is the building block of any organization, it is important to identify individualistic characteristics in order to trace potential firm-specific expertise advantages. Compared with novices, experts have superior knowledge and skills. More precisely, experts have superior knowledge and skills within the domain(s) of their expertise. Expertise is thus domain-specific: that is, one can be an expert chess player, medical diagnostician for a specific disease, or manager of an organization within a specific industry context.

The knowledge aspects of expertise are crucial for explaining competitive advantages. Competitive advantages are realized through choosing and performing costly value activities (Porter, 1985). Choosing and performing value activities require knowledge. Expert knowledge may be considered as a source, which may – when utilized properly – result in realized competitive advantages (Day & Wensley, 1988). For example, superior understanding of customers' needs and knowledge of how to satisfy those needs are required to develop superior products which enhance the organization's competitiveness.

Further elaboration is required to explain the role of knowledge in strategic tasks. Organizations operate in ever-changing environments. Conscious decision-making originates in stimuli, that is, noticing and interpreting data. An important point is that stimuli noticed must be interpreted, that is, assigned meaning in order to become information. In the psychology of perception, a distinction is made between the stimulus object and the stimulus (Crech, Crutchfield & Livson, 1974). A stimulus object is the source of the stimulus, while a stimulus can be seen as the data associated with the stimulus object which is noticed and interpreted. For example, noticing and interpreting changes in consumers' preferences need not necessarily be identical to the changes that occur. Thus what is noticed is not the real thing, as something may be added, deleted or changed as data from the stimulus object are registered.

The cognitive processes referred to as categorization are crucial for the noticing and interpretation of stimuli. Categorization is a basic cognitive activity closely related to conceptualization and understanding (Rosch 1978). The categories held by the actor are crucial for whether or not specific stimuli are noticed, and, if noticed, how they are interpreted.[1] The actors' categories develop through interaction with their environments (Rosch, 1978). From this it follows that experiences with

1. Whether a given stimulus is noticed will also be influenced by the actor's attention and preparedness as well as characteristics of the stimulus, for example, its strength (Kiesler & Sproull, 1982; Fiske & Taylor, 1991).

a specific domain should result in categories particularly suited to this domain.

Organizations and their employees do not operate in a vacuum. They are context bound. In order to adjust to changes in consumer preferences by offering superior products, knowledge of and adjustment to specific customer segments are needed. To make wise decisions and initiate adequate activities (as assumed in the strategy and management literature), knowledge about the actual context is needed. March (1978) has termed such contextual relevant actions, based on domain-specific knowledge, as contextual rationality. Knowledge about the context alone, is, however, not sufficient. In addition, the actor needs knowledge of how to structure and solve problems. In other words, procedural rationality is also required (Simon, 1978). The notions of procedural and contextual rationality can be conceived as representing different types of knowledge. This is also reflected in Andersen's (1983) distinction between procedural and declarative knowledge. Procedural knowledge refers to rules and procedures, which can be applied so as to generate behavior. Declarative knowledge means facts about events, things, their relations and states of the world. Such knowledge is of crucial importance for the interpretation and understanding of the actual domain where the procedural knowledge is to be applied.

Studies of experts show that, by comparison to novices, they have much more elaborated cognitive structures (Sanford, 1987). An important part of their knowledge base is declarative and acquired through domain-specific experiences. For example, chess grand masters have approximately 50,000 pieces of familiar chess patterns in their memory (Simon, 1987). Novices lack such knowledge.

In processing information, individuals rely on their previously developed knowledge structures. Within their domain (of expertise), experts perform better than novices because they have more elaborated and better suited cognitive structures for this specific domain. Findings also indicate that experts and novices differ in the way their schemata are structured (Lord & Maher, 1990). Experts and novices have also been found to differ in their information-processing activities. For example, experts have better recall of relevant information than novices. In addition, their recall is less biased. The knowledge structures of experts, which are stored in long-term memory, are larger and more easily accessed from short-term memory as compared with novices. This extensive store of knowledge, which is easily accessible, acts as a substitute for limited, short-term memory-processing capacity. This implies that experts often recognize immediately what novices require great effort to discover. Experts recognize relevant categories more quickly than novices; in addition, these categories are linked more strongly to relevant actions (Glaser, 1988).

In sum, past research (especially the cognitive science literature: Johnson, 1988; Shanteau, 1992) suggests that experts in many situations, as compared with novices, perform better in recognizing and making sense of stimuli, as well as in solving problems. The greater ability to recognize and interpret stimuli also indicates that experts do better at problem-finding than novices. This is important because finding the «right» problem (Dillon, 1982) is a prerequisite for solving relevant problems. Due to their greater information-processing capacity, experts are faster in their noticing and interpretation stimuli, also indicating faster and more relevant problem-solving abilities then novices.

Becoming an expert requires a substantial amount of experience within the actual domain. For example, becoming an expert in medicine often requires five years or more of extensive experience after graduation, while to become a chess grand master requires even more intensive training. Thus, becoming an expert demands energy and the investment of time in wrestling with domain-specific problems. An additional point is that expert knowledge is partly tacit in nature (Polanyi, 1967). The more effective problem-solving strategies applied by experts are difficult to trace, and experts themselves are, in part, unaware of the rules they use and how they solve problems. The tacit nature of expertise also indicates that such knowledge is difficult to imitate. A resource (in this case expert knowledge) difficult to imitate can, as such, be a source of sustainable competitive advantage. If, however, the expertise was knowledge solely residing in the head of the expert, this would not be sufficient to label it a strategic asset, as an expert is mobile and may be attracted by a competitor's offer. To be an asset which can give rise to sustainable competitive advantage, some organization-specific elements must be present.

Uniqueness in organizational expertise

This section focuses on why and under which conditions expert knowledge can be a source of sustainable competitive advantage, and thus a strategic asset. We first discuss organization-specific elements in individual expertise, and then focus on collective aspects of organizational expertise.

Organization-specific elements

A substantial amount of the expert's knowledge base is acquired in a specific context. For individuals, the organization and its surrounding environment largely frame their context. Within this context the individual is exposed to specific activities and problems which determine experiences and influence the individual's specific contextual learning. The frequently quoted study by Dearborn and Simon (1958) shows that people from different departments emphasize different aspects and problems, reflecting the fact that they focus on and learn to handle activities and problems related to different parts of the organization – environmental context in which they are embedded. For example, an important part of a marketer's knowledge relates to information about specific customers, their names, reactions and so on. However, to become valuable experts, marketers must also possess detailed knowledge of the organizations from which they come, their product offerings, and how to solve the customers' problems. Thus, an important part of marketing expertise consists of detailed knowledge about specific customers and their preferences, the actual organization, and the match between the organization's product offerings and the customers. This becomes important in facing competition. The match between a detailed knowledge of customers and organization-specific elements may give rise to unique solutions that are appreciated in the marketplace, and which, because they are nonimitable, may yield sustainable competitive advantages. This is consistent with the observation that some firms consistently perform better then their competitors (Nelson, 1991).

Individual experts in an organization do not operate in isolation. An important part of their expertise and ability to operate stems from interaction with and support from other people within the organization, and the organization-specific procedures, routines and information systems. These must be learned in order for experts to operate effectively. Organizations vary with regard to customer, people, routines, technological arrangements – even within the same industry. Because a substantial amount of the expert's declarative knowledge is acquired in an organization-environment context, crucial elements of the expertise will be organization-specific and difficult to imitate. This may constitute a rare, valuable resource (Barney, 1991).

The organization-specific elements of expertise need further elaboration. For the expert to be effective, interactions with colleagues and the use of information stored in the organization and its information system are crucial. As mentioned above, key characteristics of experts include the structure of their knowledge base, their information-processing capacity and problem-solving strategies, and their large amount of stored information. Being in a specific organizational context allows the expert to access and make use of information residing within the organization. More precisely, being an expert in an organizational context links the knowledge bases, that is, the memory of the individual expert with the memory of the organization (Walsh & Ungson, 1991), or as termed by Wilensky (1967) «the organizational intelligence». The linkage between the expert and the «organizational memory» or «organizational intelligence» thus enhances the information-processing and problem-solving capacity of the individual expert. For example, the individual uses the available data and information system to structure attention and search. New observations are discussed with colleagues. Past experiences and contextual knowledge influence interpretations. Because organizational contexts vary, and because they must be learned, such expertise is not easily imitable for the following reasons: the expertise which includes the interaction of the expert and the organization is complex and largely tacit in nature. If the expert moves out of the organizational context, parts of what made her or him successful as an expert within that organizational context is removed from the individual. Learning a new organizational context takes time. The new context may not match the former, with the result that organization-specific expertise may be difficult to transfer and imitate. In addition such knowledge may be less valuable in another organizational context. Thus quasi-fixed expertise may yield Ricardian rents (Peteraf, 1993). The following example may illustrate this point. Some managers are considered as experts based on the performance of their organizations where they apparently have made great contributions (Thomas, 1988), and thus have become attractive as managers. It has, however, often been observed that successful managers – assumed to be expert managers – often fail in new settings.

Collective aspects of organizational expertise

The above discussion of expertise as a sticky resource, difficult to imitate, can be elaborated further. So far the focus has been on the individual expert in the organizational context. This is, however, a too narrow and partly faulty perspective. In real life, as a prerequisite for organizations to exist, people work together. That is, people with expert knowledge work together. The organizational expertise thus becomes the collective of experts in their organizational context (Eliasson, 1990). Noticing and interpreting stimuli and problem-solving activities result from experts' interactions in that specific organization-environment context. The collectivity of organizational expertise also indicates that this asset is less vulnerable than that of a single expert in the organization. First, the collective organizational expertise is difficult to duplicate. Second, similar to the biological world, it is often observed that when some functions are destroyed, they are partly taken over or compensated for by others. Thus, losing a member of the organizational expert team can often be compensated for by, for instance, recruiting a new expert member or making rearrangements within the remaining expert team. For example, research teams within universities known for their excellence often lose members. Even so, the most competent research teams are often able to maintain their leading positions for substantial periods of time.

Table 1. Characteristics of organizational expertise

Level	Knowledge base	Characteristics
1. Individual	Procedural Declarative Information processing Extended memory	Organization-specific knowledge element Difficult to imitate
2. Organizational	Expert team Organization specific knowledge Interaction	Almost impossible to imitate Robust to loss of capacity

Table 1 summarizes the above discussion. Organization-specific elements in the individual expertise, including linkages to the organizational memory, may make this resource (expertise) difficult to imitate. In addition, the context may give rise to Ricardian rent. The collective (organizational) expertise may even be more protected against duplication. When this expertise is valuable, for example, in the noticing and construction of opportunities and formulation of alternatives, it may give rise to competitive advantages. The requirements of expertise necessary to yield competitive advantages will be elaborated in the next section.

Organizational experts as a source of competitive advantages

This section focuses on potential competitive advantages that can be traced to knowledge aspects of expertise. Compared with novices, experts' information is assumed to be more accurate and more relevant. Experts also have a greater knowledge base. They process information faster than novices do, which may result in earlier and more accurate noticing and interpretation of opportunities (and threats). This, in turn, can result in the more accurate formulation of alternatives and choice of actions. As is evident from the above discussion, the following two additional characteristics are needed to explain why expert knowledge may give rise to sustainable competitive advantages: first, expertise is difficult to imitate and, second, valuable expertise knowledge may be, in part, organization-specific.

Organizations are embedded in ever-changing environments. Conscious strategic decision-making originates in strategic stimuli, that is, the noticing and interpretation of environmental data signifying opportunities and threats (Ansoff, 1980; Mintzberg, Raisinghani & Théorêt, 1976). The noticing and interpretation of environmental data require knowledge. Knowledge is needed in order to know what to look for, and to make sense of such environmental data. Expert knowledge is advantageous in two ways:

- It allows for early noticing. Early warning as such is advantageous as it increases the time to prepare and to act. This is an important point due to mobility barriers. Most organizations face some type of mobility barriers. It takes time to overcome such barriers. For example, early noticing that the present market niche will change in size or form, that is, what type of activities the niche will support (Zammuto & Cameron, 1985), allows the organization at an early stage to redirect its resources and activities. It also takes time to enter and become established in a new market, to change product offerings or modes of distribution. An important, but frequently overlooked point, however, is that the required reaction time may vary substantially both across industries and across firms within the same industry, due to the firm's capability or otherwise to adjust rapidly to new situations (Porter, 1980).
- Expert noticing and interpretations are also more accurate and relevant than is the case for novices. Expertise thus results in fewer failures and more relevant conceptualizations, which are prerequisites to conscious and accurate actions. More accurate noticing and interpretation thus allow for higher hit rates, and less inaccurate actions and dramatic failures (Shanteau, 1992).

Past research also show that experts are better problem-solvers than novices. In viewing decision-making as problem-solving the following should be noted. Decisions relate to the choice of action(s). The consequences of actions chosen at a given point in time will be realized in the future. Thus, choice among action(s) is related to the envisioning of consequences projected into the future (Boulding, 1966). This requires some representation (model) of the problem, which allows for better predictions. Research findings demonstrate that experts in specific situations predict better than novices (Shanteau, 1992). The higher performance of experts in interpretation and problem-solving can thus be conceived of as superiority in problem-framing and problem representation (modeling), where the expert knowledge allows for more relevant problem representations, and thus better predictions.

Research findings demonstrate that in some cases it pays to be first, that is, first-mover advantages. This advantage may stem from technological leadership, pre-emption of assets and/or buyer switching costs (Lieberman & Montgomery, 1988). Being the first is, however, no guarantee of success. For example, in embryonic industries, substantial consumer learning is needed. Educating consumers is costly, and such education often has externalities difficult to internalize for the first mover. The history of information technology is rich in examples of first movers who have paved the way for later entrants. First-mover advantages as a result of expertise can arise for the following reasons: expert knowledge allows for early noticing of environmental data and accurate interpretation of such data, and thus early actions (when appropriate), and because of accuracy in noticing and relevancy in interpretations and problem-framing, expert knowledge allows for fewer mistakes, and thus more accurate judgment as to when it pays to be first.

An additional point is that, due to organization-specific elements in the organizational expertise, organizations possessing expert knowledge may differ in their noticing, interpretation and exploitation of new opportunities. Gaining first-mover advantages requires noticing data signifying opportunities and accurately interpreting them. Knowledge about how the organization should proceed to exploit the opportunity is needed, as well as how to maintain these advantages by not being imitated. An example may illustrate the knowledge requirements. Omnipaques, a nonionic X-ray contrast, with a market share of approximately 40% of the world market for that product category, has, for a substantial time, been a successful product of the very profitable Norwegian pharmaceutical firm, Hafslund-Nycomed. The firm, which was founded more than a century ago, became involved in X-ray contrast more than 50 years ago. The patent underlying the successful product was not developed within the firm. Rather, the idea was developed and patented by a Swedish researcher, Ahlmen, who tried without success to sell the patent to several pharmaceutical companies until Nycomed finally bought it. Here, knowledge was needed to uncover the advantages of the basic patent (innovation), to use the patent and turn it into a product, foresee market reactions, and to protect the substantial research and development and market investments against imitations. This example illustrates that highly competent firms can differ in their expertise due to specific elements[2] related to organization and knowledge and thus, that some more than others can be more competent in discovering and exploiting specific opportunities.

The organization must adapt continuously to changing environments to survive and prosper. The war-metaphor of strategy as a fight, won or lost, once and forever, may be misleading. Rather, strategy should be conceived of as a never-ending race. Some changes may be discontinuous and dramatic, where turn-arounds are needed to save the organization. The important point, however, is that changes take place all (most of) the time and that continuous, often incremental, improvements are needed to maintain the competitive edge (as reflected in Porter's (1990) quest for upgrading).

Continuous upgrading requires detailed and accurate knowledge. Knowledge is needed to note and interpret the changes taking place, and to allow for superior problem-solving to stay ahead. The greater the knowledge base and the information-processing capacity associated with expertise, the greater the advantages in the upgrading race.

Organizations differ in level and composition of expertise. The changes that are noted, and how they are interpreted, may result in different upgrading activities, even between organizations belonging to the same industry. The most adequate composition of organizational expertise is a source which, through adequate utilization (to be discussed later), can and will be reflected in sustainable competitive advantage.

Expertise may yield other competitive advantage as well. Experts and expert organizations know more about their products and services and

---

2. Other factors, such as economic resources and attitude towards risk, may explain differences in exploiting new opportunities. This however, does not seem to be the case in the above example. The firm was (and is) a relatively small pharmaceutical firm. Larger firms with substantially more economic resources exist(ed). Nor has the firm been recognized to be particular risk-prone.

how to solve customers' problems than do the customers. Searching for information and evaluating products and service providers are time-consuming, costly activities which require knowledge. For many products and services, customers simply lack adequate knowledge (and time) to search for information and accurately evaluate the offerings prior to purchase. Such situations correspond to what Nelson (1970) has termed experience goods, that is, that products and services can be adequately evaluated only after the customer has experienced the product or service. In some cases, the customers are not capable of evaluating products or services even after they are consumed (such as, credence goods, Darby & Karni, 1973).

In situations where the search for information is costly and it is difficult or impossible to assess suppliers and product or service alternatives prior to the purchase contract, customers tend to rely on actors they believe to be better informed. For example, there is ample evidence that people rely on others, for example, opinion leaders, as a strategy to cope with purchase decisions perceived as complex and risky (Bauer, 1960). An important point is that the consequences of a purchase are realized only in the future.

In some cases neither the product nor what actually is to be delivered is specified prior to the contract. This is typical when hiring an advertising company or entering into a research contract. In such situations relational contracting is prevalent (Macneil, 1980). Problems are formulated and reformulated, alternatives are elaborated, and decisions unfold over time within the relationship between the exchange partners. In such situations a key determinant is the customer's belief that the contracted party is able and willing to perform. Superior expertise, recognized by others, plays a crucial role in such situations. For example, findings from communication research show that the perceived expertise of the source is crucial for the effectiveness of communication (Hovland, Janis & Kelley, 1953; Bagozzi, 1986). In a similar vein, superior expertise adds to the organizational reputation. Due to incomplete a priori information, and because the activities to be performed will unfold in the future, expertise plays a key role to signal that the organization can perform, and can thus be a key factor in attracting new customers (Fombrun & Shanley, 1990). Because customers experience that the organization has expert knowledge and that it can perform, organization-customer relationships tend to stabilize and lock in customers. Such locked in, satisfied customers may also serve as advice givers in word-of-mouth advertising, enhancing the reputational value of expertise.

The above discussion reveals that organizational expertise can be an important source of competitive advantage. First, expert knowledge is a source allowing for superior activities, for example, through early and more accurate noticing and interpretations, and faster and more adequate problem-solving. Second, the above discussion also shows, that expertise, as such, can be a competitive advantage through its reputational effects.

Figure 1: Expertise and Competitive Advantages

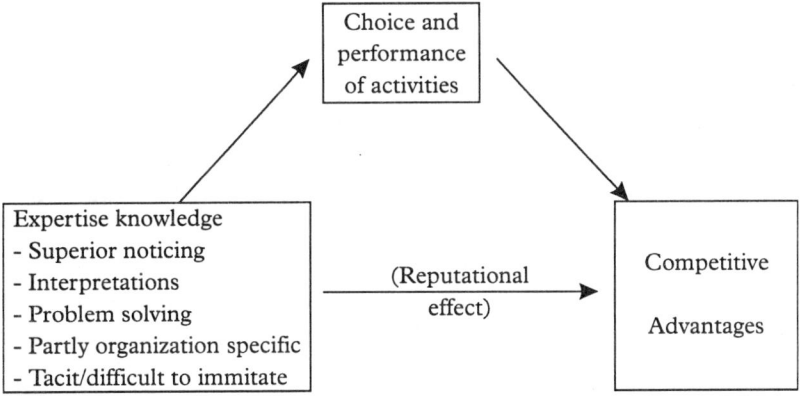

Expert dynamics

This paper views expertise as a resource and a source of competitive advantage. As demonstrated in Figure 1, this source can also, itself, be a competitive advantage. A resource is often viewed as static. However, resources may be exploited in new ways, and thus resources should be considered to be dynamic. This is true, in particular, in the dynamic capabilities approach, which is a part of the resource-based perspective forcefully argued for by Wernerfeldt (1984), Teece, Pisano and Shuen (1990) and others. Two main aspects can explain expertise dynamics: expertise may be exploited differently over time, and the expertise may develop and change over time. In the following we first untangle the dynamic mechanisms of expertise. Then the factors inhibiting the dynamic exploitation and development of expertise, which can explain the deterioration of competitiveness, are emphasized.

Mechanisms in expert dynamics

The key characteristics of expertise emphasized above relate to superior knowledge and information-processing. This superiority in knowledge allows for faster learning and updating of new information. Expert knowledge can thus be an important element in achieving learning advantages. Such learning advantages can be beneficial both in noticing and exploiting new opportunities, as well as for faster adjustments and improvements, allowing the organization a faster learning curve (Alberts, 1989).

Professional experts have professional networks (Shanteu 1992). Experts in the various fields know each other. They attend professional conferences, they meet, and they stay in contact. Through strong and weak ties, they exchange information (Granovetter, 1973, 1985). Thus, besides possessing knowledge, experts are also embedded in expert networks allowing for fast information exchange, which they can due to their knowledge base evaluate and adjust to their organizational context. An important point is that due to organization-specific elements in the expert's knowledge base, new information may be evaluated and used differently across experts, even those belonging to the same industry and professions. Because organizational expertise also includes interactions between people varying in expertise, organization-specific evaluation and utilization of new information are even more likely. Such organization-specific evaluation and utilization may be an argument for joint knowledge-producing activities as well (Ouchi & Bolton, 1989).

Experts are also assumed to possess superior problem-solving skills. New problems represent challenges. Due to superior knowledge and problem-solving skills, experts, more than others, are likely to solve the new challenges which are important in acquiring new knowledge, and further improve the problem-solving capacity. The importance of challenges in enhancing knowledge is easily understood by focusing on the research community. Knowledge production is the prime purpose of research. The problems encountered, the research setting and research expertise involved, greatly influence the quality and output of research. Fundamentally new and basic insights are produced, primarily, by expert research teams preoccupied with fundamental, basic problems. New insights into how to improve products and production to attain higher organizational performance are primarily produced by organizations close to the customers' problems. This indicates that exposure to new and challenging problems (in addition to organizational arrangements, sufficient time and resources to wrestle with the new problems) is important in enhancing both individual and organizational expertise (Amabile, 1990).

Factors inhibiting expert dynamics

As environments, and thus competition, become increasingly more dynamic, the expertise must be dynamic as well if the organization is to stay competitive. Stalk, Evans & Shulman (1992) have characterized competition as a «war of movement» and «a process more akin to an interactive video game than to chess» (p. 62). In their opinion, (Stalk, Evans & Shulman, 1992) expertise dynamics are a prerequisite for organizational dynamics.

A prerequisite for fast and adequate reactions is early and accurate notice and interpretation of environmental changes requiring expertise, that is, detailed knowledge and superb information-processing capabilities. It has often been observed, however, that organizations possessing superb expertise knowledge, and other required capabilities, lose their competitive edge. Factors inhibiting expertise development are, in part, the same as those explaining expertise dynamics.

- Expertise relates to domain-specific superior knowledge. The acquired knowledge guides and directs. Present expert knowledge may thus shadow any change of perspective. At the organization level, where the expertise resides in teams of experts, their interactions and knowledge stored in routines and information systems, the expertise rigidity may become even more profound (Leonard-Barton, 1992).

- A key premise for the organizational expert team performance is mutual interaction and understanding. Such mutual understanding and interactions may produce one-eyed dominant perspectives, hampering new and innovative perspectives and solutions due to group-think effects (Janis, 1982).

- Success both at the individual and organizational level guides and directs attention and activities. Past success, and knowledge and beliefs about cases, may inhibit new approaches. Present expertise may thus function as competence traps (Levitt & March, 1988).

- Expertise, both at the individual and organizational level needs challenges to grow. Lack of challenges – or perception of challenges – for example, by being embedded in routine tasks, resulting in a lack of stimulating challenges, may cause the stagnation and deterioration of expertise.

- Being confronted with new, partly understood challenges that may enhance the organizational expertise requires the allocation of time and other resources. As such tasks tend to be conceived of as unstructured, they must be put on the agenda in order not to be trapped by routine tasks (Gresham's law). Lack of adequate organizational arrangements that allow new and unstructured challenges to be explored and developed may thus be a threat to expertise development. (For an interesting case of internal corporate venturing, requiring new insights and expansion of present knowledge, see Burgelman, 1983.)

- New and partly understood challenges are not only time-consuming, but due to their novelty, the steps to follow to arrive at the final solution are not known in advance. The road to the solution must be sought and discovered. Time-consuming and costly detours may also occur. Successful solutions often require a substantial amount of experimentation. This requires time, and resources for experimentation are needed. Due to uncertainty, such experimentation may fail. Therefore, reward systems allowing for experimentation and the potential failure of experiments is also needed. Lack of arrangements allowing for new challenges to enter the organizational agenda and reward systems allowing experimentation and failures, may, therefore, be threats to dynamic growth of expertise.

Table 2 summarizes the above discussion. An apparent paradox is that several of the same mechanisms may both stimulate and inhibit expert dynamics. The table lists factors related to individual expertise (1a), organizational expertise (1b), challenges (2), and organizational arrangements and incentives that may stimulate and inhibit expertise dynamics, which is of crucial importance for sustained competitiveness.

The presence of individual expertise, including relevant organization-specific elements as emphasized above, may facilitate the noticing and interpretation of new data, and may thus result in new knowledge and new solutions. At the same time, the existing knowledge structure and

Table 2. Factors stimulating and inhibiting expert dynamics

	Stimulants	Inhibitors
1. Expert knowledge		
a) Individual	Facilitate	Structure/direct (specific focus)
• Knowledge base	• noticing	
• Information-processing capacities	• interpretation	
• Problem solving capacities	• knowledge update	
	• new solutions	
b) Organization	Extended knowledge and problem-	Group think
• Expert team	solving capacity	
2. Challenges	Present	Absent
3. Organizational arrangements and incentives		
• Agenda-setting, new unstructured tasks	Present	Absent
• Allow for experimentation	Present	Absent
• Allow for experimentation failures	Present	Absent

focus may hamper the knowledge update. A key challenge is to benefit from acquired expertise without strangling new learning.

The virtue of collective expertise, residing in the organization and its extended networks, as a valuable strategic resource was emphasized above. The presence of multiple, interacting individuals who are experts can expand the knowledge base and expertise beyond the sum of the individual experts. True synergy in knowledge and expertise may result. On the other hand, when caught in past solutions and mutual expectations, group think, with fatal consequences, may occur (Janis, 1982). Keeping the organizational expert team alert and motivated for continuous renewal becomes of prime importance and represents a major task for competitiveness (Amabile, 1990).

In addition to the factors related to organizational arrangements and incentives discussed above (and summarized in Table 2), the following should be noted. Organizations possess technologies and routines. Parts of the organizational setting, for example, information systems and routines, can be considered as elements of the organizational memory and, as such, an element of the organizational expertise. Organizational technologies and routines structure focus. Starbuck (1983) even claims that organizational structures, routines and procedures generate actions. Such structuring elements may sharpen the organizational focus. This is often needed to uncover and exploit opportunities. At the same time, such a structured focus may cause important problems to be overlooked (Zajac & Bazerman, 1991). A primary concern then is the balance between focus and flexibility.

Organizations often want to strengthen their expertise by recruiting newcomers with different expertise. As such, this a good thing to do. The effect on the organizational expertise, may, however, turn out to be modest. The newcomers are in a minority, and the strong and dominant perspectives already developed may cause the newcomer to comply with the dominant expertise perspective. The hoped-for expertise enhancement may thus be eliminated (March & Simon, 1958).

The organizational environments and challenges are ever changing. Of prime importance for the organization to survive and prosper is the noticing and interpretation of environmental data signifying changes in order to act accurately. Expert knowledge allows for early and accurate noticing and interpretation. As noted earlier, a key element in expertise is declarative knowledge. Also this element of expert knowledge must be updated. The most adequate way to do so, is to be close to where the changes can be noticed, as reflected in the following quote

> In large corporations ... you can't sit in the office at corporate headquarters and really develop a good feel for what's going on. You've got to go out and spend time in operating units ... if you sell through distributors or dealers, you should spend time with them. You have to know what's going on in a business and marketplace. (USA Today, May 4, 1993, 2B)

Such closeness to sources of change is needed for early noticing and interpretation, for expertise updating and necessary redirection of activities, and for access to the new expertise needed for survival and prosperity (Teece 1992).

Conclusions

This paper demonstrates that expertise can be a valuable, dynamic source of competitive advantage, and that expertise, through its reputational effects, can yield competitive advantages. In this paper the focus has been on expert knowledge, which is a prerequisite for exploiting competence and/or capabilities.

Expert knowledge is often thought of as superior knowledge and information-processing capacity allowing for faster and more accurate noticing and interpretation of data, which is of prime importance for superior problem-solving. Even though expertise is often conceived of as an individual characteristic, this paper shows that elements of the experts' knowledge base is organization-specific. Through linkages to organizational routines and information systems, which may extend the experts' memory and capacity to find and solve problems, the organization-specific knowledge of the expert may become substantial. At the collective level, including interacting expert management teams, the organization-specific expert knowledge becomes even more profound. Due to the tacit nature of such organization-specific expert knowledge, and its inherent difficulty to imitate, it may become a source of sustainable advantage. The paper also demonstrates that inherent mechanisms allow expertise to become a dynamic resource, but also that expertise may deteriorate due to the fragility of such mechanisms.

Fostering collective organization-specific expertise requires cooperation and interactions between individual experts. Superior Japanese firms have been recognized for their expertise and sustainable competitive advantage. It seems reasonable to assume that this, to a substantial degree, can be attributed to mutual understanding and interactions, that is, social aspects enhancing the collective performance of individuals, resulting in superior performance. The socializing of newcomers to Toyota illustrates this.

> The novice salarymen will spend two months on the assembly line «because they have to learn where the profit comes from». They will spend another two months in a department unrelated to their final employment destination to get a more rounded view of the company ... Their first month will be spent on ... fostering the cooperative skills considered the heart of Toyota's famous learn production system. (*Chicago Tribune*, April 26, 1993)

To maintain the competitive edge, a key challenge is to create conditions for continuous updating, development and utilization of the organizational expertise, that is, to create and sustain the best climate for organizational learning, which means being exposed to challenges, allow for challenges, agenda setting and sufficient time and resources (Argyris, 1976; Garvin, 1993).

Expert knowledge is often believed to be of importance only for high-tech firms. However, even in industries often believed to be low-tech, organizations may benefit from superior, dynamic expertise related to their domains. For example, McDonald's has been able to stay ahead and enjoy above normal industry returns for a substantial period of time. This indicates that knowledge is needed, that superior expert knowledge may be created in most (all?) industries, and that, when such expertise becomes valuable, it may give rise to competitive advantage.

References

Alberts, W.W. (1989): The Experience Curve Reconsidered. *Journal of Marketing 23*: 36-49.

Amabile, T.M. (1990): A Model of Creativity and Innovations in Organizations. In L.L. Cummings & B.M. Staw (eds): *The Evolution and Adaptation of Organizations*. Greenwich, CT: JAI Press, 231-275.

Andersen, J.R. (1983): *The Architecture of Cognition*. Cambridge, MA: Harvard University Press.

Ansoff, H.I. (1980): Strategic Issue Management. *Strategic Management Journal 1*: 131-148.

Argyris, C. (1976): Single-Loop and Double-Loop Models in Research on Decision Making. *Administrative Science Quarterly 21*: 363-375.

Bagozzi, R.P. (1986): *Principles of Marketing Management*. Chicago: Science Research Associates.

Barney, J. (1991): Firm Resources and Sustained Competitive Advantage. *Journal of Management 17*: 99-120.

Bauer, R.A. (1960): Consumer Behavior as Risk Taking. In R.S. Hamcock (ed.): *Dynamic Marketing for a Changing World*. Chicago: American Marketing Association, 389-400.

Boulding, K.E. (1966): The Economics of Knowledge and the Knowledge of Economics. *American Economic Review 56*: 1-13.

Burgelman, R.A. (1983): A Process Model of Internal Corporate Venturing in the Diversified Major Firm. *Administrative Science Quarterly 28*: 223-244.

Chi, M.T.H., R. Glaser & M.J. Farr (1988): *The Nature of Expertise*. Hillsdale, NJ: Erlbaum.

Chicago Tribune (1993): Instilling Creativity to a Point. *Chicago Tribune*, Monday, April 26.

Crech, D., R.S. Crutchfield & D. Livson (1974): *Elements of Psychology*. 3rd edn. New York: Alfred A. Knopf.

Darby, M.R. & E. Karni (1973): Free Competition and the Optimal Amount of Fraud. *Journal of Law and Economics 16*: 1-20.

Day, G.S. & R. Wensley (1988): Assessing Advantage: A Framework for Diagnosing Competitive Superiority. *Journal of Marketing 52*: 1-20.

Dearborn, D. & H.A. Simon (1958): Selective Perception: A Note on Departmental Identification of Executives. *Sociometry 35*: 38-48.

Dillon, J.T. (1982): Problem Finding and Solving. *The Journal of Creative Behavior 16*: 97-111.

Eliasson, G. (1990): The Firm as a Competent Team. *Journal of Economic Behavior and Organization 13*: 275-289.

Fiske, S.T. & S.E. Taylor (1991): *Social Cognition*. 2nd ed. New York: McGraw-Hill.

Fombrun, C. & M. Shanley (1990): What's in a Name? Reputation Building and Corporate Strategy. *Academy of Management Journal 33*: 233-258.

Garvin, D.A. (1993): Building a Learning Organization. *Harvard Business Review july-aug.*: 78-91.

Glaser, R. (1988): Expertise and Learning: How do We Think about Instructural Processes Now That We Have Discovered Knowledge Structures? In D. Klahr & K. Kotovsky (eds.): *Complex Information Processing: The Impact of Herbert Simon*. Hillsdale, NJ: Erlbaum, 269-282.

Granovetter, M. (1973): The Strength of Weak Ties. *American Journal of Sociology 78*: 1360-1380.

Granovetter, M. (1985): Economic Action and Social Structure: The Problem of Embeddedness. *American Journal of Sociology 91*: 485-510.

Grant, R.M. (1991): The Resource-Based Theory of Competitive Advantage: Implications for Strategy Formulation. *California Management Review 33*: 114-135.

Hovland, C.I., I.L. Janis & H.H. Kelley (1953): *Communication and Persuasion*. New Haven: Yale University Press.

Janis, I.L. (1982): *Groupthink*. Boston: Houghton Mifflin, 2nd ed.

Johnson, E.J. (1988): Expertise and Decision under Uncertainty: Performance and Process. In M.T.H. Chi, R. Glaser & M.J. Farr: *The Nature of Expertise*. Hillsdale, NJ: Erlbaum, 209-228.

Kiesler, S. & L. Sproull (1982): Managerial Response to Changing Environments: Perspectives on Problem Solving from Social Cognition. *Administrative Science Quarterly 27*: 548-570.

Leonard-Barton, D. (1992): Core Capabilities and Core Rigidities: A Paradox of Managing New Product Development. *Strategic Management Journal 13*: 111-125.

Levitt, B. & J.G. March (1988): Organizational Learning. *Annual Review of Sociology 14*.

Lieberman, M.B. & D.B. Montgomery (1988): First-Mover Advantages. *Strategic Management Journal 9*: 41-58.

Lord, R.G. & K.J. Maher (1990): Alternative Information-Processing Models and their Implications for Theory, Research, and Practice. *Academy of Management Review 15*: 9-28.

Macneil, I.R. (1980): *The New Social Contract*. New Haven, CT: Yale University Press.

March, J.G. (1978): Bounded Rationality, Ambiguity, and the Engineering of Choice. *Bell Journal of Economics 9*: 587-607.

March, J.G. & H.A. Simon (1958): *Organizations*. New York: John Wiley & Sons.

Mintzberg, H., D. Raisinghani & A. Théorêt (1976): The Structure of Unstructured Decision Processes. *Administrative Science Quarterly 21*: 246-275.

Nelson, R.R. (1970): Advertising as Information. *Journal of Political Economy 81*: 729-754.

Nelson, R.R. (1991): Why Do Firms Differ, and How Does It Matter? *Strategic Management Journal 12*: 61-74.

Ouchi, W.G. & M.K. Bolton (1989): The Logic of Joint Research and Development. *California Management Review 33*: 9-33.

Peteraf, M.A. (1993): The Cornerstones of Competitive Advantage: A Resource-Based View. *Strategic Management Journal 14*: 179-191.

Polanyi, M. (1967): *The Tacit Dimension*. Garden City, NY: Doubleday Anchor.

Porter, M.E. (1980): *Competitive Strategy*. New York: Free Press.

Porter, M.E. (1985): *Competitive Advantage*. New York: Free Press.

Porter, M.E. (1990): *The Competitive Advantage of Nations*. New York: Free Press.

Prahalad, C.K. & G. Hamel (1990): The Core Competence of the Corporation. *Harvard Business Review 68*: 79-91.

Rosch, E. (1978): Principles of Categorization. In E. Rosch & B. Lloyd (eds.): *Cognition and Categorization*. Hillsdale, NJ: Lawrence Erlbaum.

Sanford, A.J. (1987): *The Mind of Man. Models of Human Understanding*. Brighton, Sussex: Harvester Press.

Shanteau, J. (1992): The Psychology of Experts: An Alternative View. In G. Wright & F. Bolger (eds.): *Expertise and Decision Support*. New York: Plenum Press, 11-23.

Simon, H.A. (1978): Rationality as a Process of Product and Thought. *American Economic Review 68*: 1-16.

Simon, H.A. (1987): Making Management Decisions: The Role of Intuition and Emotion. *Academy of Management Executive 1*: 57-64.

Stalk, G., P. Evans & L.E. Shulman (1992): Competing on Capabilities: The New Rules of Corporate Strategy. *Harvard Business Review 70*: 57-69.

Starbuck, W.H. (1983): Organizations as Action Generators. *American Sociological Review 48*: 91-102.

Teece, D.J. (1992): Competition, Cooperation, and Innovation. Organizational Arrangements for Regimes of Rapid Technological Progress. *Journal of Economic Behavior and Organization 18*: 1-25.

Teece, D.J., G. Pisano & A. Shuen (1990): Firm Capabilities, Resources and the Concept of Strategy. Berkeley, CA: University of California, working paper EAP-38.

Thomas, A.B. (1988): Does Leadership Make a Difference for Organizational Performance? *Administrative Science Quarterly 33*: 388-400.

USA Today (1993): IBM's York No Wallflower. *USA Today*, May 4, 2B.

Walsh, J.P. & G.R. Ungson (1991): Organizational Memory. *Academy of Management Review 16*: 57-91.

Wernerfelt, B. (1984): A Resource Based View of the Firm. *Strategic Management Journal 5*: 171-180.

Wilensky, H. (1967): *Organizational Intelligence: Knowledge and Policy in Government and Industry.* New York: Basic Books.

Zajac, E.J. & M.H. Bazerman (1991): Blind Spots in Industry and Competitor Analysis: Implications of Interfirm (Mis)interpretations for Strategic Decisions. *Academy of Management Review 16*: 37-56.

Zammuto, R.F. & K.S. Cameron (1985): Environmental Decline and Organizational Response. In. L. Cummings & B. Staw (eds.): *Research in Organizational Behavior*, vol. 7. Greenwich, CT: JAI Press, 223-262.

Information Systems as a Secondary Strategic Resource: The Case of Bank Credit Evaluations[1]

Anna Mette Fuglseth & Kjell Grønhaug

The purpose of this paper is to enhance the understanding of information systems as a strategic resource. Our emphasis is on how such systems may improve organizational effectiveness and performance, and thus make organizations more competitive. In this paper we particularly focus on how information systems can yield advantages through improved implementation of strategies, and how such systems, when adequately designed, can improve the effectiveness of complex management processes and enhance organizational learning. Through the linking of decisions (and decision-makers) in hierarchical organizational structures, improving coordination and collective organizational learning, we argue that information systems can be a valuable resource to boost organizational performance.

First, we define basic concepts and clarify crucial assumptions underlying our paper. This section also relates and positions our paper to previous efforts to understand the potential advantages of information systems as a secondary strategic resource in management processes. The term secondary refers to the critical dependence on adequate design and competent users to reap the potential benefits of such systems.

Next, we present a case describing the credit evaluation process for business loans in a large Norwegian bank, and the effort to design an information system to support and improve this process. Comparisons with the present system show that the new design yields multiple advantages such as improved coordination of decisions and decision-makers involved in credit evaluations at different organizational levels, improved decision quality, and improved organizational learning as well. Finally, implications are highlighted.

---

1. This is a slightly modified version of a paper published in the International Journal of Information Management (1994), 14, 269-280, reprinted by permission of the publishers, Butterworth-Heinemann, Ltd. ©.

Information systems as a strategic resource

By the term resource we mean all assets, capabilities, organizational processes, attributes, and knowledge controlled by an organization that enable the organization to conceive of and implement strategies that improve its efficiency and effectiveness (Daft, 1983). This broad definition views resources from an organizational perspective, that is, the organization may possess, develop, or acquire resources, which, when adequately applied, may give rise to improved performance.

A resource, even though it may prove useful to the organization, is not necessarily strategic, that is, giving the organization specific advantages. If the resource is available to all firms within the industry, it might become a necessity, implying that the organization must possess and utilize this resource simply to keep up. Organizations not possessing the resource, for whatever reasons, for example, lack of financial resources or competence in utilizing the resource, will perform worse than firms using the resource if this deficiency cannot be compensated for in any other way. In order to be strategic, a resource must be rare among the organization's current and potential competitors and be imperfectly imitable, and it should also be difficult to find strategically equivalent substitutes (Barney, 1991). In this paper we will emphasize how information systems can be an important, necessary, resource, as well as how this resource can become strategic.

The term information system denotes computerized systems designed and implemented in order to increase the efficiency and effectiveness of information-processing in organizations. Information systems may also be termed a secondary resource, as its value is determined by organizational members' use.

Although the strategy literature emphasizes human resources as crucial to the organization (Itami & Roehl, 1987; Eliasson, 1990), there has only been a modest focus on how information systems may enhance the value of human resources, boost the organizational performance, and become strategically important. Several authors, however, have focused on information technology (Porter, 1985; Porter & Millar, 1985) as a potential source of strategic advantage. We agree that the adoption of information technology may enhance organizational performance. We doubt, however, that information technology itself can be a strategic resource. If the technology itself is to be strategically important, it must be proprietary to the organization (for example, through internal development or contracting), and imperfectly imitable, which is unlikely. Specific uses of information technology may, however, be strategically important as the organization may develop specific applications and uses which, in their actual context, may give rise to competitive advantages difficult to imitate by competing organizations. An example is the use of just-in-time technology to link value activities between organizations. Some just-in-time systems are based on relatively simple programmes and off-the-shelf technology, and can easily be imitated by competitors from a technological point of view, but they may give a first-mover advantage by attaching customers to the organization.

Barney (1991) is one of the few authors who focuses explicitly on information systems as a potential strategic resource in connection with management processes. Barney argues that an information system that is «deeply embedded in a firm's informal and formal decision-making» may hold the potential to be a strategic resource (p. 114). His argumentation corresponds to our discussion above: the specific use of the information systems and the fact that the specific design and use («deeply embedded ...») are difficult to imitate, may give information systems the status of a strategic resource.

Information systems and organization strategy

The purpose of an explicit strategy is to relate the organization to its ever-changing environments in such a way that it makes the best possible use of its resources, and adequately adjusts to and benefits from changes taking place. The value of any strategy lies in its implementation. Choice and performance of costly value activities determine whether organizations succeed or fail (Porter, 1985). The organizational resource base and the use of these resources highly influence the organizational choice and performance of value activities. Strategy can be seen as an ongoing, complex organizational decision-making process, consisting of cycles of processes involving the following phases: search for threats and opportunities, inventing, developing, and analyzing alternative strategies, choice of a strategy, implementation of the strategy and evaluation of results as part of a new search for threats and possibilities (Simon, 1977). Each strategy process is not as sequential as the description suggests, and each phase may itself be a complex decision-making process, or as noted by Simon (1977): «There are wheels within wheels within wheels». In practice the phases are interwoven in an ongoing strategy process which may include participation of members at lower levels in all phases. Where formulation of strategy ends and implementation begins is a matter of definition of the phases (Grønhaug, 1989). In this paper the term implementation means carrying out business activities according to the courses of action/guidelines which we consider part of the formulation of strategy.

The ongoing formulation and implementation of strategy take place in an organizational context. Among the key organizational characteristics are the presence of multiple members (actors), hierarchical structure, division of labor and specialization. It has long been recognized that it is the concerted effort of organization members that may result in superior performance (Drucker, 1973).

Decisions take place at various levels in the organizations and can be of different types; for example, as reflected in strategic, managerial and operational level actors and decisions. Strategic decisions are usually assumed to be made at the top of the organization, while operations, that is, the execution of the various activities needed to implement strategies, mostly take place at lower levels in the organization. To be successfully implemented, decisions and activities at the various levels should be coherent. However, as the streams of activities are implemented in ever-changing environments, the resultant outcome of such activities should be communicated to higher levels in the organization to allow for adjustments and reformulations of present strategy.

In his discussion of possible benefits that accrue to an organization that «possesses a system where computers and managers are intimately linked», Barney (1991) lists «an *efficient* flow of information among managers, the ability to consider large amounts of information *quickly*, and the ability to share this information *efficiently*» (p. 114, our italics). Barney also claims that the same benefits might accrue to organizations with «a closely knit, highly experienced management team, without an information management system» (p. 114).

We agree with Barney that an experienced management group may have a very efficient communication process, and we do not think that a management information system can substitute human interactions embedded in the team culture, probably acquired over years. The purpose of a management information system, however, is to increase the effectiveness of (strategic) planning and control activities by providing access to external and internal databases, to support analysis of data, and to support communication processes. An important purpose is also to support the managers in their understanding of the environment and the adaptation of their organization to the environment by offering modeling capabilities or specific economic models, that is, mathematical expressions of cause-effect relationships in the environment or in the organization. A management information system may thus complement face-to-face communication processes in the management team and give benefits in addition to the efficiency qualities mentioned by Barney.

Furthermore, organizations also consist of non-managers. In organizations above a certain minimum size most of the operations take place at the lower, operational levels. The activities conducted, and how these activities are conducted, reflect the realized strategy (Mintzberg, 1987), and thus to what extent and how the formulated strategy has been implemented. Information systems designed to link and monitor decisions at different organizational levels can be an advantage able to obtain the needed coherence in implementing the planned strategy. An information system may also contribute to systematic feedback allowing for adequate reformulation of the organizational strategy and collective learning.

The issue of coherence between formulated and implemented strategy is especially critical in organizations where multiple actors perform in part the same tasks, but operate almost independently of each other; for example, in insurance companies where a multiplicity of employees handle, evaluate, and issue insurance. In such organizations, implementation of the formulated strategy depends on the standards for evaluation used by the individual operators, to what extent the standards are the same across operators, and how the standards are practiced.

In stable environments, and for tasks that can be fully structured, information systems (expert systems) may be an important means to impose the same standards on the actors, thereby attaining consistency between formulated and implemented strategy. An example is the redesign of the processing of applications for insurance at Mutual Life Benefit (Hammer, 1990). In order to improve productivity, existing job definitions and departmental boundaries were swept away, and a new position called a case manager was created. Case managers have total responsibility for an application from the time it is received to the time a policy is issued. Shared databases and computer networks make different kinds of data available to the case manager, and an expert system containing the collective knowledge helps people with limited experience to make sound decisions.

In situations where the decisions involved are complex, and the organizational environments are rapidly changing, we are not able to fully structure the decision-making process. In such situations an information system alone is not adequate because complex decisions involve judgment and subjective analysis. Human judgment alone, however, may also be inadequate because of the computational power and precision needed to support understanding of cause-effect relationships required to exhibit purposeful behavior, a prerequisite to pursuing a formulated strategy. Furthermore, in turbulent environments we expect strategy to be adjusted often in order to adapt the organization to changing conditions. This implies that an information systems should also be designed to adapt to changing conditions.

In such situations the human actor plus an information systems can provide a more effective decision than either alone (Keen & Scott Morton, 1978). In order to support consistency between the formulated strategy and implementation, such an information systems should be tailor-made and integrated in the organizational decision-making processes. Integration implies that strategic, tactical, and operational decisions should be linked. Tailor-made implies that the system should be designed to handle organization-specific decision processes related to the environments where the organization operates. An organization-specific information system will thus contain elements that are primarily of value for that organization alone. When the system design is particularly suitable, and when it contributes to boosting organizational performance, the information system really becomes an important, secondary, strategic resource difficult to imitate, where a straightforward replica will be of a lesser value for the imitating competitor (Barney, 1991; Wernerfeldt, 1984).

In the next section we report on a case to illustrate the above arguments, that is, the design of an information systems to support a bank's credit evaluations.

Case: bank credit evaluation

This section reports on the design of an information system to support credit evaluation of business loans in a major Norwegian bank.

Credit evaluation is an example of a complex decision situation. A loan is a sale of money today in return for an uncertain future cash flow. Evaluation of a customer's creditworthiness is, therefore, a complex decision process which includes analysis of the future earnings of the customer. Such analysis comprises both an evaluation of the prospects of the customer's line of business and of the customer's ability to cope with the future. Credit evaluation, therefore, demands both formal education to perform a strategic analysis and experience in evaluating the reliability of the customer's accounts and budgets. Moreover, in larger banks, credit evaluation is to a substantial degree decentralized to the lower-level employees. Business loans comprise the largest single category of the earning assets of banks: that is, our chosen situation is important to the bank. The Norwegian banking industry certainly faces a dynamic environment. Since 1980 economic instability has reigned and since 1985 the banking industry has experienced a full business cycle with a period of expansion and recession (Steffensen & Steigum, 1990). During this period the banks also had to adjust to the change from operating in a market with customers queueing for loans to a highly competitive market.

Described below is our effort to develop a prototype version of a system to support the credit evaluation processes in the actual bank. The following sources served as the point of departure: the bank's credit manual (part of its strategy), the credit evaluation documents, and a tape-recorded think-aloud interview with an experienced credit consultant while observing her evaluating a specific loan application at her terminal.

The credit evaluation process

The bank is an hierarchical organization consisting of three administration levels: strategic, tactical and operational. Credit evaluation takes place at all three levels of the bank. At the strategic level, top management decides on the composition of the loan portfolio, on interest rates and pricing of risk. Their decisions are based on analyses of industries and trades in which the bank has a heavy involvement, their competitors, economic trends and their present portfolio. Their strategic tasks involve the development of two sets of plans: prescriptions for the credit evaluation and control processes, and directions for handling the composition of the portfolio. The procedures for credit evaluation are described in the credit manual (a two-volume book). The directions for handling the portfolio are changed often and at short notice to handle opportunities and threats in the dynamic environment. Examples of directions are limits to the total involvement in specific industries and special demands on shareholders' funds within specific trades and activities. The directions are communicated in written reports and memos.

At the tactical level, the credit committee decides whether to accept or reject loan applications based on the evaluation of the credit consultant at the operational level and the directions for portfolio composition from top management. The members of the credit committee also fill the role of troubleshooters, handling problematic situations and high-risk customers. Furthermore, the tactical level includes specialists monitoring and evaluating developments in industries and trades where the bank is heavily involved. Their reports are sent to the strategic level and included in the portfolio analyses.

At the operational level, the credit consultants play a key role. Loans are credit extensions, often involving ongoing personal relationships between the bank and its customers. The credit consultants are responsible for such relationships, and each credit consultant has a portfolio of customers. They monitor the performance of each customer and the value of collateral. New loan applications are evaluated according to the procedures prescribed in the credit manual and the directions for portfolio composition. The nature of the work, that is, the complex decision situations involved, implies that the given directions cannot be considered as specific decision-making rules, but rather as guidelines. The credit consultants may use their special knowledge of the customers and their business and decide to deviate from the directions. For example, in the observed case, the customer, a contractor, should not have been granted an extension of his bank overdraft facilities according to the directions, but the credit consultant judged that the bank might suffer a greater loss if extension of credit was denied. Her conclusion was that the credit should be granted on special terms, and that the customer should be transferred to the high-risk group of customers receiving special attention and advice from one of the troubleshooters at the tactical level.

A large organizational database contains historical financial data for three years and a one-year budget for each customer. The database system includes operations for calculation of the risk classification of the customers. The risk classification is based on historical cash flow and shareholders' funds (solidity), and the value of the collateral. The database updates itself every day, extracting data such as deposits and overdrafts from the transaction systems. The credit consultant communicates with the database using a tailor-made system. The system allows her to extract data on each of her customers according to a predefined standard only. The system also supports the entry of data to the database in connection with a new loan application, and it provides a framework for filling in the credit documents according to the prescriptions in the credit manual. It does not, however, support the credit consultants in their calculations or evaluations of the customer's creditworthiness.

Observations and system considerations

One of the most difficult problems in designing an information systems is to decide what it means to improve a specific decision-making process, that is, to establish a situational norm (Fuglseth, 1989). Here we used the formulated strategy as the norm and the observation of the credit consultant as a description of implementation of the strategy.

We first focused on inconsistencies between the strategy and the actual credit evaluation process. According to the credit manual, the future earnings of a customer should be emphasized when evaluating the creditworthiness of the customer. In practice, however, this was not done. There are several reasons for this discrepancy. For example, the credit manual contained no detailed instructions about how to accomplish an analysis of future earnings and uncertainty. The credit manual illustrating the results of a credit evaluation did not contain quantitative analyses of future earnings or uncertainty regarding these earnings, nor does the present system support evaluation of future earnings. Performing uncertainty analyses without the support of a computer is very time-consuming. As a consequence, the credit consultant did not perform any analyses of future earnings or quantitative analyses of uncertainty.

Use of the directions for handling the composition of the portfolio may also cause inconsistency between formulated and realized strategy. A large number of directions are given, and they are often changed at short notice. Some of the directions apply to all customers, for example, that accounts receivable should be evaluated at 60% of their face value, while some guidelines apply to specific trades only. In the present system it is left to the credit consultant to keep track of the current directions and select the set of directions relevant to the various loan applications.

The space for documentation of credit evaluations is restricted in the present system, and the credit manual emphasizes clear conclusions. The effect is that the assumptions and reasons underlying the credit conclusions are not very well documented. Also, the credit documents are filed on paper with the credit consultant. The lack of documentation of the assumptions makes it difficult both for the credit consultant and the organization to learn from past failures. The lack of centralized files makes it difficult for the organization to compare past failures and successes in order to get a better understanding of cause-effect relationships. The corporate database contains data on the yields for each loan and customer. In an ever-changing environment, however, such data may be an inadequate indicator of the quality of a specific credit evaluation process. To analyze cause-effect relationships and understand strengths and weaknesses in the evaluation processes, the assumptions and reasoning of the credit consultant should be compared with the actual developments.

In the design effort, the following aims were emphasized:

- to improve the consistency between the formulated strategy and its implementation;
- to improve the quality of the complex decision-making process; and
- to facilitate individual and organizational learning.

The three dimensions are not independent. Consistency is the primary dimension of our effort. Improving quality and organizational learning should also be consistent with the strategy. In our effort, however, we wanted to draw the bank managers' attention to the potential of information systems that is not considered in the present strategy, and not exploited in the current information systems. This part of our design effort can be regarded as an example of business process redesign with information technology (Davenport & Short, 1990).

Figure 1 shows the components of the new prototype system for credit evaluation. The present corporate database is linked to decision support systems at each organizational level. The decision support systems at each level are tailor-made to support the decision processes at that level. In the prototype version we focus on the decision support systems for credit evaluation and on the linkage of this decision support systems to strategy through the Management Control Variables.

The strategy for the credit evaluation activity is described in two sets of documents; directions for handling changing environments and procedures for credit evaluation and control processes. The two sets of documents are reflected in two different components of our system: a coordination component for communication of directions for handling the environment (management control variables), and the decision support systems for credit evaluation and credit decisions reflecting the procedures for credit evaluation and control. Support of organizational learning is implemented through a document base. Below we will describe these components: [2]

2. The prototype has been built using a spreadsheet package. The system is screen-oriented: displays are formatted to match the screen, and each display is organized so that it contains a logical unit of data. The user leafs among the screen pages by selection from a menu, but there is also the possibility for using relative paging commands.

Figure 1. Components of the new prototype system

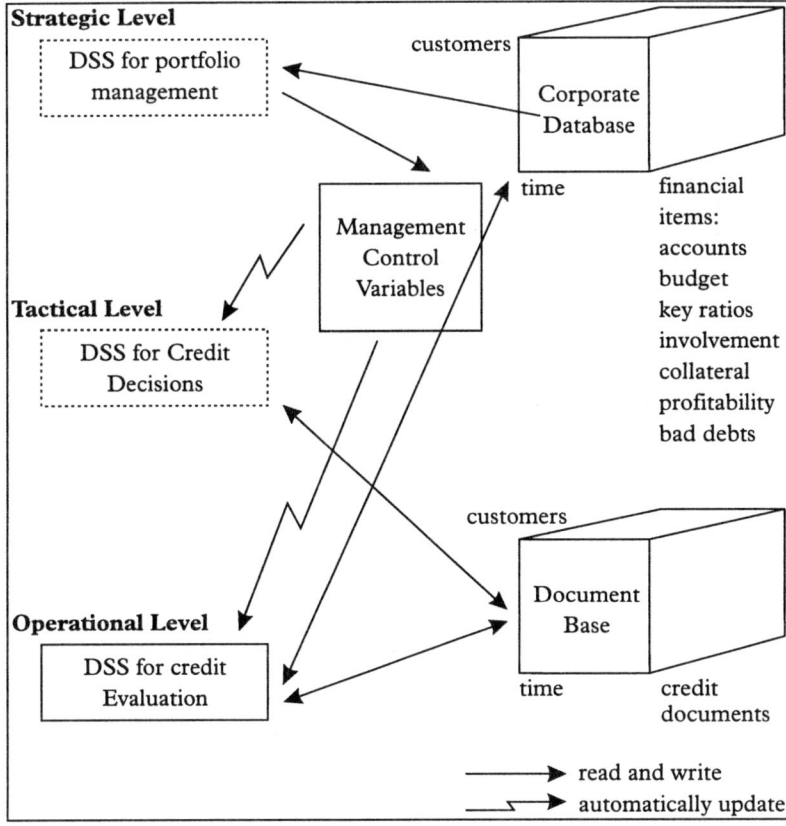

Coordination

The system should be designed so that values of control variables could be changed and forwarded to lower levels at short notice in order to obtain consistency between strategy and performance. This requirement is obtained through the coordination component (management control variables). The coordination component is a screen-oriented spreadsheet application containing the directions for handling the environment. The application contains the current values of the control variables. The control variables are grouped in two categories: general, which apply to all customers, and trade-specific variables.

The coordination component is updated by top management and linked dynamically to the decision support systems at the tactical and operational levels so that changed values are accessed by these decision support systems on activation. Furthermore, the directions for handling the environment are integrated in the system informing the credit consultant which control variables, with accompanying values, should be applied to the loan application under consideration.

In the present system, changes in directions for handling the environment are announced to the credit consultants by ordinary internal mail. One advantage of the coordination component compared with today's procedure is that changes are announced faster, but that could have been handled in the present system by electronic mail. The real advantages of the coordination component are the dynamic link to the credit evaluation decision support systems and the integration of the directions in the system. These qualities ensure that the values of the management control variables are always consistent with organizational strategy, and that all relevant directions are considered.

Credit evaluation

The credit manual describes the procedures to be followed in the implementation and control processes, and structures the credit evaluation process, also emphasizing the items to be included in the credit documents. The present system does not, however, support the credit consultants in their evaluation of the customer's creditworthiness. The quality of the evaluation is dependent on the ability to evaluate the present position and the future performance of the customer. The prototype decision support system illustrates how the computational power and the graphical qualities of a modern personal computer can support credit consultants in their decisions.

From the corporate database, the credit consultants can extract account and budget data. They can also extract data on financial key ratios. In order to support the credit consultants in their evaluation of the present position of the customer, external bench marks for comparison are provided. An example of such bench marks are data for comparing a contracting customer's results with the average results of 50 contracting firms of approximately the same size (sales, number of employees).

According to the credit manual, the future earnings of a customer should be emphasized when evaluating the creditworthiness of the customer. In practice, however, this is not done, mostly because the present information system does not support evaluation of future earnings and mainly focuses on historical data.

In the prototype we designed a screen page for five-year budgets in addition to historical data. In order to support the credit consultant in establishing estimates of future earnings for the customer, trend data were also included. The trend figures serve two purposes: they are useful when discussing future earnings with the customer, in particular when the customer does not deliver budgets, and they may also be useful in the evaluation of the realism of budgetary figures from the customer.

In addition screen displays for a standard set of analyses of the uncertainty of future earnings (what-if and sensitivity analyses, goal-seeking analysis, and analysis of the probability that the company will be put into compulsory liquidation) were implemented.

We have also designed a more formalized credit evaluation process. The new prototype provides a framework for evaluations with text fields for assumptions, reasons, and conclusions. The credit consultants are not allowed to save their credit evaluation as a final credit report until all fields are filled in. If they are unable to fill in certain fields, they must explicitly state why they cannot: for example, that data from the customer are not available. The reason for this pressure is to stimulate reflection, to have more thorough evaluations, and to have better documentation of the evaluations.

Document base

Credit evaluation is a knowledge-intensive process demanding both education and experience in interpreting the customer's data. The prototype system proposes a document base where all documents are filed electronically; in contrast to the present system where all credit reports are filed on paper. The reason for this document base is to stimulate individual and organizational learning. The prototype was designed to stimulate individual learning in two ways: the above-mentioned pressure on the individual credit consultant is an attempt to stimulate reflection, also with the experienced credit consultant. The document base will also serve as an organizational knowledge base that makes it easier for the novice credit consultant to learn from experienced colleagues. The document base facilitates the search for experienced credit consultants' handling of similar cases.

The document base was also designed to stimulate organizational learning. By organizational learning we mean adaptation of goals, environmental attention, and procedures as a function of experience (Cyert & March, 1963). The corporate filing system, together with evaluations which are better documented, make it easier for the organization to learn from past successes and failures, to understand why things went wrong, and what it should have done in order to prevent or repair the damage. The results of such learning would be changes in the values of the management control variables and in the credit evaluation and control procedures.

Discussion

At the outset we argued that information systems can attain the status of valuable secondary, strategic resources. In the case we emphasized the design of a system to improve the consistency between formulated strategy and implementation, the quality of complex decision-making processes, and individual and organizational learning. Table 1 contrasts the present system and the new prototype system.

Inspection of Table 1 reveals that we have attempted to improve the consistency between the formulated strategy and the realized strategy through a system design emphasizing formalization of procedures and coordination between decision levels. The analysis processes have been formalized by the system asking for in-data and calculating and presenting a standard series of analyses of historical accounts and future earnings. The evaluation processes have been formalized by the system specifying in detail which variables must be considered, and demanding that assumptions, reasons, and conclusions must be specified. Improved coordination between top management's adaptation of instructions and the credit consultants' use of these instructions has been designed by integrating the management control variables in the decision support system to support the credit consultants.

The quality of the credit evaluation process is improved by supporting the credit consultants' judgment. The new system offers a better basis for their judgment. Evaluation of the customer's present performance is supported by external benchmarks allowing the consultants to compare their clients with other firms of the same size and in the same line of business. The considerations of future development of a customer's firm are supported by quantitative analyses, allowing the credit consultants to consider not only whether prospects are very good/good,

Table 1. The present and the new prototype systems

	Present system	New prototype
Consistency/ quality	Analysis of historical accounts • detailed guidelines • table presentation	Analysis of historical accounts • formalized process through system design • table presentations • graphic presentations

	Analysis of future earnings
	• no guidelines
	
	• qualitative considerations
	  – one year budget data
		Analysis of future earnings
		• formalized analyses through
		  system design
		• support of quantitative analyses
		  – five year buget data
		  – trend analysis
		  – what if- and sensitivity analysis
		  – goal seeking analysis
		  – indicators of compulsory liquidation

	Evaluation of customer
	• communicatons of Management
	  Control Variables
	• formalized process through
	  system design
	  – pattern for filling in
	    credit documents
	  – text fields of limtied space
	
	• no external benchmarks
		Evaluation of customer
		• integration of Management
		  Control Variables
		• formalized process through
		  system design
		  – pattern for filling in
		    credit documents
		  – text fields for reasons
		  – and assumptions
		  – text fields for conclusions
		  – all fields must be filled in
		• external benchmarks
		  – trade standards

Learning	No support of learning	Stimulation of individual learning
		• formalized process through
		  system design
		  – all text fields must be filled in
		
		Facilitation of organizational learning
		• corporate filling system
		• better documented evaluations

poor/very poor, but to develop an understanding of the uncertainty of the loan project.

Finally, both individual and organizational learning is facilitated and stimulated. Organizational learning is facilitated by a corporate document base that is easy to access and use and includes all credit documents. The improved documentation of the credit evaluation process in the new system makes it possible to compare expectations with actual developments, thereby gaining a better understanding of cause-effect relationships and individual strengths and weaknesses. The prototype also provides an efficient flow of data, which allows consideration of large amounts of data quickly and the ability to share the data efficiently.

Information technology is the technology that makes information systems possible. The information technology used in the proposed prototype is neither rare nor imperfectly imitable. The competitors of the bank may implement the same information technology and use the same system architecture, that is, a corporate database, a coordination component, and decision support systems at each organizational level linked to the database and coordination components. Furthermore, all software packages for the system components can be bought off the shelf. Most of the structure of the prototype may also be imitated, that is, the screen page design, the kinds of analyses, and the integration of control variables.

The content of the prototype, however, is firm-specific: The corporate database contains financial data for the customers of the bank. The decision support system consists of screen pages that reflect the bank's procedures for credit evaluation. The management control variables and the values of these variables depend on the composition of the bank's loan portfolio, and the ability of top management and trade specialists to analyze and evaluate the environment. The relevant external bench marks are dependent on the portfolio of customers.

The above discussion shows that the system has been tailor-made to reflect the strategy of the organization and support a specific decision process. The system is the result of an explicit design process based on an analysis of the decision-making behavior of the organization. The quality of the information systems depends on the quality of the strategy, and it has been designed to reflect strategy. Information systems cannot replace knowledge or human judgment in complex situations. In complex organizational processes the primary potential of competitive advantage is embedded in the knowledge of the organization (Itami & Roehl, 1987). The usefulness of information systems depends on the knowledge for handling the activity in question. However, a firm-specific information system, as in the present case, may improve the performance of the activity in question and, because of facilitating and stimulating learning both at the individual and organizational level, it may also enhance the organizational knowledge accumulation process. Moreover, the firm-specific elements of the proposed information system are almost impossible to imitate successfully. Thus, the designed information system has the potential to become a valuable secondary strategic resource for the organization.

As noted at the outset, few contributions have addressed the question of how information systems may give rise to competitive advantages in management processes. More research, both theoretical and empirical, is needed. In our opinion, future research should focus on the recursive relationship between information systems and information technology and strategy (Davenport & Short, 1990). Thinking about information systems and information technology should be in terms of how such resources may improve the effectiveness of the organization, and thinking of strategy should be in terms of the capabilities that information systems and information technology can provide in knowledge enhancement, improved implementation, as well as exploiting opportunities that would otherwise be impossible.

References

Barney, J. (1991): Firm Resources and Sustained Competitive Advantage. *Journal of Management 17*: 99-120.

Cyert, R.M. & J.G. March (1963): *A Behavioral Theory of the Firm*. Englewood Cliffs, NJ: Prentice-Hall.

Daft, R. (1983): *Organization Theory and Design*. New York: West.

Davenport, T. & J. Short (1990): The New Industrial Engineering: Information Technology and Business Process Redesign. *Sloan Management Review, Summer*: 11-27.

Drucker, P.F. (1973): *Management, Tasks, Responsibilities, Practices*. New York: Harper and Row.

Eliasson, G. (1990): The Firm as a Competent Team. *Journal of Economic Behavior and Organization 13*: 275-289.

Fuglseth, A.M. (1989): *Decision Support: Method for Diagnosis of Managerial Information and Situation Perceptions*. Dissertation (in Norwegian). Bergen: Norwegian School of Economics and Business Administration.

Grønhaug, K. (1989): Strategy: Idea, Concretion, and Implementation (in Norwegian). In T. Reve & K. Grønhaug (eds.): *Strategy and organization:* 30-47. Oslo: TANO.

Hammer, M. (1990): Reengineering Work: Don't Automate, Obliterate, *Harvard Business Review July-August:* 104-112.

Itami, H. & T.W. Roehl (1987): *Mobilizing Invisible Assets*. Cambridge, MA: Harvard University Press.

Keen, P. & M.S. Scott Morton (1978): *Decision Support Systems: An Organizational Perspective*. Reading, MA: Addison-Wesley.

Mintzberg, H. (1987): The Strategy Concept (I+II). *California Management Review 30*: 11-52.

Porter, M.E. (1985): *Competitive Advantage*. New York: The Free Press.

Porter, M.E. & V.E. Millar (1985): How Information Gives You Competitive Advantage. *Harvard Business Review, July-August*, 149-160.

Simon, H.A. (1977): *The New Science of Management Decision*. Englewood Cliffs, NJ: Prentice-Hall.

Steffensen, E. & E. Steigum (1990): «The Business Cycle and the Bank Crisis» (in Norwegian), Working paper no. 1/1990. Bergen: Center for Research in Economics and Business Administration.

Wernerfeldt, B. (1984): A Resource Based View of the Firm. *Strategic Management Journal 5*: 171-180.

Escaping the Iron Cage: Where it Goes and What it Takes

Martin Gjelsvik

The purpose of this paper is to investigate how a firm in a highly institutionalized market may develop resources and capabilities as a foundation for sustainable competitive advantage. In these markets firms are characterized by isomorphism, and we expect that firms competing in such markets will have difficulty in elaborating and maintaining sustainable competitive advantages.

Resource-based theory implies that firms are able to develop and sustain heterogeneous resources as a basis for competitive advantage. Survival is based on differential positions and internal resources. Competitive forces and isomorphic pressure will both countervail those efforts. Will organizations in these environments succeed in developing and sustaining heterogeneous resources and differential competitive positions, or are they doomed to enter the iron cage?[1]

The paper uses elements of institutional theory to explicate relevant aspects of the functioning of financial markets and their environments. It then draws heavily on resource-based theory to explain how firms in institutionalized environments can develop and utilize internal competence as a basis for sustainable competitive advantage. Resource-based theory is thus brought into a well-defined environmental context. The paper rests upon an analysis of a specific field study. If a resource-based view of strategy can explain how firms may viably differentiate in highly institutionalized markets, that theory passes an important test.

The paper begins by discussing the conditions of firms in a highly institutionalized market. We then discuss possible competitive strategies for change to overcome competitive and isomorphic pressure by drawing heavily on resource-based perspectives. Our example is drawn from

---

1. Max Weber claimed that under capitalism, the rationalist order had become an iron cage in which humanity was imprisoned (Weber, 1952: 181-182). Bureaucracy, the rational spirit's organizational manifestation, was so efficient and powerful that, once established, the momentum of bureaucratization was irreversible.

the banking industry, specifically Norwegian savings banks. The reason is straightforward: the banking industry is embedded in a highly institutionalized environment and is known to strive vigorously to gain new market shares, with only modest and short-lived success. The intent of this paper is to help practitioners in this field to better appreciate the more intangible and invisible resources they command.

Institutional theory

The foundation for institutional theory was made by Selznick (1949, 1957). He argued that organizational rationality is constrained by «the recalcitrance of the tools of action», and that organizational procedures become valued as ends in themselves (1949: 253-259). An organization becomes institutionalized as it is «infused with value beyond the technical requirements of the task at hand» (1957: 17). Managers of organizations employ co-option as their strategy to obtain legitimacy and support. Co-option is a mechanism by which external elements are incorporated into the decision-making process of an organization. Contemporary efforts towards the further development of the theory rest on the foundation built by the sociologist Peter Berger. His most comprehensive body of ideas is to be found in his work with Luckmann (Berger & Luckman, 1967). They argue that social reality is a human construction created by social interaction. The process by which actions are repeated and given similar meaning by oneself and others is defined as institutionalization. These ideas were introduced to the theory of organizations at the micro level, but were later brought up to a macro level. It is noteworthy that Berger argues that the very concept of bureaucracy is a meta-institution, which depicts in a generalized manner a portrait of orderliness, predictability and, in its emphasis on the formalization of relations, moralized anonymity. Zucker has pursued and elaborated this theme, arguing that «organizations are the pre-eminent institutional form in modern society» (Zucker, 1983).

This paper uses the term organizational field. It is defined as «those organizations that, in the aggregate, constitute a recognized area of institutional life: key suppliers, resource and product consumers, regulatory agencies and other organizations that produce similar services and products» (DiMaggio & Powell, 1983: 148). Once disparate organizations in the same line of business are structured into an actual field, powerful forces emerge that lead them to become more similar to one another. Organizations may change their goals or develop new practices and new organizations enter the field. In the long term, however, organizational actors making rational decisions construct around themselves an environment that constrains their ability to change further in later years (DiMaggio & Powell, 1983). As an innovation spreads, a threshold is reached beyond which adoption provides legitimacy rather than improved performance (Meyer & Rowan, 1977).

Isomorphism has been introduced as a mundane term to describe the homogenization of firms. Hawley (1968) defines the term as «a constraining process that forces one unit in a population to resemble other units that face the same set of environmental conditions». As suggested in the introduction, two main types of isomorphism coexist: competitive and institutional. Competitive isomorphism assumes efficiency and economizing efforts by managers in fields with predominantly free and open competition. Firms compete not only for resources and customers, but for trust, influence and legitimacy as well. Thus, DiMaggio and Powell (1983) claim that institutional isomorphism is a useful tool for understanding the politics and ceremony that pervade much modern organizational life. They identify three mechanisms of institutional isomorphic change:

- coercive isomorphism that stems from political influence and the problem of legitimacy;
- mimetic isomorphism resulting from standard responses to uncertainty; and
- normative isomorphism, associated with professionalism.

Organizational fields can be recognized by density of interaction, information flows, and the fact that members identify themselves with the field. Suppliers of products and services that meet the same needs and demands as the object of study should be included as competitors. The virtue of this unit of analysis is its ability to include all relevant actors. It directs our attention not only to competing firms, as does the population approach of Hannan & Freeman (1977), or to networks of organizations that actually interact, as does the interorganizational network approach of Laumann, Galaskiewicz & Marsden (1978), but to the totality of relevant actors. The term organizational field includes both connectedness (the existence of transactions tying organizations to one another: such transactions might include formal contractual relationships, participation of personnel in common enterprises such as professional associations, labor unions, or boards of directors) (Laumann, Ga laskiewicz & Marsden, 1978) as well as structural equivalence (similarity of position in a network structure) (White, Boorman & Breiger, 1976).

Competitive isomorphism is associated with technical environments, a term that may be defined as «those in which a product or service is produced and exchanged in a market such that organizations are rewarded for effective and efficient control of their production systems» (Scott & Meyer, 1983). Organizations adopt efficient structures and practices or risk defeat by relatively better-adapted rivals. Institutional environments are characterized by the elaboration of rules and requirements to which individual organizations must conform if they are to receive support and legitimacy. The requirements may stem from regulatory agencies, from professional or trade associations, and from generalized belief systems that define how specific types of organizations are to conduct themselves (Meyer & Rowan, 1977). Organizations in a common institutional environment begin to look like each other as they respond to similar regulatory and normative pressures, or as they copy structures adopted by successful organizations under conditions of uncertainty (Orrù, Biggart & Hamilton, 1991).

We claim that banks find themselves in highly institutionalized and technical environments. In a seminal article, Scott & Meyer (1987) combine them (Table 1).

Table 1. Combining technical and institutional environments

		Institutional environments	
		Stronger	Weaker
Technical environments	Stronger	banks, airlines	general manufacturing
	Weaker	schools, legal agencies	restaurants

Resource-based theory

In the section above, we argued that banks find themselves in environments of competitive as well as institutional forces. The competitive forces compel banks to economize on their resources. To survive, their behavior must be compatible with the efficient and effective use of resources and capabilities, which is the starting-point for a resource-based approach to strategic management. Resource-based strategy focuses on costly-to-copy attributes of the firm as sources of economic rent. These attributes are the fundamental drivers of performance and competitive advantage (Barney, 1986; Rumelt, 1987). According to this perspective, an organization's ability to attain viable market positions depends on its ability to develop and maintain advantageous positions in underlying resources important to production and distribution.

Traditionally, strategy and resource-based theory are discussed separately. Strategy is carried out to develop and sustain competitive advantage through a unique and nonimitable product/market mix. The resource-based theory posits that the firm's resources are unique. However, in the service industry, it is often impossible to separate the two. The literature on the service industries claims that the employees (a resource) are part of the perceived product. In the banking industry it holds true that the quality of the customer representatives determines the quality of the product. Although conceptually and theoretically separable, in practical life we agree with Wernerfelt (1984) that «for the firm, resources and products are two sides of the same coin». (p. 171).

Heterogeneous resources in firms are a core premise for resource-based theory. On the basis of our above discussion, where we posit that banks are subject to strong isomorphic competitive and institutional processes of change, it may seem contradictory to rely upon resource-based theory. However, our intention is to spell out how organizations in this environmental setting may escape isomorphism. Our purpose is to investigate how firms may succeed in creating sustainable competitive advantages in an environment pressing for homogeneous products, structures and technologies. The theory is therefore beneficial; even more so than Porter's (1980) general, generic strategies.

How do we define resources? Daft (1983) includes all assets, capabilities, processes, attributes, information and knowledge controlled by a firm that enable the firm to understand and implement strategies that improve its efficiency and effectiveness. Barney (1991) makes these distinctions:

- *Physical capital resources.* Physical technology, plant and equipment, geographic location, access to raw materials.

- *Human capital.* Training, experience, judgment, intelligence, relationships, and insight of individual managers and employees.

- *Organizational capital.* Formal reporting structure, formal and informal planning, controlling and coordinating systems, informal relations among groups within a firm and between the firm and those in its environment.

This list is not complete. Grant (1991) has added intangible resources such as reputation, brand knowledge and goodwill. In an empirical study in England, Hall (1992) finds that firm and product reputation seem to be the primary intangible resources contributing to a firm's success.

Not all resources are of equal strategic importance. Some resources may even put constraints on a firm's ability to attain its goals. Examples are a historically contingent poor location or an unhappy composition of the management team. Other resources may prove to be neutral in relation to competitive advantage because they are homogeneous or tradable. Resources become of strategic relevance and importance when they enable a firm to conceive of and implement strategies that improve its efficiency and effectiveness, thereby creating value to customers.

What do we mean by stating that some resources are attributes of sustainable competitive advantage? Barney (1991) posits that a competitive position is sustained only if it still exists after attempts to duplicate it have come to a halt. That definition is misleading, because its implicit premise is that of rational actors and full information. In practical life, firm A may not have complete knowledge of firm B's resources because of limited access to information or limited capacity to handle information. At the end of the day, a firm possesses competitive advantages to the extent that they sustain a value-creating strategy that, in turn, produces added value (for example, rent) compared with its competitors. Contrary to Barney's definition, such a conception lends itself to operationalization.

Resource-based theory may explain lasting differences between firms that cannot be ascribed to the actual industry. The need to explain these differences at a firm level is well documented (Rumelt, 1991; Hansen & Wernerfelt, 1989). The theory may also help practitioners to identify resources at home base as a viable foundation for developing competitive advantage, resources of which they are aware. Advantageous positions based on history, luck and other accidental circumstances may be further developed through more conscious and goal-oriented processes. Measures to protect existing positions are also of vital importance. This is particularly evident for resource combinations and intangible resources that are not valued in formal reports or profit and loss statements. Barney (1986) argues that firms may achieve exceptional advantages by analyzing existing assets.

Access to special resources in a firm may constitute a foundation for cost leadership as well as differentiated products. In other words, resource-based theory may be of service in the analysis of both input and output markets. It is appropriate for our purpose to make use of Rumelt's (1987) isolating mechanisms. These mechanisms protect individual firms from imitation and preserve their income streams.

According to Rumelt the firm's mission is to capture and protect an extra entrepreneurial rent. Property rights are vital, but numerous innovations are not susceptible to protection by that mechanism. Rumelt introduces the term quasi-rights, which he relates to lags, information asymmetry and friction. There is no unambiguous, mutually exclusive list of isolating mechanisms.

Rumelt's suggestions are as follows:

- *Information impactedness.* Innovators can inhibit effective imitation when they can prevent potential competitors from obtaining the knowledge gained from successful operations, either through conscious secrecy or tacit knowledge. The latter implies that the firm itself does not know the causes of success.

- *Response lags.* Competitors may be slow in responding to an innovator due to the time it takes for competitors to recognize, evaluate, and formulate a response to the innovation. Competitors may also be unwilling to cannibalize existing high-rent business by offering competing substitutions.

- *Economies of scale.* Traditional entry barriers may occur if the minimum efficient scale of a business is comparable to the size of the market, and if the assets required are specialized to this use.

- *Producer learning.* The producer becomes more efficient as experience is gained. The experience is cumulative, and a first mover may gain a lasting edge if the organization has developed an efficient internal climate for learning.

- *Buyer switching costs.* This phenomenon is particularly relevant in markets known to have large switching costs, and where search or evaluation costs are high, or buyers invest substantial specialized human capital in learning how to use or consume the product.

- *Reputation.* Many products, and services in particular, cannot be accurately evaluated by buyers until after they have been purchased and used. As Klein & Leffler (1981) show, a producer's ability to sell high quality versions of such experience goods depends on its reputation. To the extent that buyers' beliefs about reputation depend on the length of time the product or service has operated reputably, first movers can obtain advantages.

- *Communication good effects.* Some products and services increase in value as the number of adopters or users increases. Conner & Rumelt (1986) term these communication goods. The effect arises because the product serves as a means of social coordination (standardization) or because a larger base attracts a larger number of complementary goods. The upshot is the *de facto* standard, where a particular brand or manufacturer's product becomes the means of coordination. These competitive positions are very powerful and offer the promise of large entrepreneurial rents.

The ATM card may serve as an example. The benefit of the card is greatly enhanced by the number of places it may be used: for example, number of ATMs, EFTPOS terminals at filling stations and retail stores, etc. The proliferation of cards grew rapidly with the diffusion of easy-to-use EFTPOS terminals in Norway.

- *Buyer evaluation costs.* As buyers face increasing problems in evaluating competing products, they seek ways of economizing on evaluation costs. The most common tactic is to free-ride on presumed analyses of the well informed and to buy the market leader. Such behavior provides advantages to the market leader as long as the follower's product or service is not significantly better.

- *Advertising and channel crowding.* Early entrants into a market sometimes face less crowded advertising message spaces and distribution channels. This asymmetry allows an early entrant to build customer awareness less expensively than later entrants.

We have now presented the two strands of theory, which are summarized in Figure 1.

Figure 1. The relationship between resources, institutional and competitive pressure and competitive advantage

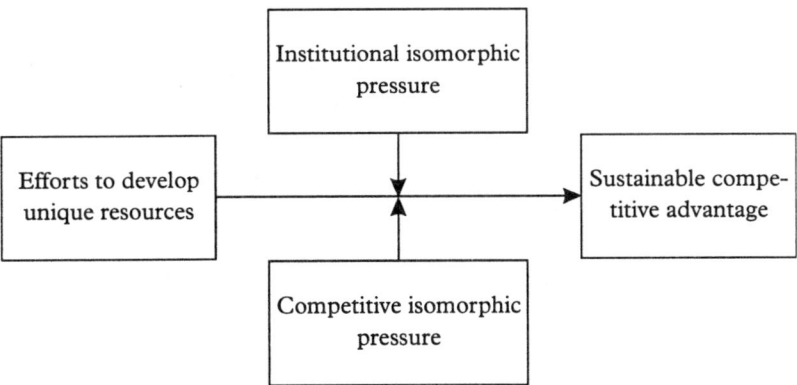

Organizations and their managers will make continuous efforts to develop unique resources to achieve entrepreneurial rent through sustainable competitive advantage. Some efforts succeed, others fail. Success is enjoyed to the extent the organization manages to escape the institutional and competitive isomorphic pressures. In the next sections we investigate the contingencies and processes available for managers to escape from this iron cage. Before doing so, we need to introduce our players: the Norwegian savings banks.

The playing field

Empirical studies of highly institutionalized environments are mainly focused on the non-private sector. In this study we focus on an industry where the survival of the firms is contingent not only on efficiency, but on the adaptation to the constraints of institutionalized factors and claims. In this organizational field we will not only study the influence of the state, which has been the common focus, but membership of various associations common to Norwegian savings banks. These organizations and associations play a dominant role in the isomorphic process of change. In the Norwegian market, commercial and savings banks are very similar. Consequently, the terms savings banks and banks may be used interchangeably. The two banking groups operate in the same markets, ingratiate themselves with the same customers and are supervised by the same state agency (Kredittilsynet). They do, however, have a somewhat different ownership and governing structure. As in some other European countries, the savings banks have a very strong domestic position.

The primary role of banks is to mediate resources from savers to borrowers. In this respect we may say that the market is homogeneous with banks as price takers. In the long run, it can be argued, banks with superior cost efficiency will survive in a deregulated market. However, the real world is more complicated. In the service sector, the premise of a homogeneous market excludes the submerged part of the iceberg. Building lasting and stable relationships with your customers requires differential, internal capabilities.

The organizational field of Norwegian Savings Banks is illustrated in Figure 2:

Figure 2. The organizational field of Norwegian savings banks

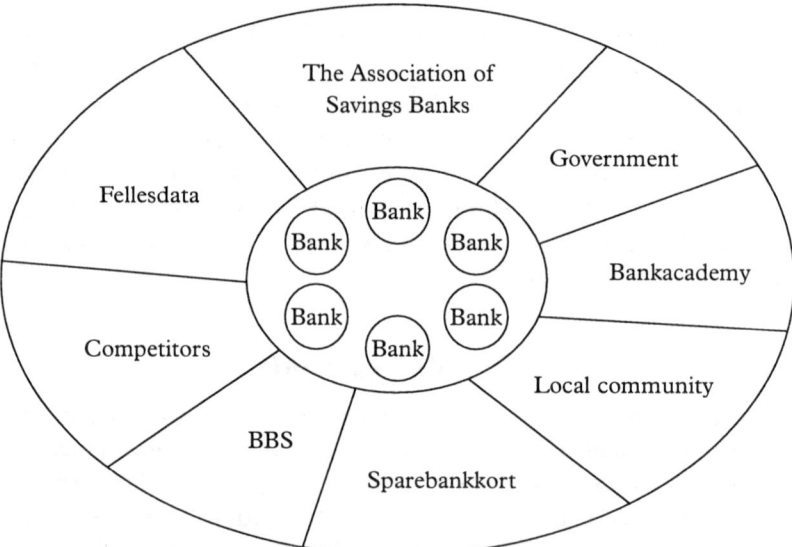

The financial markets are highly institutionalized. Legal requirements are numerous and constrain the banks' options for competitive action. Central areas such as equity ratios, ownership, assets investments and organizational forms are all subject to regulation. The banks' participation in more or less voluntary joint associations is another important –

and underestimated – constraining factor. For example, the ability to differentiate products is substantially curtailed by membership of the BBS (the banks' payment system that regulates all payment transactions between banks), Fellesdata (joint computer company) and Sparebankkort (the savings banks' joint debit and credit card company). Most attempts to differentiate products can therefore easily be copied.

The Association of Savings Banks

All Norwegian savings banks are members of the Association of Savings Banks in Norway. The association advocates the interests of the savings banks industry. It handles the relationship between the industry and the government, interpreting and monitoring weak and strong signals from relevant actors and bodies in the political environment (for example, the Parliament, the Central Bank, and other regulatory authorities).

The association represents a common normative order, and the savings banks have traditionally complied loyally with its recommendations. To some extent, the association takes on a role as an extension and interpreter of the state's jurisdiction, including the distribution of legitimacy on behalf of the authorities. The banks are awarded legitimacy and trust in exchange for loyal behavior.

Organizations' conformity to a common normative order increases and secures societal resources and long-term survival (Meyer & Rowan, 1977). We should therefore expect that banks would comply with the statements and the normatively stronger recommendations of the Savings Banks Association. In addition, a large number of savings banks demonstrate a strong feeling of belonging to the savings bank system. Against this background it might be expected that savings banks would go through parallel processes of change. However, savings banks are, in fact, not identical, but they do look alike from a general outsider's point of view. In the same sense as we discussed bureaucracy as a metaphor, we may interpret bank as a meta-term.

Legal requirements

The savings banks are regulated by the Savings Banks Act. This act constrains the savings banks, as well as granting some privileges such as the right to carry out certain banking activities, for example, to accept deposits from the general public. In addition, savings banks are subject to regulation under other acts. The act lays the foundation for the savings banks to develop into full-service financial institutions. In Norway there are only minor differences between commercial and savings banks. Apart from their disparate form of ownership, the differences are negligible.

The Financial Activities and Institutions Act is of great relevance, as it regulates future trends in the financial services market such as holding companies comprising both bank and insurance companies. The latter was revised at the end of 1991 to facilitate procedures for concession, organizational structure, transactions and consolidation. We will not go into details of regulation, but the various acts put severe constraints on existing activities as well as future diversification trends through financial holding companies.

Payments transaction

The transmissions of the customers' and the banks' payment transactions are carried out through a national network. Standardization of the network has been accomplished by means of BUS (the Banks' Development Company). Traditionally, the transaction medium has been the organizing unit: BBS has taken care of the paper-based transactions and the computer companies the electronic ones. This distinction is being blurred, however, because BBS, partly to rationalize its own operations, partly to expand its line of business, now offers electronically based products (for example, autogiro).

According to figures from the Association of Savings Banks, the operation of payment transactions is responsible for a large part of a bank's resources. They indicate that 40% of the costs are tied to payment transaction activities. The development of improved procedures and new products is arranged through BBS, if necessary in collaboration with the computer companies (Fellesdata and Nordata).

As a coordination mechanism for commercial and savings banks, BBS's sphere of influence is expanding. As already mentioned, a new company was recently established, BankAxept, to coordinate and operate the banks' card products. The company is organized as a subsidiary of BBS. The third bank group, the Post Bank, runs its own payment network. The two networks are to some extent connected, as customers can pay their bank giros in the post offices and vice versa. For years, state agencies have pressed for an integration of the two networks. Most likely, an integration will eventually result as a consequence of the deregulation of the Post Bank, in which process all services must be priced so as to recover the costs incurred.

For payments transactions, another important fee and income generator, we may conclude as for products: standardization across bank groups will increase rather than diminish, with greater isomorphic institutional change as the likely result.

Employees

To a large extent, bank employees share the same educational background from the Bank Academy (an industry-wide joint company). The banks have, in association with the employees' organizations, facilitated basic banking education as well as more advanced formal training. Through centrally arranged agreements, employees have a right to study within a defined number of office hours. To a large extent an internal labor market has developed within the banking industry and in the various banks.

Within the banks, where size permits, great efforts have been made to develop internal career paths, thus ruling out the recruitment of employees with a radically different background. The employees' own organizations (the unions) have been extremely skeptical about outsiders. The supply of new and different talents has been minimal. Mainly to secure legitimacy and harmony in the work place, the savings banks have agreed to minimize external recruitment. Entry has been very hard for potential employees external to the organizational field.

This process holds true for bank managers as well. In small and medium-sized savings banks, the career path for managers has been through the Bank Academy. Recently, however, there has been a growing tendency to recruit bank managers externally. Traditional manufacturing industries have been among the suppliers. There is reason to believe that new viewpoints will penetrate and permeate the banking organizations. Fresh (to banking) models and world views will be imported, and will challenge the conservative bank culture. At this point in time, one can only speculate on probable consequences. Organizations permeated by institutionalized rules, procedures and norms are hard to change. Even new managers will relate to influential and conservative formal and informal networks that will affect their strategic thinking.

Nearly all (96-97%) bank employees are organized in the Union of the Financial Services. The union exerts its influence, but in a somewhat subtler, less vociferous, way than in manufacturing industries. A core competitive element, the banks' opening hours, is regulated by centrally negotiated agreements between the union and the bank employers' association. The agreements are based on a typical Scandinavian industrial-democracy model.

Comprehensive systems, such as deposits, loans and internal and external accounting, are all developed by Fellesdata. As a rule, the training of procedural skills is arranged by BBS or the joint computer companies, that is from those who developed the routines. The training is technically oriented, and not adjusted to possible local organizational needs. Through this standardized training, the employees will eventually interpret the meaning of the system in a common manner. This way of organizing training will constrain the employees' cognitive processes. If we accept that bank employees have similar backgrounds and formal education from the outset, the common training and implementation of identical procedures surely will cement these traits.

Product development

Organizations embedded in an institutional context are subject to isomorphic pressure. DiMaggio and Powell (1983) have identified three mechanisms leading to isomorphism: coercion, imitation and normative pressure. In our case, all of these processes are prevalent. The regulatory bodies exert coercive power, the Association of Savings Banks normative power and even imitative pressure. Norms are prevalent in the networks of managers, and banks openly copy products and organizational structures and technologies from each other.

However, none of this prohibits the banks from developing proprietary products. The banks always face the possibility of intense imitation of the products' technical and tangible attributes. In that respect there is hardly any difference between banks and other firms in the service industries. The prospects of local product development, however, are further restricted by the fact that innovations as a rule are advanced in cooperation with joint computer companies or other collaborating companies. This brings up another important institutionalizing sphere: the banks' collectively owned companies.

The savings banks are connected to one of two competing computer companies: Fellesdata or Nordata. The former is wholly owned by the savings banks. Representatives of these banks are members of the board of directors, together with the manager of the Association of Savings Banks. The vast majority of the savings banks are connected to Fellesdata.

Regardless of their data connection, the banks' dependence on them in their product development cannot be over-exaggerated. There is good reason to express this view even more strongly: much product development in the 1970s and 1980s was technology-driven, particularly in Fellesdata. ATMs, EFTPOS terminals at filling stations and retail stores, and home banking concepts, are examples. At the outset, these product categories were identical for all savings banks connected to Fellesdata. They were important innovations; banking became more convenient for the customers, the new services generated income (fees) for the banks and the technology was cost-effective as the need for personnel was reduced.

For our thesis the following is highly noteworthy: the savings banks were the first to develop and commercialize these innovations. The commercial banks tried hard to copy or develop similar products – and succeeded – after a time lag of 1-2 years. In Norway, plastic cards used in ATMs and various other terminals are based on local, Norwegian standards. Contrary to most other countries, debit cards dominate the market. With debit cards, withdrawals are deducted from an account instantaneously, as opposed to a credit card, where the customer is billed later. Most Norwegians have a wage account with a bank into which the salary is automatically transferred. The domestic market is too small to sustain differentiated, proprietary card technologies. State agencies have put extensive coercive pressure on banks to coordinate their technologies in this field and even demanded that the state-owned Post Bank be let into the same network of terminals, a prime example of institutional isomorphic pressure in this organizational field.

Furthermore, banks are all connected to a national infrastructure. Long-lasting normative pressure from the Central Bank and the authorities to coordinate these services (between commercial, postal and savings banks) have also played a major role. Newly established banks are allowed to enter this network by paying a fee. The costs of alternative developments have been prohibitive.

The savings banks' efforts to gain competitive advantage in the period 1977-1987 are instructive. The intention was to establish, elaborate and sustain competitive advantages in electronic payments' transmissions. Thus, the savings banks were first to the market with ATMs and EFTPOS terminals at filling stations and retail stores. The group of savings banks and the commercial banks invested in a disparate infrastructure. The savings banks stuck to their magnetic strip technology, whereas the commercial banks leap-frogged to so-called smart card technology (based on a chip technology). These investments were intolerably high. Under the present circumstances, this strategy has been abandoned. The development and implementation of common, standardized procedures is secured through a newly formed joint venture (BankAxept, a subsidiary of BBS).

It is worth elaborating somewhat on the income-generating function of cards and card-based product innovations. The income generated is in the form of fees. Most income in banks is interest, the net interest margin being the major source of profit. Interest rates are very volatile, and thus represent an unstable and, importantly, unpredictable income stream. In recent years banks have fought tough battles with their customers to gain acceptance for fee-based products. Fees are a more predictable and steady source of income. Uncertainty is reduced as banks become less vulnerable to changes in the interest level and the variable institutional regimes of interest fixation. The basis for fees, this increasingly important income generator, is becoming standardized in the organizational field of the banking industry, thus seriously constraining the potential for discriminating income streams. Not competitive, but institutional forces limit the possibilities for building competitive advantage.

The same argument goes for cost efficiency. Cost reductions are being realized by replacing manual and costly services and procedures with electronically based activities and products. However, technology and procedures are being standardized across banks and banking groups. To a large extent, they are also implemented in the same fashion and at the same time. Again, the potential for differential cost reductions is being hampered by isomorphic change processes. A potential differentiation is attainable by adding different services to the bank cards. However, in practice this is ruled out. The cards have an international and close connection with either VISA or the Eurocard system. This implies a series of constraints to the banks' choices. Secondly, the savings banks have chosen to develop their card products through a shared effort in Sparebankkort, a company wholly owned by the savings banks. Recently, the savings and commercial banks have joined forces in a new jointly owned company for future development of card and terminal technology.

In developing the loan and deposits products, the computer companies again are playing a decisive role. Proprietary development has been blocked because all programming has to be carried out in Fellesdata subject to their priorities. It is problematic for an individual bank to establish an alternative list of priorities. The organizing principles of data, formatting and programming language, are elements constraining radically new solutions. One example may be illuminating: a bank wanted to develop a deposit product with appeal to the family, and demanded that the interest be calculated on an accumulative basis. This turned out to be impossible as the data was grouped around an account concept, not a customer concept.

Tangible products in banks are similar, often identical. Original and successful innovations are open to imitation.

A model for sustainable competitive advantage

Some organizations present themselves as meta-institutions. We have suggested that bureaucracy and banks both qualify for that tag. The environment's expectations of a bank are almost identical. These expectations represent a common public image of the bank that helps the customers to understand what a bank may offer. In addition, this public image helps the employees and the managers in the banking industry to identify with the industry and its organizations. In other words, a bank is a bank is a bank. Individual perceptions of a bank display minor deviations. The banking industry is perceived as one category. An organization's image and identity guide and activate individuals' interpretations of them, and those interpretations and motivations affect patterns of organizational action over time (Dutton & Dukerich, 1991). An example of the strength of this identification process is the fact that leading banks have established identical goals for the development of costs. The common goal of the dominant banks in the industry is that operating costs are not allowed to exceed 50% of the sum of the net interest margin and other income (for example, fees and commissions).

The institutional theory of organizations recognizes that not all firms in an industry have the same structure. Some firms have the ability to withstand pressure because they were established under different conditions. Organizations tend to become what they are. A new company will put to use the prevailing technology and organizational forms and strategies at the time of establishment. This imprinting remains as a dominant feature throughout the firm's lifetime, which explains why newly established banks may have competitive advantages, either cost leadership or differentiation, as opposed to the established banks. Having defined their market segments, new banks may invest in the latest technology, marketing tools and systems for credit evaluation. Banks establishing themselves today, decide on strategies and methods acceptable and adjusted to present sentiments. For example, it is acceptable for a new bank to charge fees for payment transactions. When well-established banks made such attempts, there was a vast public outcry. The public expects banks to act as they always have.

A bank needs to break through this general public perception in order to differentiate itself successfully. Indeed, even if a bank on an objective, factual basis should differentiate, it is not an easy task to communicate this to the customers and the public at large because the general perceptions of bank are universal.

Above, we have posited that banks are subject to strong institutionalized pressure from many quarters: the authorities, the Association of Savings Banks, joint companies, employees and customers. These groups act as agents to influence the bank through direct and indirect processes such as normative strain, as suppliers of standard operational procedures, products and educational programmes. All organizational levels are thus affected.

In addition to the tangible product or procedure, the joint companies offer legitimacy and trust as well, which is being marketed strongly in relation to the banks. A reciprocal legitimizing process takes place. On their side, the joint companies emphasize the true collaboration with the banks in the development process. To achieve legitimacy in a cost-effective way, the joint company will ensure that the participation from the banks is representative, consisting of participants which enjoy a high status in the banks. To sum up: the joint company acts as a guarantor for the new products.

These jointly owned companies act very differently, however, from those intermediaries Zucker has in mind: «Intermediaries smooth transactions via a quasi-insurance of completion without opportunism or malfeasance by focusing on the transaction itself and remaining indifferent to the outcome» (Zucker, 1986). In our case the joint companies take a great interest in the outcomes and tend to behave opportunistically. These companies are interested in retaining their monopoly role in relation to the savings banks. As part of deregulation, independent competitors are making efforts to enter the organizational field, and thereby gaining access to the savings banks as potential suppliers.

To escape isomorphic features, a savings bank could find other partners to develop products and procedures. The joint companies' role as guarantor and supplier of legitimacy will increase considerably the transactions costs connected to such attempts. The fact that alternative suppliers do exist will in itself result in efficiency improvements in the joint companies.

Nevertheless, the banks may conceive of themselves somewhat differently. The recruitment of non-bankers, access to literature and professional journals, conferences and external consultants, are all elements meant to differentiate the competence and world views of the bank managers. For obvious reasons banks can be conceived of as service companies wishing to develop and sustain long-term relations with profitable market segments. Within such a conceptualization of business strategy, the establishment of customer loyalty is a vital and decisive task. A bank will therefore enhance its potential to survive to the extent that the communication process between the bank and its customers can be understood and utilized efficiently. A bank needs to learn how to use this communication process optimally, partly by discovering and interpreting the customers' needs, partly by increasing the sales of products and services. The organization needs to facilitate internal learning, establish knowledge structures among those organizational memories, in order to disseminate knowledge to the participants in the organization and to customers.

In a highly institutionalized market permeated by stringent isomorphic forces of change, a single one of these elements will not suffice to create and sustain a competitive position (Figure 3). Several elements

Figure 3. Model for sustainable competitive advantage

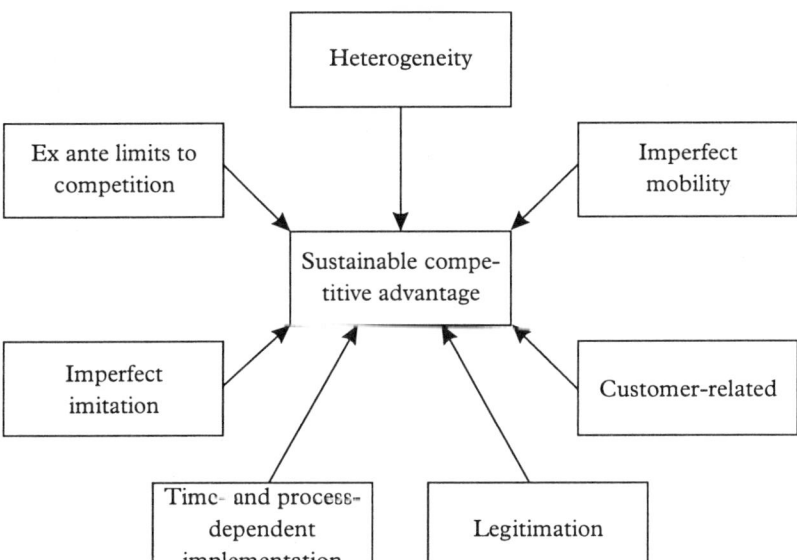

must work together for mutual reinforcement and elaboration. Our purpose is to present a prescriptive model for a bank by including two perspectives:

- Banks operate in an institutionalized environment.
- Banking is a service industry.

Heterogeneous resources

As already stated, the basic assumption of resource-based theory is that the resources underlying production are heterogeneous across the relevant firms (Barney, 1991). Rumelt (1974) states that «a firm's competitive position is defined by a bundle of unique resources and relations». Heterogeneity is a necessary, but not sufficient condition. This is particularly true in banking for several reasons; the isomorphic pressure for change will tend to mold resources into homogeneous categories, which implies that *ex ante* heterogeneous resources must be consciously elaborated to be sustained.

The bank management's conceptualization of what they actually offer their customers is also of vital importance. If that conceptualization is limited to «transmission of money and payment transactions», the product will be conceived of as being homogeneous among competitors. If the mission is to «offer our customer peace-of-mind in all financial issues», the perspective is expanded in many directions. Such a conceptualization implies a much more comprehensive bundle of essential resources, not least human and organizational capabilities. All consultancy should be individually adjusted and performed. Part of the service design will take place in a joint effort between bank and customer.

This broad perspective opens up the possibility of the employment of resource-based development strategies. First-mover advantages and entrance barriers depend on the deployment of heterogeneous resources.

Imperfect imitation

The heterogeneity will be short-lived if the resources lend themselves to easy and rapid copying or imitation. By borrowing Rumelt's (1987) terms, information impactedness and response lags, we can explain why innovations are not copied or imitated, at least in the first place.

For managers bombarded with information in their daily work, what competitors do may actually escape their notice. In today's financial market there is hefty competition for the best customers. An interest offer, which evidently is easily copied, may remain secret from competitors if it is not made public. Some banks have embarked on this tactic by offering their superior customers so-called drawer-products. Sometimes, but not always, the competitor banks may be notified by customers playing the role of carrier pigeon. This simple example illustrates what kind of intelligence effort it takes to survey the competitors.

A lag may also occur because the competitors are of the opinion that imitation will cannibalize their own customer base. In that case, the competitor may adopt a waiting attitude, praying that the innovation will be unsuccessful or aborted. In this case, the manager makes a conscious decision of what not to imitate, not that imitation in itself is hard to execute. The issue belongs here, nevertheless, because the innovator may have staged the initiative with the intention of tempting the competitor to copy with cannibalizing consequences.

So far, we have discussed features preventing or holding up imitation in the short run. To sustain competitive advantages over a longer period of time, the resources must not lend themselves to easy imitation. These issues will be discussed in more detail later («time- and process dependent implementation» and «customer-related»).

Ex ante limits to competition

Normally, firms will compete for particularly valuable and useful resources. If these are accessible in the open market, severe competition may be expected to raise costs among the buyers. Costs may rise prohibitively, ruining every expectation of future entrepreneurial rent. An example, a bank may have secured a superior location at a time when no competition existed. Later demographic trends have helped to make the location extremely suitable and convenient. It may be a result of sheer luck or conscious planning.

Rumelt (1987) calls our attention to the general fact that a positive entrepreneurial rent depends on an *ex post* value of a new venture which exceeds the *ex ante* costs by securing and deploying the necessary resources. Barney (1986) posits a similar argument in reminding us that the performance of a strategic choice not only depends on the expected rent from the strategy. The costs related to implementation must be included.

Banks are very dependent on reputation and must be universally trusted to survive. Banks that continually lead the market in developing confidence-creating measures will establish and reinforce a superior reputation.

Imperfect mobility

Resources are perfectly immobile if they are nontradable (Peteraf, 1993). These resources may be categorized as a sub-group of non-perfect mobility. Belonging to this group are specialized resources which are idiosyncratic to the extent that they are of no value outside the firm. More common are resources that are partly tradable, but are of greater value to the firms where they are in use than to the wooing firm. Resources are imperfectly mobile when their full value only can be realized dependent on internal, firm-specific circumstances or relations. They cannot be traded without losing part of their value on the way.

The value of a single resource is typically dependent on certain fertile resource combinations. The mobility is constrained when at least one of the resources in a combination is firm-specific. Efficient cross sale in a bank may be achieved through a combination of an updated register of the customer base and a customer representative (adviser) where the pair of them define the true needs of the customer. Apparently, the register of the customer base will not do the job by itself. Without an updated register, however, to tell the adviser who the customers are, what products they already have, etc., the adviser risks really irritating the customers by wanting to sell the same products twice. The communication process will be more efficient and expedient if the relevant data are in place in advance.

The transmission or exchange of resources may be so costly that mobility is prohibited. In the mid-1980s, transfer or refinancing of loans from one institution to another was associated with considerable establishment costs. These fees exceeded by far the real costs to the bank of the establishment or transfer of the loan to the competing institution. This practice constituted a major barrier to competition for well-established prosperous customers (who are a valuable resource). Institutional coercive pressure, producing a new regulation, ended that practice. Competition is at present fierce for sound customers. An institutional rule has contributed to more efficient resource allocation.

Time and process-dependent implementation

Resources and innovations that depend on considerable internal, time-consuming processes, are imperfectly mobile and hard to imitate. Note the emphasis on internal processes as a prerequisite for making resources ever more firm-specific. Such processes imply complex social settings that often escape full conceptualization and description, especially for outsiders. According to Itami and Roehl (1987), all successful organizations have as a distinguishing characteristic an understanding of learning processes running parallel to the operational tasks. Consequently, all activities embrace the potential to increase or degrade the knowledge components tied to resources. It follows that wise managers will pursue strategies that enrich and expand the knowledge base of core competence in the firm. The value of resources for future deployment may increase considerably by coupling them to an internal knowledge base through learning at the individual level as well as at the organizational level.

Barney (1991) emphasizes three relations: dependence on unique historical conditions, causal ambiguity between the firm's resources and its sustained competitive advantage, and social complexity. Most contingency models presume that a firm's performance can be discussed independently of the firm's heritage and other idiosyncratic attributes. Porter (1980) claims that these backgrounds are of no relevance to the understanding of the performance of firms. The resource-based perspective, however, in line with institutional views, not only argues that firms are historical and social entities, but points out that the ability to secure and utilize resources depends on their place in time and space.

This view also finds support with traditional strategy researchers like Ansoff (1965), and is transparent in path-dependent models (Stinchcombe, 1965). These models indicate that institutionalized rules and procedures are indeed inflexible. March & Olsen (1989) claim that institutionalized features are not always being reshaped according to environment changes. Instant adjustments, as economic theories of organizations suggest, are few and far between.

In a firm, self-reinforcing feedback mechanisms supporting prior decisions, and thus blocking off alternative views, are plentiful. A strategic resource acquired at the time of establishment may consequently be highly valuable. Managers are not always conscious of this fact. Students of culture will share this perspective: a unique and valuable organizational culture created and well established at an early stage of the life of the firm can hardly be copied.

The ambiguity rests upon the assumption that the causal relationship escapes comprehension or is only partly conceived (Lippman & Rumelt, 1982). As Demsetz (1973) has observed, sometimes it is hard to understand why one firm consistently outperforms others. Lack of understanding is not incomprehensible in a busy, complex competitive market. The comprehension could be advanced by taking the time and resources to systematically survey the competitors through market research.

Competitive positions may be embedded in complex, social phenomena like particular relations, company culture, confidence and reputation. Physical hardware may easily be copied, but the actual utilization may demand considerably larger efforts due to the social context in which it is embedded. For example, it has been proved that the location of an ATM has a strong influence on the psychological well-being of the user. In open spaces some users feel insecure.

Customer-related

Sustainable competitive advantages can only be conceptualized as part of the communication with the customer. In the end, the resource transformation process must result in products and services through a service delivery system with attributes that meet the buyer criteria with the majority of the market segment.

The service management literature claims that the experience with the product or service cannot be evaluated separately from the encounter with the producer. Translating this to the banking industry, implies that the customer representative will be an integral part of the service. These employees may be turned into resources that have powerful potential for creating sustainable competitive advantage.

We have seen that the bank's standard procedure is to recruit employees from the Bank Academy. That institution represents a hallmark and offers normal legitimacy. This procedure is cost-efficient in itself, but certainly presents a drawback as well: it creates no competitive position. Firm-specific internal training may gradually have a differential effect. Such measures may create additional entrepreneurial rent if they focus successfully on the bank's existing customers.

Compared with other service industries, banking enjoys a relatively stable customer base. In view of this, we point out that the existing customer base represents a potentially lasting and profitable firm-specific resource. A more efficient utilization and cementation of the relation between the bank and its customers may result in an improved and stronger competitive position. The full exploitation of the communication process between individual customers and their bank representatives, may be turned into a core capability.

This view can be further elaborated. Market surveys carried out on behalf of the bank over an extensive period of time indicate the cost-effectiveness of acquiring additional business from existing customers rather than the acquisition of new customers. For comprehensive and long-term financial transactions, search and evaluation costs are considerable. To establish a lasting and satisfactory bank relationship, the customer must invest time and effort to get acquainted, learn procedures and rules, etc. Switching a bank relationship is thus not only an economic transaction, it is also a social enterprise.

The degree of success in such a venture can only be evaluated in hindsight. The choice of a banking partner will, to a large extent, be decided on reputation. A superior reputation can be established through satisfied customers built on a communication process of high quality. The quality of this process must certainly outperform those of competitors, and be of consistent value to the customers. To the extent reputation is built over time, first-mover advantages are viable through this process.

The process also facilitates a more effective and goal-oriented communication in bank-customer relations, through learning by experience. The experience is cumulative on both sides, and a consistent first mover will hardly be overtaken. For the customer, switching costs will eventually reach considerable heights for a corresponding level of service in other financial institutions.

All existing, well-established banks have a broad focus. Certainly, most banks operate within limited geographical markets, but they aim at servicing all the customers in that market. The customer base is broad, typically consisting of a large number of retail and commercial customers from most industries. Given this base historically, it is next to impossible to follow a focused strategy. Ending long-term customer relations on the bank's initiative is a complicated task. The reasons are hard to explain to the customers in question, and to the local community, including the media. Loss of general trust and legitimacy is a highly likely outcome, together with a high risk of losing good customers as well.

Legitimacy

Using resources from the organizational field is the most obvious method to gain and sustain legitimacy. In that case, legitimacy is acquired for free, as a bandwagon effect. But there is no such thing as a free lunch.

This procedure does indeed have a major disadvantage: these resources cannot be transformed into a basis for a sustainable competitive position. When resources are being brought in from outside the organizational field, the challenge of legitimacy meets the firm head on. If, however, the measures are barely visible or intangible, the need for external legitimacy will diminish. Measures hardly observable for competitors enjoy the best chance to succeed as bases for viable differentiation.

Utilizing resources supplied by contractors with a peripheral relationship to the savings banks industry may represent a possible trade-off. The supplier may, for example, have a relationship with a few banks, or offer a very limited number of its products to banks. This category of suppliers may lie beyond the normal border-scanning horizon of competing financial institutions. For the banks, it will be advantageous if suppliers exhibit some knowledge of the industry's special needs.

Preliminary conclusions

Differential strategies are hard to achieve in institutionalized, organizational fields. Joint development of procedures, products and services points in that direction. In addition, the customers in fact expect similar products from the various banks. They conceive of a bank in a similar manner. Visible products and services are susceptible to rapid copying or imitation, and temporary competitive advantages are difficult to attain in the long run.

To make a differentiation strategy viable, the bank needs to establish, develop and maintain unique and nonimitable advantages. Evidently, efforts within such a strategy cannot be carried out in open cooperation with the jointly owned companies or others included in the organizational field. Attention needs to be focused on potential partners outside of, or peripheral to, the organizational field. Firms in a highly institutionalized environment may well develop heterogeneous resources, despite continuous isomorphic competitive and institutional pressure. They are not merely passive, conformers; strategic options are available and managers do make strategic choices.

In this paper we have tried to indicate why even banks are different, and how a viable competitive position may be created and sustained. Most of the elements here touched upon are mutually reinforcing. Capabilities being time-consuming to evolve, and implying complex and consistent processes, are hardly imitable and mobile. Modest *ex ante* competition may lead to sustainable first-mover advantage. However, exaggerated originality, a visible and radical departure from established, institutionalized rules and culture, may lead to problems of legitimacy. Compromises may be necessary.

Isomorphic pressure can be avoided if resources are invisible or intangible. The prospects of competitive advantage will be further improved if the causal links between measures and performance are ambiguous to the competitors. The possibilities will be strengthened even more when the elaboration of resources is dependent on a complex social interplay of elements at an individual and organizational level, activities so subtle that perfect registration and conceptualization by outsiders is prohibited.

When the organization moves into nonisomorphic territory, a need for organizational adjustment is likely. The organizational field is relatively homogeneous with similar models of organization and standard operating procedures. A consequence of importing new organizational elements from the periphery of the organizational field will probably be organizational changes to accommodate efficient implementation.

References

Ansoff, H. I. (1965): *Corporate Strategy*. New York: McGraw-Hill.

Barney, J.B. (1991): Firm Resources and Sustained Competitive Advantage. *Journal of Management 17*: 99-120.

Barney, J.B. (1986): Strategic Factor Markets: Expectations, Luck and Business Strategy. *Management Science 42*: 1231-1241.

Berger, P. & T. Luckman (1967): *The Social Construction of Reality*. New York: Doubleday.

Conner, K. & R.P. Rumelt (1986): *Software Piracy*. Working paper. Los Angeles, CA: UCLA.

Daft, R. (1983): *Organization Theory and Design*. New York: West.

Demsetz, H. (1973): Industry Structure, Market Rivalry, and Public Policy. *Journal of Law and Economics 16*: 1-19.

DiMaggio, P.J. & W.W. Powell (1991): The Iron Cage Revisited: Institutional Isomorphism and Collective Rationality in Organizational Fields. In W.W. Powell & P.J. DiMaggio (eds.): *The New Institutionalism in Organizational Analysis*. Chicago: University of Chicago Press.

Dutton, J.E. & J.M. Dukerich (1991): Keeping an Eye on the Mirror: Image and Identity in Organizational Adaptation. *Academy of Management Journal 34*: 517-554.

Glasberg, D.S. & M. Schwartz (1983): Ownership and Control of Corporations. *Annual Review of Sociology 9*: 311-332.

Grant, R.M. (1991): *Contemporary Strategy Analysis: Concepts, Techniques, Application*. Cambridge, MA: Basil Blackwell.

Hall, R. (1992): The Strategic Analysis of Intangible Resources. *Strategic Management Journal 13*: 135-144.

Hannan, M.T. & J.H. Freeman (1977): The Population Ecology of Organizations. *American Journal of Sociology 82*: 929-964.

Hansen, G. & B. Wernerfelt (1989): Determinants of Firm Performance: The Relative Importance of Economic and Organizational Factors. *Strategic Management Journal 10*: 399-411.

Hawley, A. (1968): Human Ecology. In D.L. Sill (ed.): *International Encyclopedia of the Social Sciences*. New York: Macmillan, 328-337.

Itami, H. & T.W. Roehl (1987): *Mobilizing Invisible Assets*. Cambridge, MA: Harvard University Press.

Klein, B.K. & K.B. Leffler (1981): The Role of Market Forces in Assuring Contractual Performance. *Journal of Political Economy 89*: 615-641.

Laumann, E., J. Galaskiewicz & P. Marsden (1978): Community Structure as Interorganizational Linkage. *Annual Review of Sociology* 4: 455-484.

Lippman, S.A. & R.P. Rumelt (1982): Uncertain Imitability: An Analysis of Interfirm Differences in Efficiency under Competition. *Bell Journal of Economics 13*: 418-438.

March, J.G. & Olsen, J.P. (1989), *Rediscovering Institutions: The Organizational Basis of Politics*. New York: The Free Press.

Meyer, J.W. & B. Rowan (1977): Institutionalized Organizations: Formal Structure as Myth and Ceremony . In W.W. Powell & P.J. DiMaggio (eds.): *The New Institutionalism in Organizational Analysis*. Chicago: University of Chicago Press.

Orrù, M., N.W. Biggart & G.G. Hamilton (1991): Organizational Isomorphism in East Asia. In W.W. Powell & P.J. DiMaggio: *The New Institutionalism in Organizational Analysis*. Chicago: University of Chicago Press.

Peteraf, M.A. (1993): The Cornerstones of Competitive Advantage: A Resource-Based View. *Strategic Management Journal 14*: 179-191.

Porter, M.E. (1980): *Competitive Strategy*. New York: Free Press.

Rumelt, R.P. (1991): How Much Does Industry Matter? *Strategic Management Journal* 2: 167-186.

Rumelt, R.P. (1987): Theory, Strategy, and Entrepreneurship. In D. Teece (ed.): *The Competitive Challenge*. Cambridge, MA: Ballinger, 137-158.

Rumelt (1974): *Strategy, Structure and Economic Performance*. Boston: Harvard Business School.

Scott, W.R. & J.W. Meyer (1991): *The Organization of Societal Sectors*. In W. Powell & P. DiMaggio: *The New Institutionalism in Organizational Analysis*. Chicago: University of Chicago Press, 123-124.

Selznick, P. (1957): *Leadership in Administration*. New York: Harper & Row.

Selznick, P. (1949): *TVA and the Grassroots*. Berkeley, CA: University of California Press.

Stinchcombe, A. (1965): Social Structure and Organizations. In J.G. March (ed.): *Handbook of Organizations*. Chicago: Rand McNally, 142-193.

Weber (1952): *The Protestant Ethic and the Spirit of Capitalism*. New York: Scribner.

Wernerfelt, B. (1984): A Resource-Based View of the Firm. *Strategic Management Journal 5*: 171-180.

White, H.C., S.A. Boorman & R.L. Breiger (1976): Social Structure from Multiple Networks in Block Models of Roles and Positions. *American Journal of Sociology 81*: 730-780.

Zucker, L. (1983): Organizations as Institutions. In S.B. Bacharach (ed.): *Research in the Sociology of Organizations*. Greenwich, CT: JAI Press vol. 2, 1-47.

Zucker, L. (1986): Production of Trust: Institutional Sources of Economic Structure: 1840 to 1920. In L.L. Cummings & B. Staw (eds.): *Research in Organizational Behavior*. Greenwich, CT: JAI Press vol. 8, 60-65.

Concluding Remarks

The focus of this book was on rethinking the boundaries of strategy. In these concluding remarks, we will reflect on the new boundaries we have drawn around strategy with the inclusion of the resource based perspective. We conclude by cautioning our readers that while the boundaries have been rethought, the new boundaries are not permanent.

Have the boundaries of strategy been redrawn? Reflecting on the chapters in this book as well as the enormous attention being given to the resource based perspective, we would answer the question of redrawn boundaries by a resounding «yes». However, an important thesis of this book has been that the resource based perspective is an additional, rather than an alternative, perspective in understanding strategy. The articles in this book have focused on an integration of the resource based perspective into the boundaries of strategy.

What is achieved by this integration? The resource based perspective has given new insight into the answer of the basic question of strategy: «Why do some firms succeed and others fail?» as exemplified in the articles in this book. The implications of integrating the resource based perspective are that we need to rethink how strategies are formulated, changed, how competencies are identified and used, etc. This has further implications for how strategy is studied. In this book we have faced some of the challenges presented by this integration.

And, finally, we must recognize that the boundaries of strategy need to be continually «rethought». This can be done by being aware of the benefits to understanding strategy that can be gained from both the past and the future. The past may provide us with a rediscovery of the newest «Penrose». The field of strategy has benefited from rediscovery of theoretical perspectives from many different fields. We need to be open to rediscover other perspectives which can help us better understand strategy. The future holds many uncertainties making us unable to permanently draw the boundaries of strategy. As students of strategy we need to be open to the changes that may come in terms of new questions to be answered by strategy and new boundaries to be drawn.

We know what the boundaries of strategy have been in the past; this book helps explain the boundaries of the present; we will need to be open to rethinking the boundaries in the future.

The Authors

Bo Eriksen, Odense University, Odense, Denmark.

Joyce Falkenberg, Norwegian School of Economics and Business Administration, Bergen, Norway.

Anna Mette Fuglseth, University of Bergen, Bergen, Norway.

Martin Gjelsvik, Rogaland Research, Stavanger, Norway.

Paul C. Godfrey, Brigham Young University, Provo, Utah, USA.

Kjell Grønhaug, Norwegian School of Economics and Business Administration, Bergen, Norway.

Sven A. Haugland, Norwegian School of Economics and Business Administration, Bergen, Norway.

Charles W. L. Hill, University of Washington, Seattle, Washington, USA.

Christian Knudsen, Copenhagen Business School, Copenhagen, Denmark.

Randi Lunnan, Norwegian School of Economics and Business Administration, Bergen, Norway.

Bente Løvendahl, Norwegian School of Mangement, Oslo, Norway.

Odd Nordhaug, Norwegian School of Economics and Business Administration, Bergen, Norway.

Øyvind Revang, Norwegian School of Mangement, Oslo, Norway.

Torger Reve, Norwegian School of Economics and Business Administration, Bergen, Norway.